BUILDING EMBODIMENT

Building Embodiment: Integrating Acting, Voice, and Movement to Illuminate Poetic Text offers a collection of strategic and practical approaches to understanding, analyzing, and embodying a range of heightened text styles, including Greek tragedy, Shakespeare, and Restoration/comedy of manners.

These essays offer insights from celebrated teachers across the disciplines of acting, voice, and movement and are designed to help actors and instructors find deeper vocal and physical connections to poetic text. Although each dramatic genre offers a unique set of challenges, *Building Embodiment* highlights instances where techniques can be integrated, revealing how the synthesis of body, brain, and word results in a fuller sense of character experiencing for both the actor and the audience.

This book bridges the gap between academic and professional application and invites the student and professional actor into a richer experience of character and story.

Baron Kelly is the Vilas Distinguished Professor in the Theatre and Drama Department at the University of Wisconsin–Madison. He is a four-time Fulbright scholar and has traveled extensively as a cultural specialist for the United States Bureau of Education and Cultural Affairs teaching and lecturing on the theatre in Russia, Scandinavia, Africa, Europe, London, and Asia. His teaching of acting has led him to teaching and lecturing residencies in more than a dozen countries on five continents.

Karen Kopryanski is an Assistant Professor and the Head of Voice and Speech at Virginia Commonwealth University. She has coached more than 80 theatrical productions in the United States and spent ten years on the faculty of The Boston Conservatory. A 2003 graduate of the ART/MXAT Institute at Harvard University, she is also Reviews Editor for the *Voice and Speech Review*; an associate teacher of Fitzmaurice Voicework; a recently appointed US Fulbright specialist; and has taught and led workshops in Russia, Italy, Canada, Singapore, Austria, and Turkey.

BUILDING EMBODIMENT

Integrating Acting, Voice, and Movement to Illuminate Poetic Text

Edited by
Baron Kelly and Karen Kopryanski

NEW YORK AND LONDON

Designed cover image: Kala Ross and Isaiah Hein in *Our Country's Good* by Timberlake Wertenbaker at the University of Louisville, 2017. Photo by Tom Fougerousse.

First published 2023
by Routledge
605 Third Avenue, New York, NY 10158

and by Routledge
4 Park Square, Milton Park, Abingdon, Oxon, OX14 4RN

Routledge is an imprint of the Taylor & Francis Group, an informa business

© 2023 selection and editorial matter, Baron Kelly and Karen Kopryanski; individual chapters, the contributors

The right of Baron Kelly and Karen Kopryanski to be identified as the authors of the editorial material, and of the authors for their individual chapters, has been asserted in accordance with sections 77 and 78 of the Copyright, Designs and Patents Act 1988.

All rights reserved. No part of this book may be reprinted or reproduced or utilised in any form or by any electronic, mechanical, or other means, now known or hereafter invented, including photocopying and recording, or in any information storage or retrieval system, without permission in writing from the publishers.

Trademark notice: Product or corporate names may be trademarks or registered trademarks, and are used only for identification and explanation without intent to infringe.

Library of Congress Cataloging-in-Publication Data
Names: Kelly, Baron, editor. | Kopryanski, Karen, editor.
Title: Building embodiment : integrating acting, voice, and movement to illuminate poetic text / edited by Baron Kelly and Karen Kopryanski.
Description: New York, NY : Routledge, 2023. | Includes bibliographical references and index.
Identifiers: LCCN 2022060754 (print) | LCCN 2022060755 (ebook) | ISBN 9781032068329 (hardback) | ISBN 9781032068312 (paperback) | ISBN 9781003204060 (ebook)
Subjects: LCSH: Movement (Acting) | Voice culture. | Acting—Problems, exercises, etc. | LCGFT: Essays.
Classification: LCC PN2071.M6 B85 2023 (print) | LCC PN2071.M6 (ebook) | DDC 792.028—dc23/eng/20230130
LC record available at https://lccn.loc.gov/2022060754
LC ebook record available at https://lccn.loc.gov/2022060755

ISBN: 978-1-032-06832-9 (hbk)
ISBN: 978-1-032-06831-2 (pbk)
ISBN: 978-1-003-20406-0 (ebk)

DOI: 10.4324/9781003204060

Typeset in Bembo
by Apex CoVantage, LLC

For all of our students.
You are what inspires us to keep searching for answers.

CONTENTS

List of Contributors ... ix
Acknowledgments ... xi
Preface ... xii

Introduction ... 1

PART 1
Acting ... 5

1 The Natural Elements ... 9
   Peter Allen Stone

2 Leading Center, Super Objective, and Style ... 21
   Josh Chenard

3 Tackling Heightened Text ... 29
   Miriam Mills

4 (3" × 5") × 40: A Journey to Embodiment ... 38
   Louis Fantasia

5 The Words: Golden Keys to the Inner Life of the Character ... 50
   Baron Kelly

6 Embodiment Through Breath and the Voice   58
   Josephine Hall

7 Playing the Persian Queen   67
   Stratos E. Constantinidis

PART 2
Teaching   81

8 Sculpting and Imaging the Text: An Equitable and
   Inclusive Approach to Speaking Heightened Language   83
   Peter Zazzali

9 The Sound in the Silence; the Movement in the Stillness:
   Discovering Embodiment in Presence   96
   Karen Kopryanski and Peter Balkwill

10 Grace, Gravitas, and Grounding – Approaching Greek
   Tragedy: Through a New Translation of *Hecuba*   110
   Tamara Meneghini

11 Animating the Ancients: A Scaffolded Approach to
   Physicalizing Greek Theatre   119
   Doreen Bechtol

12 Naughty, Bawdy Characters and Comedy of Manners   131
   Candice Brown

13 "O, Villain, Villain, Smiling, Damned Villain": *Hamlet*
   and the Rhetoric of Repetition   141
   Matt Davies

14 Agamemnon's Homecoming: Using Active Analysis to
   Explore Ancient Theatre   153
   Sharon Marie Carnicke

   Conclusion   164

Index   *165*

CONTRIBUTORS

Peter Balkwill is an assistant professor of acting and drama in the School of Creative and Performing Arts at the University of Calgary; he studied under Steve Pearson and Robyn Hunt at the University of Washington, Seattle; additional research as co-artistic director of the Old Trout Puppet Workshop in Calgary.

Doreen Bechtol is an associate professor in the MLitt/MFA Shakespeare and Performance program at Mary Baldwin University where she directs Shakespeare and contemporary work along with teaching acting, movement, collaborative company practices, and devising with Shakespeare.

Candice Brown is an associate professor of voice and acting in the Musical Theater Division of the Boston Conservatory at Berklee, a proud member of the Actors Equity Association, and a Boston-based actor, director, voice and dialect coach.

Sharon Marie Carnicke is a professor of dramatic arts at the University of Southern California and internationally known for her groundbreaking research on Stanislavsky.

Josh Chenard is a director, educator, associate teacher of Fitzmaurice Voicework, Certified Teacher of the Michael Chekhov Technique, and proud member of the Stage Director and Choreographers Society.

Stratos Constantinidis was born and educated in Greece. He lives and works in the United States. His latest book on Greek drama is *The Reception of Aeschylus' Plays through Shifting Models and Frontiers* (Leiden and Boston: Brill, 2017).

x Contributors

Matt Davies is a professional theatre maker and an associate professor in the Shakespeare and Performance graduate program at Mary Baldwin University.

Louis Fantasia was the first American to direct on the reconstructed London Globe stage, with a workshop production of *Much Ado About Nothing* in 1996; he has directed over 250 plays and operas worldwide.

Josephine Hall has been a professional actor for over 30 years and currently teaches acting and voice at Greensboro College, North Carolina.

Baron Kelly is the Vilas Distinguished Professor of Theatre and Drama at the University of Wisconsin, Madison; he is a four-time Fulbright scholar and a member of the College of Fellows of the American Theatre.

Karen Kopryanski is the head of voice and speech at Virginia Commonwealth University, where she teaches in the BFA and MFA programs; she is also an associate teacher of Fitzmaurice Voicework, a 2022–25 Fulbright Specialist, and the Reviews Editor for the *Voice and Speech Review*.

Tamara Meneghini is a professional actor, director, and coach, who serves on the theatre and dance faculty at the University of Colorado Boulder where she teaches performance styles and movement and voice-based practices, including Fitzmaurice voicework, Williamson physical technique, mask work, and intimacy coordination.

Miriam Mills has directed over 100 shows nationally and currently teaches acting, directing, acting for the camera, comedy techniques, and advanced performance classes in auditioning for Rider University Westminster School of the Arts.

Peter Allen Stone is the head of acting at the University of Kentucky Department of Theatre and Dance, the former chair of acting for film at the New York Film Academy, and the author of *Acting for the Camera: Back to One*.

Peter Zazzali is an internationally recognized actor-trainer who is currently director of the School of Theatre and Dance at James Madison University. He was formerly head of the BA (Hons) acting program at Singapore's LASALLE College of the Arts and is the author of two books: *Acting in the Academy* and *Actor Training in Anglophone Countries*.

ACKNOWLEDGMENTS

Baron Kelly would like to thank Dr. Stan Kahan, Murray Lebowitz, Joanne Joseph, and Ross Shenker for their support.

Karen Kopryanski would like to extend her deepest gratitude to Rocky Sansom, whose advice ("be empowered") has become a mantra; to Beth Wren Elliott, who helped edit her first attempts at writing and made her feel like she could; to friends, loved ones, and colleagues for cheering her on, to Robyn Hunt and Steve Pearson for their gracious support and boundless inspiration; and to Barbara Seidl, keeper of the longitudinal memory.

PREFACE

We met in 2020, only a month before the COVID-19 lockdown. At the time, we (along with Washington, DC actor Steven Carpenter) were adjudicating the semifinal round of the Irene Ryan Scholarship competition at the Kennedy Center American College Theatre Festival in College Park, Maryland. As we shared observations and feedback with actors, our conversations kept returning to the idea of embodiment, which we broadly defined in the moment as the ability to synthesize voice and movement skills into one's acting. The whole may be more than the sum of its parts, but underdeveloped skills in voice or movement have an undeniable impact on an actor's overall performance. That day in Maryland, we witnessed the work of many gifted students, but many of them also relied on similar habitual behaviors (both vocal and physical) and pedestrian gestures that didn't match the stakes of their scenes and monologues. This occurred whether they were performing contemporary pieces or heightened, poetic text and was evident in locked knees, leaning forward at the waist, generalized shouting, devoicing the ends of words and thoughts, or barreling through text without leaving room for moments of inspiration. All of these tendencies indicated, rather than *revealed*, the actor's emotional connection to a character or scene, and our observations – over and over – were centered on ways actors might return to their bodies, use their voices more fully and creatively, and be more present, not just with their scene partner, but with their fluid, spontaneous responses to the given circumstances (rather than relying on contrived or rehearsed behaviors that masked their individuality).

The conversation continued beyond the competition, and we recognized that the skills required for poetic text would have addressed many of the issues we witnessed, especially those related to the voice and body. The formality of heightened language incorporates a wide range of poetic elements and often involves epic, or at least intensified, circumstances, which distinguishes it from everyday speech. When an actor builds the embodiment essential for performing poetic text, they develop the skills to communicate complex thoughts with greater clarity of meaning and intention. Their breath, body, and vocal expression are able to meet the demands of the text which, in turn, helps them illuminate the story for the audience. In our own classrooms, we have seen how this physical and vocal work can then be translated to more contemporary plays and acting roles.

Additionally, we recognized that the skills required for one style of poetic text (i.e., Shakespeare) are not completely irrelevant to other styles, such as Greek tragedy and Restoration theatre, or comedies of manners. It might be possible, for example, to treat the citizens in Shakespeare's *Coriolanus* like a Greek chorus, or to turn the lens of operative word analysis, which is so helpful for speaking the intricate text in plays like Congreve's *The Way of the World*, toward messenger speeches in Greek tragedy.

We have many colleagues who have their own approaches to this work, so we turned to some of the scholars, directors, actors, and instructors whose work we know and admire and asked if we could tap into the ways in which they are building embodiment in their own rehearsal halls and classrooms. We gathered a group and posed the central question: how can we help actors get *inside* of, and viscerally connected to, language? Several themes arose that helped unify the vision for this anthology:

Innovation. There is something of the scientific method in how theatre-makers work: we observe a problem, examine existing methodologies, hypothesize about new ways to solve the problem, and then test those hypotheses through experimentation. How might it be possible to interrogate pedagogies that have become commonplace? Which ideas and exercises do we prioritize because they yield powerful results? Which pedagogical approaches might complement each other? We asked our contributors to focus on how their work expands and builds upon existing actor-training techniques. In sharing their approaches, we hope to spark even further exploration and invite the reader to make leaps of their own.

Synthesis. In keeping with our original observations about the essential nature of voice and movement, we also wanted to examine how actors, directors, and teachers can reach beyond acting methodologies and across the disciplines of voice and movement to construct more holistic approaches to teaching, acting, or directing. Acting, voice, and movement are often taught separately, siloed from each other. How might these core disciplines be considered in concert, rather than in isolation? Emotion manifests in the body as a physical experience, even though intellectual thought may accompany those feelings, and both thought and feeling are communicated via the mechanisms for voice and speech. All three must work together toward a broader palette of playable acting choices. When they do, a curious and beautiful thing happens: their subconscious is afforded a moment of *character experiencing*, and the text begins to work on them in a way that is deeply present, highlighting that particular actor's unique embodiment of the role.

Poetry. The concept of character experiencing reaches far beyond Shakespeare. We wondered how experiments across the previously mentioned disciplines might transfer across dramatic genres and harmonize with other complex text structures, each of which offer unique challenges for the actor. In Greek tragedy, we are confronted with issues of translation, poetry, the epic size of the dramatic action, and the complexity of the Greek chorus. In Shakespeare, we are challenged by unfamiliar words and idioms, editions of the plays that alter spelling and meter, and approaches that fixate on adhering to rigid rhythmic structures (or eliminating them altogether). Restoration plays and comedies of manners offer another set of challenges, where the actor must navigate formal costumes and complex body language on top of intricate grammatical structures and, quite probably, dialect work. This anthology assembles exercises and approaches to these three types of poetic text, considering both the challenges and rewards in mining a wide range of rich, complex language for connections and clues.

Usefulness. We also wanted the book to be practical for both teachers and actors – a collection of essays that would encourage specificity of language, the creation of vivid, evocative, profound imagery, and full engagement of the body in expressing thought – while also being simple to follow and understand. Some of the chapters here are written directly for the actor, while others focus on the perspective of the teacher or director. An essay might appear in one section but still be relevant to another, so we encourage you to consider how the exercises in *Acting* might be applied in the classroom, or how an analysis in *Teaching* might complement the artistic process. We know the work outlined here will lead to acting with greater energy and intensity, richer embodiment, and an openness to the possibilities in language and movement.

As the theatre community has returned to live performances, we have both recognized that embodiment has suffered greatly. We especially notice this among younger actors who had to quarantine at the very moment they were learning who they are, what they like about themselves, and what their artistic preferences are. Many of them were, perhaps, just beginning to investigate the vast range of possibilities for how they might use their bodies and voices in their acting. Cultivating these skills in an online forum is antithetical to practicing in a live classroom or performing on a live stage. Technique has the potential to become as reflexive as muscle memory, but it requires diligent practice to build confidence and proficiency. Embodied practices shape the actor's skills in synthesizing the intellectual, emotional, and physical nuances of text. When we encourage assimilation of everything that comes within the grasp of the five senses, the actor's work can reflect the flexibility of their voice, sense of rhythm, responsiveness to imagery, and empathetic connection to character.

We hope you find inspiration in these pages and that building your own embodiment will take your work in exciting new directions.

INTRODUCTION

In the theatre, each actor must find a way of embodying a character and a certain degree of latitude is inevitable, the result of the individuality of the actor. Each actor allows their experiences to filter through their work, influenced by the capacities and limitations of their bodies and voices. Physical manifestations are revealed through tempo, rhythm, gesture, and body language. Voices vary in prosodic combinations of pitch, volume, inflection, resonance, and rhythm. Individual expression is determined by endless combinations of these vocal and physical characteristics, so that even if two actors visualize a character in exactly the same way, their performances must vary. Two different oboes may play the same melody, but the sound will have variation because of the inherent differences in the composition of the wood, the construction of the instruments, and the skill and experience of the musician.

Experience is also subjective and a result of the unique history of the individual. None of us sees or reacts in the same way because the process entails more than just the physical act of seeing; it involves a *way* of viewing something, which influences the details we notice, our thoughts and judgments about what we observe, and the ways we respond. Playwrights choose and arrange words with deep craft, and the actor must be able to investigate (and replicate) the intangible moments of inspiration that will help give birth to the thought on stage. This can be a daunting process, but when it happens, even moments of listening to other characters become more interesting. Rather than *portraying* a character, the actor begins to *experience* them. Character experiencing is often revealed when an actor is able to remain present to the shapes, meanings, and imagery behind the words they are speaking. When words are seen, tasted, touched, and felt, they break up assumed or habitual patterns of thought. A skillful actor may present an adequate representation of character and a reasonable interpretation of lines; a brilliant actor will reveal the subtleties of dialogue and character that result only from the fullest embodiment of the text.

In many ways the task has always been, in the words of William Gillette,

> for an actor who knows exactly what he's going to say to behave as though he *doesn't*; to let his thoughts apparently occur to him as he goes along, even though they're in his mind already; and to apparently search for and find the words by which to express those thoughts, even though those words are at his tongue's very end throughout.[1]

The only way to arrive at this well-crafted illusion is to actually be in the moment, or embodied, as it unfolds. The path to being fully present in mind, body, and voice is as individual as the actor. One might be inspired when they apply a physical gesture to an action they are trying to play, while another might discover that paying attention to punctuation helps them articulate thoughts more clearly. Any entry point *is* acting. In playing a piano, the performer is making music whether their attention is primarily focused on finger flexibility, pedal dynamics, or sight reading. Phrasing, mood, gesture, volume, and structure are all involved in performance – theatrical or musical – so working on one will inevitably affect the whole.

How to Use This Book

This anthology features a collection of essays that all have different entry points into building embodiment. Some contributors begin by setting the stage for movement first, while others dive deeply into specific elements of language. This is not a book that must be read from front to back.

The book features two sections. The first, *Acting*, features chapters that were written in direct conversation with the actor; many of these will encourage you to jump in and play right from the start. The second part, *Teaching*, centers the perspective of the instructor or director, outlining exercises that might be used in a classroom or rehearsal hall. We have organized the chapters so that each section begins with broad concepts (exercises that integrate skills across disciplines and even styles of poetic text) and gradually narrows to focus on essays that dive more deeply into a single style, a single play, and even a single figure of speech.

We encourage you to let yourself be drawn to what is interesting or useful for you *right now*. In our classrooms, we nudge actors and students toward working on their feet because impulses and reactions get clearer when the work is lifted off the page and centered in the body. We invite you to do that here, whether you are reading as an actor or an instructor – do the gesture, make the noise, and let yourself have the reaction so that you can fully experience each chapter.

Note

1. William Gillette and George Arliss, *The Illusion of the First Time in Acting* (New York, NY: Scholar's Choice, 2015), 40.

PART 1
Acting

As actors, we are sometimes unaware of how our life experiences and habitual behaviors might predetermine our interpretation of a character. The opportunity to explore interesting, original choices can be murky territory. Because we are using ourselves as the instrument that plays the music, it can be difficult to objectively discern where to begin, what is or isn't working, or to know if we can fully trust, enjoy, and feel confident with the choices we've made.

Two of the greatest challenges in working with poetic text lie in the complex structure of the language and in how we can express the physical experience of a world that would have been very different from our own. Intellectually, we might understand what is happening, but often we struggle to bring the words off the page in a way that feels and sounds connected and authentic. Some styles of poetic text may involve formalized, yet expansive, expressions of emotion that require a fullness of voice and body we are not used to. Others use unfamiliar words, concepts, and phrasing. Some give the illusion of being rehearsed speeches. We need to pull apart the language to get at the heart of the meaning and employ somatic practices to create open, expressive bodies that can communicate with specificity and clarity. We must find moment-to-moment inspiration and allow our artistic choices to manifest fully or else the epic nature of the themes (i.e., love, justice, power, disorder, conflict, loss, family) become lost.

In our experience, the most reliable solution to these problems is to center the actor's voice and body as a primary source for artistic choices. Visceral responses to sound, text, and imagery arise in uniquely individual ways that can spark deeper understandings of the characters we play and the stories they are featured in. Through this work, we might discover a version of Euripides' Helen that has

DOI: 10.4324/9781003204060-2

6 Acting

trouble completing a sentence, or a version of Constance, from Shakespeare's *King John*, who is circling the drain of grief for her son, both physically and verbally.

The chapters in this part of the book are written in direct conversation with the actor. They invite the reader to step outside themselves, engage with poetic text from various physical and vocal vantage points, and see if those frames of reference can bring logic and meaning to their acting choices. The section progresses from broad explorations that may be applied to a wide variety of poetic text styles, to finely detailed analyses of meaning, prosody, gesture, and given circumstances.

We begin with Peter Allen Stone's "The Natural Elements," an examination of how engaging with an element's physical and aural qualities drops us into a full-body experience of a character; giving an element permission to speak through the actor can spark new ideas about embodiment, motivation, and intention.

Next, Josh Chenard's "Leading Center, Super Objective, and Style" walks us through a process to combine Michael Chekhov's principles of Leading Center and Super Objectives by blending in the usage of idiomatic expressions. His recipe helps us get precise about physical and vocal choices, and creates vibrant, authentic characters in a way that is both playful and profound.

From here, we shift toward the blending of foundational acting techniques as, in "Tackling Heightened Text," Miriam Mills layers the work of Stella Adler and Jerzy Grotowski into an approach that can invite artists to discover the imaginative and physical truth of a character through imagery and animal associations.

Louis Fantasia's chapter, "(3" × 5") × 40: A Journey to Embodiment," offers a shorthand method for connecting to Shakespeare's text that doesn't shortchange the depth of analysis. His process brings characters to vivid life by layering microscopic, line-by-line discoveries with macroscopic interpretations of the play as a whole.

We follow this up by diving more deeply into the meanings of words. In "The Words: Golden Keys to the Inner Life of the Character," Baron Kelly examines how each word's multiple layers of meaning can help actors create paraphrases that are both innovative and genuine, revealing the depth of a character's frame of mind and intention.

Jo Hall's chapter, "Embodiment Through Breath and the Voice," dives even deeper into language by inviting us to identify operative words and marry them to inflection in a way that honors complex structure and improves storytelling through clarity of thought.

The final chapter in this section, "Playing the Persian Queen," by Stratos Constantinidis, zooms in on the moment the Queen enters in Aeschylus' *Persians*; it examines the historical context for details that would have been familiar to contemporary audiences and offers clues in the text that can inform our acting choices and enhance our understanding of the central conflict of the play.

Remember that there is no need to read this section from beginning to end. As you peruse these titles, consider what will be most useful to guide your own discoveries. You will discover the total organism by attending to your voice and movement throughout.

1
THE NATURAL ELEMENTS

Peter Allen Stone

Inside/Out or Outside/In?

What does it mean to work from the Outside/In? For me, the term indicates a process that focuses on using the actor's physical instrument as a starting point for character development. It is an approach that helps the actor find inner rhythm and emotional life without using the substitution method, which can be problematic for several reasons.

Substitution was popularized by actor and director Lee Strasberg in the 1950s. It encouraged actors to use personal experiences to create a character that was more emotionally "believable." Strasberg wanted actors to experience real emotions on stage by substituting the character's given circumstances with their own, and his approach focused on mining the psychology of the actor to work from the Inside/Out. His idea was that when the actor focuses on creating the inner or emotional life first, the physical and vocal choices will follow. If the actor has a lived emotional experience similar to the character's, they can recall that memory and relive it again as the character. For many actors, the substitution method is exhausting. Recalling dark memories in every performance is potentially re-traumatizing, especially if the actor is using the memory of an emotional event that hasn't yet healed. This reveals another obstacle: if the actor isn't careful, they can be pulled out of the character's circumstances and begin to drown in their own past, steering the actor away from the details of the character's experience by projecting their own onto the circumstances of the play; suddenly, the actor's interpretation is no longer serving the story.

Working from the Outside/In is the opposite. It is a technique that begins by focusing on the actor's instrument instead of their personal experiences. It invites

DOI: 10.4324/9781003204060-3

physical and imaginative freedom and sparks spontaneity in performance. When the actor works from the Outside/In, they begin by committing to physical and vocal choices first, and then letting these choices grow into a new emotional experience. This commitment helps the actor avoid habitual tendencies and gets them out of their head quickly, since the body responds to stimuli in more reliable ways. On any given night, the actor can be in any particular emotional state; they don't have to have lived a similar emotional experience to create a believable moment that aligns with the character's circumstance. Instead, a series of physical and vocal tasks sparks their imagination and guides them into uncharted emotional and creative territory. Working from the Outside/In supports actors of all ages and lived experiences. This is especially useful when the character in question is experiencing heightened circumstances or an intense emotional situation. *When the actor fully commits to the physical form, the emotional life is ignited.*

Exploring the Natural Elements

This particular variation of the Outside/In approach invites actors to use their imagination to embody one of four elements found in nature: *Tree, Water, Fire,* or *Air*. The training acts as a springboard by igniting a muscle memory that is easy to replicate in the future. Here, we will apply this process to four characters from Shakespeare, conjuring connections between their stories and the natural elements.[1] These explorations are suggestions, and the actor is invited to personalize the work, with full commitment to their physical and imaginative process, in order to discover new modes of self-expression.

The elemental world is powerful, primitive, and alive; it leads us back to the core of energy, life, and human evolution. Each element possesses unique qualities actors can use to channel energy and embody a character. We will examine the characteristics that comprise each element and then step inside our physical selves to fully embody it. The element will begin to speak through them, taking them on an emotional journey. Through experimentation and repetition, actors will develop an internal muscle memory for each element and cultivate a creative practice they can call on at a moment's notice. They will begin to discover their own internal rhythms and invent a system for working with the differences between elements. The ultimate goal is a process for creating dynamic characters by embodying an element and blending it with text. We will attempt to physically and vocally express each element across a magnitude from 1–10, which will lead to new physical interpretations and surprising emotional places. The work is fun, spontaneous, and liberating.

As you experiment with these exercises, use the form of each element that is the most available to you. As you explore *Fire*, for instance, you might physically embody the small popping of a candle flame or the irregular burn of a raging forest fire. Once you understand the basic concept, you may seek out more unique forms that fit the characters you are working on, like the steady flame of a lantern or the playful dance of a campfire.

Tree

Trees are grounded. They are rooted. They can be tall or short, but they are always strong. Invisible to us, beneath the earth, their roots spread far and wide. These roots intertwine and stretch deep into the soil. In a sense, they are immovable. Every tree is different, and their branches have unique forms. They can be straight, twisted, rigid, and more.

Open up your imagination while you explore the *visual*, *physical*, and *aural* qualities of *Tree*. Take note of any creative impulses or emotional responses.

Characteristics of a Tree

Rooted, Grounded, Sturdy

The Elemental Scale – Tree

1 (Human/Subtle) – Small backyard tree   *10 (Abstract)* – Giant redwood tree

Exercise 1A – Tree

1. Select a tree from nature that you would like to practice with.
2. Study its structure and form. Imagine the tree roots traveling far underground, connecting it to other plants and trees and giving it strength. Does the tree's branches stretch far and wide across the sky? Is the tree narrow, without any leaves, standing alone in a field? Are there birds and squirrels running across its branches? Write down any words, thoughts, or feelings that come to mind.
3. Feel its texture. Is it rough? Smooth? Thick? Twisted?
4. Use your hand to knock or tap on the tree. What do you hear? Is the element making any sound? Is the tree hollow? Solid?
5. Take a photo of the tree to use later as a reference.
6. After having studied your tree, stand still and close your eyes. From your memory, create the physical shape of the tree. Breathe. For a few minutes, use your imagination to physically become the tree. Feel your wide or narrow base. Imagine the roots that go through your feet and deep into the ground. Use your arms as the branches – do they grow straight up, or do they spread out wide? Breathe.
7. Gently open your eyes and see the world from your tree's perspective.
8. When you have the impulse, begin to sigh and find the quality of your tree's sound. Consider its pitch, resonance, and how the physical characteristics of

your tree impact its ability to make sound before adding words. Read the speech in the next section and choose a verse line to explore. Begin to improvise those words or simple lines of dialogue using the voice of the tree: this may be abstract and the sound nonhuman.
9. After a few minutes, begin to slowly walk around the space, as the tree, continuing to speak in its voice. Is it difficult to move the deep-rooted legs of the tree? Begin to find different physical shapes of your tree with your arms, legs, and torso as it moves.
10. Note any emotional responses you might be experiencing.
11. Note where your tree falls on a scale of 1–10: is your tree subtle and nearly human, or are you embodying the physical and vocal qualities of a giant redwood?
12. Read the speech in the next section, noting whether the tree you chose seems appropriate for the character. If it doesn't feel like a good match, what qualities do you need to add to your tree – size? roughness? shape?

Character Example – Tree

This speech of Queen Margaret's is from *Henry VI*, part 3, act 1, scene 4 (487). Sustain the feeling of being *Tree* as you read the passage aloud.

Margaret: Brave Warriors, Clifford and Northumberland,
Come make him stand upon this Mole-hill here,
That raught at Mountains with out-stretched Arms,
Yet parted but the shadow with his Hand.
What, was it you that would be England's King?
Was't you that reveled in our Parliament,
And made a Preachment of your high Descent?
Where are your Mess of Sons, to back you now?
The wanton Edward, and the lusty George?
And where's that valiant Crook-back Prodigy?
Dickie, your Boy, that with his grumbling voice
Was wont to cheer his Dad in Mutinies?
Or with the rest, where is your darling, Rutland?
Look York, I stained this Napkin with his blood
That valiant Clifford, with his Rapiers point,
Made issue from the Bosom of the Boy:
And if thine eyes can water for his death,
I give thee this to dry thy cheeks withal.
Alas poor York, but that I hate thee deadly,
I should lament thy miserable state.

There are many characters in Shakespeare, Greek, Restoration, and contemporary theatre that exhibit treelike characteristics and even though each of them will be unique (willowy, gnarled, hollow, soaring, evergreen, heavy with flowers), they will also have some qualities in common. As you analyze your character and circumstances, use your imagination and explore using different trees (or different *Water*, different *Fire*, different *Air*) until you find what is appropriate for your character. Trust your gut instinct, and it will guide you in the right direction. Perhaps what you will walk away with is that your character isn't at all like a tree. Maybe your character is more like water.

Water

Imagine standing on the end of a pier looking out at the enormous sea, or observing the water that sits in a glass on a table, or listening to water dripping from a kitchen faucet. Is the water still or in motion? Is it powerful? You will notice that in all of these forms, water can be heavy. It can be nurturing. Water takes up the space that it desires and goes where it wants, unless you build a dam, but even if the surface is still, water is always moving. That motion can be large or very subtle: the tide of the ocean ebbs and flows, and even a swimming pool slowly stirs. What would it be like to move like water?

Open up your imagination while you explore the *visual*, *physical*, and *aural* qualities of *Water*. Take note of any creative impulses or emotional responses.

Characteristics of Water

Heavy, Powerful, Nurturing, in Motion

The Elemental Scale – Water

1 (Human) – A small glass of water   *10 (Abstract)* – A tidal wave

Exercise 1B – Water

1. Select the form of water you would like to use as your model.
2. Observe the water. Study its weight and movement: are there giant waves on the surface, or is there a swift current underneath? Is it crystal clear, or does it appear murky and muddy? Does the light dance on top of it, or can you see your reflection in it? Write down any words, thoughts, or feelings that come to mind.
3. Touch the water and feel it run through your fingers. Is it shockingly cold or like a warm bath? Does it feel salty or fresh? Does it have a pungent smell, like a pond covered in algae, or is its surface icy?
4. Listen closely. Does the water make any sound? Are the waves of the ocean crashing loudly against a wall of jagged rocks? Is the dark lake quietly breathing? Is the mountain stream steadily whistling?
5. Take a photo or video to use as a reference.

6. After having studied your subject, stand still and close your eyes. Create the physical shape, weight, and inner movement of the water. Feel the weight of the water moving inside of you, even on a cellular level. Breathe. For a few minutes, use your imagination to physically embody water. Imagine channels or expansiveness. Imagine saltiness or clear freshness.
7. Gently open your eyes and see the world from the water's perspective. Be sure to keep the element moving within you.
8. When you have the impulse, begin to explore the voice of water; sigh and make sounds to discover musicality and rhythm. Discover where the voice of water lives in your body. Begin by slurring a few words as your body undulates or stirs. Experiment with your words being heavy and sloshing around. Just like *Tree*, *Water*'s voice can be abstract and nonhuman. Look at the speech in the next section and choose a verse line to experiment with, or improvise simple lines of dialogue using the voice of water. Remember that when using the voice of any element, the character must always be understood, and clarity is essential.
9. After a few minutes begin to move around the space as *Water* and improvise with your abstract voice. Notice how heavy and sluggish or swift and flowingly the water moves.
10. Note any emotional responses that you may experience.
11. Note where your water falls on a scale of 1–10. One being the most human (subtle) physical and vocal expression, and ten being the enormous abstract physical and vocal representation of an ocean wave.
12. Read the speech in the next section, noting whether the water you chose seems appropriate for the character. If it doesn't feel like a good match, what qualities do you need to add or subtract – weight? vastness? speed? temperature?

Character Example – Water

Sustain the feeling of *Water* as you read the following speech aloud, spoken by Trinculo in act 2, scene 2 of *The Tempest* (9).[2]

Trinculo: Here's neither bush, nor shrub to bear off any weather at all: and another Storm brewing, I hear it sing i' th' wind: yond same black cloud, yond huge one, looks like a foul bombard that would shed his liquor: if it should thunder, as it did before, I know not where to hide my head: yond same cloud cannot choose but fall by pailfuls.
[Sees Caliban.]
What have we here, a man, or a fish? dead or alive? a fish, he smells like a fish: a very ancient and fish-like smell: a kind of, not of the newest poor-John: a strange fish: were I in England now (as once I was) and had but this fish painted; not a holiday-fool there but would give a piece of silver: there, would this Monster, make a man: any strange

beast there, makes a man: Leg'd like a man; and his Fins like Arms: warm o'my troth: I do now let loose my opinion; hold it no longer; this is no fish, but an Islander, that hath lately suffered by a Thunderbolt: Alas, the storm is come again: my best way is to creep under his Gaberdine: there is no other shelter hereabout: Misery acquaints a man with strange bedfellows: I will here shroud till the dregs of the storm be past.

[Crawls under Caliban's gaberdine.]

Fire

Have you ever known someone with a fiery personality? Do they run around angry and screaming all of the time, or does their temper flare dangerously and unexpectedly? Could fire imply someone who is romantic or burns with passion? What about someone who *moves* like fire? Imagine lighting a match: when you strike that little stick against the flint, an explosion occurs. It may seem small, but a powerful explosion does take place. How could you physicalize that? Or imagine a volcano erupting, venting hot ash, and sparking a raging forest fire. What would it look like if you embodied that powerful outburst? What are the physical characteristics of fire? When we observe different forms of fire, we begin to see consistent qualities emerge; regardless of form, fire moves quickly. It jumps around. It is explosive. It is exciting, hot, emotional, romantic, passionate, and most of all, unpredictable.

Open up your imagination while you explore the *visual*, *physical*, and *aural* qualities of *Fire*. Take note of any creative impulses or emotional responses.

Characteristics of Fire

Unpredictable, Spontaneous, Explosive, and Passionate

The Elemental Scale – Fire

1 (Human) – Cigarette lighter trying to ignite   *10 (Abstract)* – Raging forest fire

Exercise 1C – Fire

1. Select any form of fire that you would like to use as your model.
2. Study the fire – its colors, shapes, internal tempo, and sound. Watch it sporadically explode. Can you see the intense energy that fuels it? At what speed and rhythm does it spread? Is it a deep red? Light amber? Can you locate the eye or epicenter of the flame? Observe what occurs with an initial spark, as compared to a fire that is steadily burning. Write down any words, thoughts, or feelings that come to mind.

3. Put your hand near the flame, carefully, and feel the heat. Is it darting around? Can you feel the boiling heat over the red coals?
4. Listen to the fire spontaneously crackle and pop. Are the hot coals humming with intensity? Are the flames of the forest fire roaring as the trees fall crashing down? Is it quietly hissing?
5. Take a photo or video to use as a reference.
6. After having studied your subject, stand still and close your eyes. Breathe. Sense the darkness inside your body, and imagine the initial explosion or spark that occurs to bring the fire into being. How can you physically express that unpredictable, spontaneous moment? Once lit, is your fire playful? jumpy? volatile? or even comforting? Use your imagination and explore embodying the burning fire.
7. Open your eyes and begin to see the world from the fire's perspective. With your body, continue to physicalize the sporadic movements of fire.
8. On the impulse, breathe and begin to find the voice of fire, remembering that oxygen *fuels* fire. As previously, fire's voice may be abstract and sound nonhuman. What sounds does it gravitate toward? How might the sporadic physicality be reflected in a sporadic voice? Improvise simple lines of dialogue, or use a line from the speech in the next section, to explore the voice of fire.
9. After a few minutes, begin to move around the space as fire, communicating with the objects around you. Notice if you land in one spot and smolder more hotly, or if you move more quickly from place to place.
10. Note any emotional responses that you may experience.
11. Experiment on a scale of 1–10. One being the initial explosion of a match igniting before the flame gently calms. Ten being the physical and vocal expression of a raging forest fire. Notice how your eyes may dart around and how your movements are quick, sporadic, and spontaneous.
12. Explore different levels of the elemental scale while performing the classical speech in the next section. Fire's unpredictability may make it possible to move from level to level quite quickly!

Character Example – Fire

This is Cassius' speech from act 1, scene 2 of *Julius Caesar* (701). As you read it aloud, sustain the feeling of being *Fire*.

Cassius: Why man, he doth bestride the narrow world
Like a Colossus, and we petty men
Walk under his huge legs, and peep about
To find ourselves dishonorable Graves.
Men at sometime, are Masters of their Fates.

The fault (dear Brutus) is not in our Stars,
But in ourselves, that we are underlings.
Brutus and Caesar: What should be in that Caesar?
Why should that name be sounded more than yours?
Write them together: Yours, is as fair a Name:
Sound them, it doth become the mouth as well:
Weigh them, it is as heavy: Conjure with 'em,
Brutus will start a Spirit as soon as Caesar,
Now in the names of all the Gods at once,
Upon what meat doth this our Caesar feed,
That he is grown so great? Age, thou art sham'd.
Rome thou hast lost the breed of Noble Bloods.
When went there by an Age, since the great Flood.
But it was famed with more than with one man?
When could they say (till now) that talked of Rome,
That her wide Walks encompassed but one man?
Now it is Rome indeed, and room enough
When there is in it but one only man.
O! You and I, have heard our Fathers say,
There was a Brutus once, that would have brooked
Th' eternal Devil to keep his State in Rome,
As easily as a King.

Air

Have you ever met a person that accidentally sneaks up behind you and startles you? That is one manifestation of air. How might air shake hands with another character? Do they quickly reach out and grasp the other character with a firm grip? Probably not. Air might wait for the other character to initiate the handshake and then gently offer their hand. Imagine a feather slowly floating from the sky down to the earth. What if you used your body to physicalize the air that propels that feather? How would your body move? If you jumped, would you land lightly onto the floor? Would it affect the way that you feel? Would your inner rhythm and emotional life change? Perhaps you may feel a sense of childlike play and joy as your troubles float away. Like all of the elements, air can come in many different forms. It can be a gentle summer breeze, or it can be the powerful wind in a hurricane. However, there are some common characteristics. Air is light. Often, it is silent. Air has suspension.

Open up your imagination while you explore the *visual*, *physical*, and *aural* qualities of *Air*. Take note of any creative impulses or emotional responses.

Characteristics of Air

Suspension, Light, Hovering, and Quiet

The Elemental Scale – Air

1 (Human) – Feather gently blowing in a breeze   *10 (Abstract)* – Powerful, massive tornado

Exercise 1D – Air

1. Select any form of air that you would like to use as your model.
2. Observe a light breeze or strong wind. Notice how it suspends objects. Do the leaves twist and turn as the wind blows them around? Does the dirt swirl like a tornado? Does it gently support a seagull as it hovers over the ocean? Does it speed up and then suddenly slow down? Write down any words, thoughts, or feelings that come to mind.
3. Feel the light wind gently pass through your fingers. Or feel the powerful wind hold you up as you lean your body weight against it. Or feel the wind swirl around you.
4. Listen to it silently move, or gust, or howl. Is the wind whistling? Is it thumping?
5. Study the qualities of air: its weight, speed, power, stillness. Observe how air can suspend an object – a feather, a bird, an airplane. Write down any words, thoughts, or feelings that come to mind.
6. Take a photo or video to use as a reference.
7. After having studied your research, stand still and close your eyes. Breathe (which is also air). Imagine your body becoming the air that moves the feather. Feel the lightness and power in suspension.
8. Open your eyes and begin to see the world from the air's perspective. With your body, continue to physicalize the light moments of suspension.
9. On the impulse, use your breath and begin to find the voice of air. As always, the voice you discover may be abstract, or whispery, or sound nonhuman. Begin to speak a few words quietly, perhaps a line from the speech in the next section, or by improvising simple lines of dialogue using the voice of air. Explore soft and hushed qualities of your voice.
10. After a few moments, begin to move around the space as you make sound, noticing how gentle and forceful you can be, in turn, even though you are almost always invisible to the naked eye. Does this feel playful or stealthy? Lonely or aggressive?
11. Note any emotional responses that you may experience.
12. Experiment on a scale of 1–10. One being a feather floating in the sky. Ten being the physical and vocal expression of a tornado. Notice the

playfulness, joy, and lightness that you may feel. Try not to make a sound as you move.
13. Read the classical speech in the next section, noting whether the air you chose seems appropriate for the character. Like fire, air can move quickly – and sometimes unpredictably – from level to level. Unlike fire, it can also not move at all.

Character Example – Air

Experiencing your being as *Air*, read aloud Puck's speech from act 2, scene 1 of *A Midsummer Night's Dream* (148).

Puck: Thou speak'st aright;
I am that merry wanderer of the night:
I jest to Oberon, and make him smile,
When I a fat and bean-fed horse beguile,
Neighing in likeness of a silly foal,
And sometimes lurk I in a Gossip's Bowl,
In very likeness of a roasted crab:
And when she drinks, against her lips I bob,
And on her withered dewlap pour the Ale.
The wisest Aunt telling the saddest tale,
Sometime for three-foot stool, mistaketh me,
Then slip I from her bum, down topples she,
And tailor cries, and falls into a cough.
And then the whole quire hold their hips and laugh,
And waxen in their mirth, and neeze, and swear,
A merrier hour was never wasted there.
But room Fairy, here comes Oberon.

Putting It All Together

Using the elements as a tool to create a character is an enlightening approach; it will certainly help you get out of your head and into your body. But what happens when you feel torn between different elements for your character? Is this character fire or air? Maybe this character is water? Is this character rooted like a tree? Don't get discouraged; this is part of the process. Characters have many layers, but if you can tap into the character's core element, you will have a foundation for bringing the entire being to life. Focus strongly on one element as the driving force, and commit to it with all of your energy. Mixing the elements can lead a character away from specificity and toward generality. As in any good play, characters will change, but choosing a good dominant element will also allow that character to evolve over the course of the play.

As with all creative acts, use your imagination and explore. Approach the elements with questions rather than answers. Commit physically and vocally to the elements and allow them to lead you. Challenge yourself to let go of what you think the character needs to be and open up your creative channel to new possibilities. Experiment with different elements for your character; when you find the appropriate one, you will know. The process of discovery is where you will find the greatest reward. Trust your instincts and try to avoid getting too analytical. Rely on your instrument and devote yourself to working from the Outside/In. The element is a starting point, and the goal is to create an original physical and vocal expression for the character. One that is different from your habitual movements and tendencies. An expression that will spark the physical and emotional life of the character in each performance without focusing on the psychology of the actor. Through practice, you will build a believable and viscerally engaged character that is specific, emotional, and dynamic, and the results are both freeing for the actor and enjoyable for the audience.

Notes

1. All texts have been edited slightly, and the spelling of some words have been modernized.
2. *The text has been edited slightly, and the spelling of some words have been modernized.*

Bibliography

Shakespeare, William. 2001. *The Applause First Folio of Shakespeare in Modern Type*. Annotated by Neil Freeman. New York: Applause.

2
LEADING CENTER, SUPER OBJECTIVE, AND STYLE

Josh Chenard

Working with or on any theatrical style piece can be intimidating for even the most talented actors. The language is complex, the physical demands rigorous, and crafting dynamic, entertaining characterization that is also honest and nuanced is a challenge. Whether teaching an acting class exploring styles or directing a classical production, I begin the work by providing the words of seminal theatre practitioner and director, Konstantin Stanislavski: "You can kill the king without a sword, and you can light the fire without a match. What needs to burn is your imagination" (Stanislavski 1948, 49). This advice serves as a gentle reminder to treat the text, the parameters of style, and the specificity of the language as a sail for creation, not an anchor of weighted limitation; the key to doing so? Imagination. This chapter shares my process for guiding actors as they tackle heightened text and classical characterization to harness their imagination and inspiration into bold, specific, and physical acting choices.

One of Stanislavski's greatest pupils, Michael Chekhov and Stanislavski shared a common interest in a limitless and rich imagination. Creating an approach to performance rooted in active physical choices, Chekhov understood that the body radiates intangible, invisible information to the audience. His technique provides actors with specific, dynamic tools to develop that radiant energy and cultivate the ability to channel thoughts and imagination into shape. Some popular Michael Chekhov exercises include a series of *Archetypal Gestures* that physicalize character motivation, such as pushing or pulling. Explored in large fully embodied expressions, the external presentation can grow or shrink based on the style of the work, but the internal desire must remain large and immediate. Another well-known Chekhov tool is *Psychological Gesture*: a single fluid, physical expression that has a beginning, middle, and end and encapsulates the journey of the character during the life of the play. Often abstract and personal in nature, the Psychological Gesture is used to move the actor into the spirit of the character, rooting the external expression of the actor in the internal existence of the character. One of my favorite tools to employ is *Leading Center*. This tool, which is not often written about, is perfect for physicalizing style as it encourages the actor to creatively and logically analyze both character and text then synthesize thoughts and ideas into form. Although working with a center is a familiar concept within most beginning acting classes, Chekhov deepens this practice with a few simple guiding principles that move beyond mere physical location within the body. Additional principles include that the Leading Center should consist of a quality, a vivid image or description that infuses the center with movement potential, such as luscious red lips or weak, quivering knees, two examples I will continue with later. Another aspect of this approach is that the center has mobility or motion linked to the location and quality. These additional principles add complexity and energy to the Leading Center choice; the difference is between an actor choosing their lips as their Leading Center, and thinking of those same lips not only as their center but also as red ripe cherries that grow and get close to bursting every time the character's love interest enters the room. Another example would be the knees as a character's Leading Center. If the character is clumsy, perhaps the quality of the left knee is a scared kitty cat and the quality of the right knee is a loud, rabid dog. Whenever the character becomes nervous or scared, the dog begins to chase the cat, creating a silly, jagged, unique walk for the character! The possibilities are limitless.

Later in the chapter, we will examine a variety of characters and examples in the context of these principles, but first, let's introduce and weave Leading Center and Super Objectives together by understanding how they can inform and feed off one another to enrich and enliven your physical storytelling. The next section illustrates the basic principles of Leading Center and how they can inform and feed off Super Objective to enrich and enliven your physical storytelling.

Leading Center in Molière

Let's begin by examining Argan, the bombastic hypochondriac in Molière's *The Imaginary Invalid*. Argan is cheap, paranoid, sickly, conniving, and prone to temper tantrums as he plots to marry his daughter off to a doctor to meet his own selfish needs. In the first act of the play, he explains his selfish choice to his daughter, who pleads with him that she would rather marry for love, not paternal convenience:

> My reason is, that seeing myself infirm and sick, I wish to have a son-in-law and relatives who are doctors, in order to secure their kind assistance in my illness, to have in my family the fountain-head of those remedies which are necessary to me, and to be within reach of consultations and prescriptions.

Where might an appropriate location be for Argan's center? Due to the consistent worry and hand wringing he displays, we might choose his hands. His belly might also be a good choice, reflective of his constant gastrointestinal worries and woes. Or his nose, due to his need to insert himself into relationships and situations where he does not belong. Any of these would be valid choices, depending on which feels the most exciting and connected for the actor playing the role. For the sake of this example, let's select Argan's belly as his leading center. Following Chekhov's principles, we need to assign the center a quality and mobility. Is the belly a beehive (quality) with bees constantly stinging (mobility) him if he moves too quickly? Is it a heavy bowling ball (quality) always slowly rolling (mobility) into one of the lane gutters and forcing him to jerk awkwardly left and right? Is it a ticking time bomb full of fire and heat that explodes during fits of rage? Any of these options would be rooted in the text, entertaining to watch, and would guide the actor into clear, dynamic character building and storytelling.

Once a viable and exciting Leading Center is chosen, the character will begin to take shape. Allowing the Leading Center to affect the rest of the body begins to clarify or heighten moments within scenes, based on the degree to which the Leading Center is on display. The actor might minimize the Leading Center during agreeable conversations but then play it up when the character is confused or complaining. Imagine Argan wandering around the stage clutching his belly and staggering from side to side, just like a bowling ball headed for the gutter. Allow it to build (perhaps bowling a strike!) during arguments. Allow it to roll at a crawl, barely moving, down the alley when complaining of ailments or when feigning illness for sympathy. When Argan dramatically tosses himself into his chair, might the action resemble said bowling ball gently careening into the gutter? After the center and its components have been decided upon, there are limitless creative options, levels, degrees, and directions one can investigate. You can and should explore a variety of images, concepts, and possibilities before finalizing any choices.

Super Objective in Molière

The concept of Super Objectives harkens back to the work of Konstantin Stanislavski and is typically described as what the character wants to accomplish over the span of the play (versus scene-to-scene, or moment-to-moment objectives). The Super Objective serves an important purpose, adding momentum, complexity, and a dramatic spine to the overall performance; if it is too abstract, or lacking in emotional power, it will fail to influence the actor's portrayal of the character. Though truthful, Super Objectives such as "I want to be happy" or "I want to survive" are not specific or evocative enough to serve as a driving force for the character's existence. Here, we will deepen the connection to the Leading Center by considering a unique take on Super Objectives.

When thinking about your Super Objective, consider utilizing a metaphor, idiom, simple saying or turn of phrase that directly relates to the Leading Center; a well-placed figure of speech tied into a statement about "what the character wants" or "what I want" creates unique and rich physical opportunities. A few examples might include my character wants *to get down to the bottom of it* (Miss Marple or Inspector Poirot) or *to leave their mark on the world* (Happy Loman). Returning to the Leading Center we chose for Argan, perhaps his Super Objective becomes *I want to bowl everyone over*, or *I want to "strike" down any troublemakers in my path*. In layering the Super Objective with the Leading Center, the imagery of a bowling ball comes to full fruition! Argan spends much of the play verbally, and sometimes physically, battling with the feisty maid, Toinette. Here is one example of an exchange between them as Toinette tells Argan she will not allow him to marry off his daughter to a doctor (Moliére n.d., 1.5):

Argan: What have we come to? And what boldness is this for a scrub of a servant to speak in such a way before her master?
Toinette: When a master does not consider what he is doing, a sensible servant should set him right!
Argan: Ah, impudent girl, I will kill you! Come here, come here, let me teach you how to speak.

If the performer playing Argan has a Super Objective of I want to "strike" down any troublemakers and a Leading Center of a bowling ball in the belly, this fusion will create both physical and psychological reasons to move forward with great force, sway side to side, or "roll over" Toinette – just as a bowling ball would careen down the alley, spin in the gutter, or smash through the pins to zany comic effect. In contrast, the actor playing Toinette – a character who uncovers, discovers, and holds many secrets throughout the course of the play – may decide that her Super Objective is "*I want to spill the beans.*" Paired with a Leading Center of frying pan-hands full of hot beans, this choice lends itself to outrageous, bold, and unique physical choices. Even more wonderful is that the audience won't know the inspiration for the dynamic, comical acting choices they are enjoying; they will simply revel in the highly stylized performances.

Two Steps

Before exploring other examples, I want to revisit the two steps of how to approach this technique and offer a list of idioms/sayings to guide you into Super Objective possibilities. Allow your creative instinct to lead the way; you will know when you find the right pairings because they will help you step into the character with ease, feel deeply connected to the text, and move with precision, vigor, and inspiration. As stated earlier, some characters will be better served by starting with step one; others with step two. The ultimate combination of both steps is what matters, not the order!

STEP ONE: Choose an idiom, saying, or phrase that encapsulates the spirit of the character paired with an "I want" or "I need" statement to become your Super Objective. Here is a short list you can choose from if you are simply looking to experiment:

KILL TIME	TASTE YOUR OWN MEDICINE
LET THE CAT OUT OF THE BAG	GIVE THE COLD SHOULDER
GO DOWN IN FLAMES	HIT THE NAIL ON THE HEAD
JUMP ON THE BANDWAGON	ON THIN ICE
CUT SOME SLACK	RAIN ON YOUR PARADE
GETTING OUT OF HAND	THROW CAUTION TO THE WIND
GET YOUR ACT TOGETHER	BURN BRIDGES
HANG IN THERE	HAVE YOUR HEAD IN THE CLOUDS
WRAP YOUR HEAD AROUND	RUN LIKE THE WIND
ADD INSULT TO INJURY	CUTTING CORNERS

STEP TWO: Choose a Leading Center that has a clear location on or within your body, a quality linked to your Super Objective and mobility. If the Super Objective is *I need to get my head out of the clouds*, your Leading Center might become an umbrella extending out of the crown of your head that snaps shut during a windy argument, or lifts you deeper into the clouds when daydreaming, or shields you from the rainy attitude of a negative character.

Putting It All Together With Macbeth

Shakespeare's tragedy *Macbeth* is full of complex characters, bloody murders, and heightened emotions. Macbeth himself transforms from a brave and ambitious man to a guilt-ridden and paranoid one. If we focus on his desire to rise up through the ranks and seize the Scottish throne, an idiom I would offer up as Macbeth's Super Objective is that he wants "*to carve out a niche for himself*." We hear of his ambition throughout the play in speeches such as this one from act I, scene 3:

Macbeth: The Prince of Cumberland! That is a step
On which I must fall down, or else o'erleap,
For in my way it lies. Stars, hide your fires;
Let not light see my black and deep desires.
The eye wink at the hand; yet let that be
Which the eye fears, when it is done, to see.

In light of the idea of carving, let's consider Macbeth's Leading Center to be swords for arms creating rigidity, a physical stoicism as he receives unbelievable prophecies from the Three Witches. When suddenly named the Thane of Cawdor, perhaps Macbeth's sword arms grow; suddenly he is sharpening those "swords," rubbing his arms scene to scene, swinging his arms around as his ambition grows. The physical metaphor becomes literal as he stabs Duncan, fights off Banquo's ghost, then attempts to take on MacDuff. The Super Objective of *"carving out a niche for himself"* paired with the physical manifestation of swordlike arms for Macbeth's Leading Center allows for defined characterization, specific movement qualities, and a distinct physical approach to one of Shakespeare's greatest tragic figures. You'll notice with Argan, the example began with choosing a Leading Center, then a Super Objective; the opposite order with Macbeth. Either makes a valid entry point to character creation. Begin with the image, idea, word, or concept that stirs your imagination and lights up your creative fire.

As ambitious and bold as Macbeth is, Lady Macbeth remains one of Shakespeare's most fierce and vicious characters. With a taste for power and a ruthless nature, she threatens, cajoles, seduces, and manipulates her way to eventual ruin. The expression *"bite the bullet"* urges us to push through something unpleasant. The origins of the phrase are rooted in battlefield surgery, where wounded soldiers were often treated without anesthesia and needed something malleable to bite down on. Here, the saying becomes a dangerous and appropriate Super Objective for Lady M: *I need to bite the bullet*. If her Leading Center then becomes a gun (personal guns called matchlocks were available from fourteenth century onward) shooting outwards from her mouth, suddenly shouting can become launching cannonballs, quietly spitting her words at Macbeth can become tiny piercing bullets, and her rage can fire off threats like a machine gun. Perhaps the "gun" even turns on itself sometimes, creating moments of a personal Russian roulette. You can find multiple moments to explore this Leading Center/Super Objective in one of Lady Macbeth's most famous monologues from act I, scene 5:

Macbeth: The raven himself is hoarse
              That croaks the fatal entrance of Duncan
              Under my battlements. Come, you spirits
              That tend on mortal thoughts, unsex me here,
              And fill me from the crown to the toe top-full
              Of direst cruelty! make thick my blood;
              Stop up the access and passage to remorse,
              That no compunctious visitings of nature
              Shake my fell purpose, nor keep peace between
              The effect and it! Come to my woman's breasts,
              And take my milk for gall, you murdering ministers,

Wherever in your sightless substances
You wait on nature's mischief! Come, thick night,
And pall thee in the dunnest smoke of hell,
That my keen knife see not the wound it makes,
Nor heaven peep through the blanket of the dark,
To cry 'Hold, hold!'

In this scene from act 1, scene 7, consider how this approach heightens the intensity of the conversation! Perhaps Macbeth has his hands at his own throat, worried about their murderous plot and, potentially and metaphorically, slitting his own throat; he is grasping to maintain his Super Objective. Lady Macbeth, frustrated and desperate, could be quietly whispering in his ear, firing tiny bullets like threats into his brain, clinging to her Super Objective.

Macbeth: We will proceed no further in this business.
He hath honored me of late, and I have bought
Golden opinions from all sorts of people,
Which would be worn now in their newest gloss,
Not cast aside so soon.

Lady M: Was the hope drunk
Wherein you dressed yourself? Hath it slept since?
And wakes it now, to look so green and pale
At what it did so freely? From this time
Such I account thy love. Art thou afeard
To be the same in thine own act and valor
As thou art in desire? Wouldst thou have that
Which thou esteem'st the ornament of life
And live a coward in thine own esteem,
Letting "I dare not" wait upon "I would,"
Like the poor cat i' th' adage?

Macbeth: Prithee, peace.
I dare do all that may become a man.
Who dares do more is none.

Lady M: What beast was 't, then,
That made you break this enterprise to me?
When you durst do it, then you were a man;
And to be more than what you were, you would
Be so much more the man. Nor time nor place
Did then adhere, and yet you would make both.
They have made themselves, and that their fitness now
Does unmake you. I have given suck, and know

	How tender 'tis to love the babe that milks me.
	I would, while it was smiling in my face,
	Have plucked my nipple from his boneless gums
	And dashed the brains out, had I so sworn as you
	Have done to this.
Macbeth:	If we should fail –
Lady M:	We fail?
	But screw your courage to the sticking place
	And we'll not fail.

Conclusion

The combination of a carefully selected idiom, saying, or phrase-based Super Objective paired with an evocative, active Leading Center can certainly extend beyond Shakespeare or Molière to Greek tragedy, absurdism, naturalism, or any theatrical "ism," style, or genre, but lends itself to classical pieces and physical style due to the text-driven, metaphor-based Super Objective and the physical specificity of the Leading Center. Let the text, and your gut, be your guide. When you find the right combination(s), the physical storytelling takes on a life of its own and you are moving, thinking, and reacting as the character versus the actor creating the character. One final thought as you dive into this approach: make a choice and try it! Out loud and on your feet. The intellectual exploration of Leading Centers and Super Objectives, while interesting and certainly part of the process, is only one step. As the Asaro Tribe of Indonesia and Papua New Guinea so beautifully claims, "knowledge is only a rumor until it lives in the muscle" (Brown 2017, 7).

Bibliography

Brown, Brené. 2017. *Rising Strong: How the Ability to Reset Transforms the Way We Live, Love, Parent, and Lead.* New York: Random House.
Moliére. n.d. "The Imaginary Invalid." *StageAgent.* Accessed February 20, 2022. https://stageagent.com/shows/play/1939/the-imaginary-invalid/script.
Shakespeare, William. 1974. *Riverside Shakespeare.* Edited by G. Blakemore Evans. Boston: Houghton Mifflin Co.
Stanislavski, Konstantin. 1948. *An Actor Prepares.* New York: Routledge.

3
TACKLING HEIGHTENED TEXT

Miriam Mills

There have been significant changes in acting styles over the past 100 years. We have gone from a robust, theatrical style to what feels to us as a more internalized, subtle, and physically connected technique. This evolution was, at least in part, a consequence of the advent of television. Human behavior that comes into our living rooms is going to require a more reserved imprint. What we taught in the classroom has also evolved substantially. In our theatrical history, actors often utilized set movements and gestures. Today, we find actors searching for individualized integrated movement choices that are discovered and adapted during the rehearsal process. As with many things, the successes also bring challenges: how can these techniques help us when we have to be broad and dynamic? Do these techniques work for all styles of theatre? Are these techniques reliable when dealing with texts that are heightened? What will help guide the actor to the strongest possible performance when tackling Elizabethan or Greek scripts? Considering *King Lear* and *Medea*, this chapter will explore several modern acting pedagogies that might serve actors as they create highly emotional – yet still truthful – performances when given the opportunity to tackle these challenging characters. Truthful implies that the actor expresses the character's humanity within the context of the world of the play.

At my university, I teach a course titled Great Performances in Film. Early in the semester I show excerpts from the silent films of the twenties and thirties, including a scene from *Phantom of the Opera* starring Lon Chaney. Invariably, when I show the unmasking scene, my students begin to laugh. They find the melodramatic style of acting to be, at best, amusing, and offer critiques such as "way over the top" and "weirdly melodramatic." Lon Chaney, who was known as the Man of a Thousand Faces, defended his choices and referred to his Phantom role

DOI: 10.4324/9781003204060-5

as "an extraordinary characterization" (Ebert 2004). "*The Phantom of the Opera* is not a great film if you are concerned with art and subtlety, depth and message . . . but in its fevered melodrama and images of cadaverous romance, it finds a kind of show-biz majesty" (Ebert 2004). Perhaps this is true. If you look carefully, you see Chaney's power and his physical control are evident, and he captivated the audiences of his time. The performance is huge; it is also highly stylized and theatrical but perhaps not believable for today's audiences. How might we proceed with maintaining a believability while still finding a feeling of immenseness in an emotionally charged performance that our students will take seriously?

Let us first define the term "heightened." Often when we refer to heightened text we are referring to more complex language. For the sake of this chapter, heightened text will refer to texts that require a more complex emotional state. The emotions are not hidden or subtextual; they are transparent and expressed to the highest peak of feeling. The "storm scene" (act 3, scene 2) in *King Lear* is a clear illustration.

Lear: Blow, winds and crack your cheeks! rage! blow!
You cataracts and hurricanoes, spout
Till you have drench'd our steeples, drown'd the cocks!

Throughout this scene, we hear the king's helplessness, frustration, suffering, and his intense feelings of defeat, all expressed with great humanity. The backdrop of the storm mirrors the chaos of Lear's mind. For many Lear portrayers, the scene begins at a "10." If the actor portraying Lear chooses to create the highly emotional storm scene in high dramatic fashion, the actor portraying him must find the pinnacle of rage somewhere in the two pages of dialogue between Kent and the Gentleman that precede his entrance. The actor challenged with playing King Lear must find the balance between a twenty-first century believability coupled with a stage dynamic that will captivate and convince the audience.

Where can we begin? Most experts would agree that we start with the text. From what little we know about Elizabethan acting processes, actors did not consider concepts of motivation and relied instead on instinct. Of course, they had the Bard to guide them, as well as clear acting traditions. I suspect that they did not try to be "natural" but to be *real*. Is there a difference? I believe so. What if we just immerse ourselves in the given circumstances of the script? Can we simply delve into the characters' reality? In Stanislavski's method, actors attempt to call up the memory of a similar situation within their own lives and then recreate that situation on stage, thereby realizing the playwright's intent. I maintain that Affective Memory will not help when playing characters like Medea or King Lear. Medea has a wonderful response when asked by Jason why she murdered their children, which translates roughly to "I loathed you more than I loved them" (Euripides 1955, 107). This is not in my memory. Of course, I have felt hate and even wished to hurt those who wronged me, but the hatred expressed by Medea is of a completely different quality and magnitude. It leads to actions that are so heinous, so stunningly awful I can barely comprehend them. Now, I do not have any parallel experiences in my life that could be used to make such given circumstances believable. Having such hatred is not in my memory. In a discussion once with respected acting teacher Anthony Abeson, he likened this to the line in act 1 of *The Crucible* when Abigail says, "I saw Indians smash my dear parents' heads on the pillow next to mine" (Miller 1959, 17). Personally, I do not even have that level of loss in my psyche. To use a situation that brings you a different kind of pain, such as "I saw my dog get run over by a car" is, in Abeson's estimation, not nearly strong enough. It essentially demeans the reality of the character.

If we accept the premise that Affective Memory might not serve us adequately, we then need to focus on using our imagination. Most actors realize that they have an ability to empathize with and transport themselves in any character's given circumstances. Stella Adler attempted to find a way to merge Affective Memory with imagination through Adler's "magic if." In her text on *The Technique of Acting*, she offers, "You must not take yourself and put that into Hamlet. . . . The truth of the character is not found in you, but in the circumstances" (Adler 1988, 32). Adler further asks the American actor to realize that they "greatly underestimate the wealth of their collective consciousness." I believe that she means we are so much more than just our immediate memory. "You must be made aware of how rich your memory is, for the collective memory of Man is such that he forgets nothing he has ever seen, or heard, or read about or touched" (Adler 1988, 17). It is not just what we know that we know, it is also what we are not even aware of that we know.

Imagination is a skill that must be mastered. In one exercise, Adler asks the actor to imagine a list of things you can see in your mind that are not currently present. Looking out through a window, actors imagine a number of scenarios – a child skipping rope, a man pulling a wagon – and describe what they look like, what they are wearing, even what the weather might be like. The process begins with observation and then evolves into more dynamic scenarios. For instance, imagine a vicious dog barking at a small boy or seeing a serious car crash. Developing imaginative skills is vital in marrying the text to your performance.

Let's use our imagination toward the character of Medea. Her history is essential in tackling her character. Medea is the daughter of King Aeetes, who is a son of the god Helios and brother to the goddess Circe. When Medea falls in love with Jason, she decides to help him betray her father and may have killed her brother Absyrtus in the process. Even with an abbreviated background story, the questions you begin asking might include, What was it like to grow up in a family of immortals? What was her relationship with her father? With her brother? What did they look like? What did her future look like before Jason arrived? What was the land of Colchis like? Imagine the women and children. Try to picture the houses and the land. And what of Jason? What qualities drew her to him? What was Jason wearing? Why would she betray her father? What was it like having to flee her home? Did she actually kill her brother, or did something else happen to him? What does she remember most about Colchis? Does she miss it? These questions and many more begin the process of bonding with the given circumstances of the play.

In my mind, Medea is not a play about vengeance but rather about love gone horribly wrong. In order to discover the depths of her hate, you first have to review the circumstances of her love. Medea gives so much of it to Jason only to have him betray her and have her banished. Most of us have felt the pain of betrayal. In Act One, she says the following:

> It's all over my friends; I would gladly die. Life has lost its savor. The man who was everything to me, well he knows it, has turned out to be the basest of men. Of all creatures that feel and think, we women are the unhappiest species. . . . Woman in most respects is a timid creature, with no heart for strife and aghast at the sight of steel; but wronged in love, there is no heart more murderous than hers.
>
> *(Euripides 1936, 37)*

Her rage and pain are so clear, so deep. Her cries are rooted in the depth of her love. Jason's smell, his body, his lips, his taste, and his touch all must be created in the mind of the actor. The actor playing Medea must consider what it feels like to lose hope; only then can we begin to recreate her heinous acts.

Connecting With Medea

1. Consider Medea's full story. Answer the questions posed previously. Considering Medea's history, it is unlikely that you have anything to compare with this. You, therefore, search your collective memory for horrors from our past. Using a newspaper, television images, or reading of the history from that specific time, consider what this looks like. Imagine, for example, that you are in a war zone. It does not need to be Colchis. What about Vietnam or Ukraine or Afghanistan? Create the smells, the colors of destruction, the blood. Consider the loss of life and how it might impact you if the loss included someone you love very much. By placing yourself in this environment, you begin to feel that there is so much at stake. You might begin to understand Medea's choices.
2. Medea begins the play in almost unimaginable pain. The actor needs to recreate pain in their imagination. It does not mean that the actor hurts themselves, but imagining the pain will bring the actor closer to the reality of Medea's pain. Discovering what imaginative hurt triggers your own pain, you begin to embrace the character's pain. To start embracing her pain, try to use an

"as if" to imagine the sensation of pain. Perhaps start with something physical – a needle in the eye, a broken knee, passing a kidney stone. When coupling that with her sense of total betrayal and abandonment, you begin to specify her agony. There is a marriage between physical and emotional pain. What if the person I have given all to decides to betray me? What does that look like? Do not base this on your real life but create an "as if." I find that imaginative pain can be much more theatrical and dynamic then substitution, in these circumstances.
3. Justify the circumstances. So many heinous acts are done with justification, and we shape our visions in so many self-centered ways. Medea might view Jason as deserving of pain. Actors can become blocked when they start judging the actions of a character, but in searching for a "first-person" justification, you spark the vital empathy needed to create the character. You, of course, would never hurt your children, but Medea believes that her choices are right. "I will not allow you to continue on as if nothing has happened. I will stop your scheme. I will not allow the indignity of your treatment to go unanswered."
4. Locate the character in your body. Do her movements begin in a specific physical center? How is that center different from yours? How might that influence her posture? Her walk? How does she gesture as she speaks? How does she express affection?

The emotional dynamic of Adler's techniques are not just mental exercises. They help to guide us in finding ways to explore the emotional dynamic that is required for a King Lear or a Medea. It is not enough to imagine the given circumstances. How does the actor begin to locate the character in the body? It does not just come from thought. Therefore, in conjunction with Adler, let's consider how we might layer Adler's work with the physical manifestations of Jerzy Grotowski's actions to approach the physical truth of heightened character choices. Grotowski urges us not to search for the emotional state but for the physical. Grotowski always stresses that the work on physical actions is the key to the actor's craft. An actor must be able to repeat the same score many times, and it must be alive and precise each time. How can we do this? What can an actor fix, make secure? His line of physical actions? (Richards and Grotowski 1995, 31).

Grotowski was wary of over-emoting without a solid foundation in truth. "It is not just the heightened emotions but the connection to the actions and the body and the given circumstances" (Richards and Grotowski 1995, 66). Grotowski viewed truth as a marriage between the body and the inner core in his psycho-physical technique. We often hear about actors needing to "be in their body," and there is an implied expectation that we agree on what those words mean. Most of us would define that as creating a physical form of expression that might include stillness or full movement. Being in the body implies mindfulness of choice. Thomas Richards, Grotowski's "essential collaborator," reminds the reader that physical form is not just movement. The actors must be "linked to the inner logic of the persons in their specific circumstances" (Richards and Grotowski 1995, 76). To begin the process of finding the physical form, we begin from a position of readiness and evolve stretches and observations referred to as "watching" before learning to move silently and, of course, attentively.

This is, of course, very difficult on many levels. Actors worry about portraying emotions and are commonly taught that what the other actor on stage is doing should have a profound effect on our own actions and reactions. With Grotowski, these individual character objectives are not connected to your partner but more squarely focused on your own connection to your body and actions. Grotowski referred to this as the "seeds of organicity" (Richards and Grotowski 1995, 77).

> I understood it to mean not forced, something natural, in the way that a cat's movements are natural. If I observe a cat, I notice that all of its movements are in their place, its body thinks for itself. In the cat, there is no discursive mind to block immediate organic reaction, to get in the way. Organicity can also be in the man, but it is almost always blocked by a mind that is not doing its job, a mind that tries to conduct the body, thinking quickly and telling the body what to do and how.
>
> *(Richards and Grotowski 1995, 66)*

When the actor gives up intellectual control of the body and allows the body to function freely, the truth is allowed to emerge.

Physical actions are not activities, such as cleaning the floor, washing the dishes, smoking the pipe. Grotowski says,

> It is easy to confuse physical actions with movements. If I am walking toward the door, it is not an action but a movement. But if I am walking toward the door to contest "your stupid question," to threaten you that I will break up the conference, there will be a cycle of little actions and not just a movement.
>
> *(Richards and Grotowski 1995, 76)*

It is interesting that Grotowski and Adler agree on allowing your fantasies to guide your physical actions.

> Through acting you might be remembering some moment in your life or someone close to you, or a concrete event from your fantasy that never happened, that you always wished had happened.... What did I do in the circumstances of this memory? Or: What, precisely, would be my line of physical behavior if this fantasy had actually happened?
>
> *(Richards and Grotowski 1995, 77)*

Discovering the physical truth of imagination can bring the actor to the heightened emotion required for the text. If you concern yourself with the emotion instead of the physical action, you risk diminishing the very truth and power you seek.

How, specifically, can actors use the Grotowski method in their rehearsal process.? Grotowski suggests a combination of spontaneity and discipline (1968, 39). In his text *Towards a Poor Theatre*, he spells out his process. He requests that the actor do warm-ups, then loosen up the muscles, followed by what he refers to as "plastic" exercises using the techniques of Emile Jacques-Dalcroze to study *opposite vectors*, when the body creates two opposing movements at the same time – for instance, taking with the hands and rejecting with the feet. He then asks the actor to do exercises in composition, such as creating an association with an animal.

How does the actor begin to locate the animal that would work for the character? If playing King Lear, you might associate Lear with a lion, or a rabid or wounded dog, embodying relevant, non-stereotypical physical characteristics. Creating the body of the animal in a nonrealistic way embeds the image of the animal in the actor's mind. This allows the actor to strengthen their objectives and discover the freedom of play, using the behavior of an animal as a starting point.

Losing one's inhibitions is essential to creating an uber-character. The actor must move beyond who they think they are and be willing to expose themselves to the character's truth, circumstances, and psyche (Grotowski 1968, 44). It is about rehearsing, and then rehearsing some more; in discipline, the actor finds the creative path.

Using King Lear as an example, let's examine how playing with an animal prototype leads the actor to discover the character's gait, body, and center. Starting at the forehead and ending with the toes, we will explore one lead at a time, coupling animal movements with the text of the character. As you explore, pay attention to what feels right, instinctively. You might even discover that the lead evolves over the course of the play. Lead refers to what body part "in front" and leads the rest of the body in movement. Perhaps Lear's lead starts in the nose (revealing his imperious and conceited nature) and moves to his knees by the end of the play (when he is broken and has lost everything); maybe he starts in his groin (full of himself and focused only on his own pleasure) and slowly shifts to his shoulders (as the weight of his decisions fall on him more heavily). This analysis allows the actor to explore how emotional changes evolve in the body. In act 1, scene 1, Lear feels betrayed by his youngest daughter, Cordelia, who will not publicly proclaim her love for him. Lear disinherits and shames her, but the King of France offers to marry her anyway, provoking this response:

Lear: Thou hast her, France. Let her be thine, for we
 Have no such daughter, nor shall ever see
 That face of hers again. *[To Cordelia.]* Therefore begone

Without our grace, our love, our benison. –
Come, noble Burgundy.

Physicalizing Lear

1. Discover the body impulses and work to create stretches that bring you to a state of readiness. Imagine, for instance, that you are working to attack someone. Do not move to the attack but to the position of being ready to attack. What is the stretch in that position? How does your body prepare to respond to whatever happens? Lear, in his first scene with his daughters, demands evidence of their love, and when it is not received, he pounces. Perhaps Lear is expecting one of them to refuse and is ready for a fight. The state of readiness allows the actor to physically and emotionally come into total focus. It is about being prepared to respond to whatever happens.
2. Decide on an animal that will invite discoveries in how, abstractly, the animal is akin to the character. Is Lear, in the opening scene, a wounded bird? A charging rhino? A hungry lion? A patient, venomous snake? Find the animal in your body, being as specific as possible; a crow is not an eagle. Do you find that King Lear is stubborn like a mule or obstinate like a badger? Does his stubbornness define him? Really search for the details that will serve you in this discovery process by considering how the nature of the animal connects to the nature of Lear.
3. Work the character objectives into the body structure by considering how the animal moves. Are there specific subtle movements in the spine or limbs or head that will help marry the animal with the human? Do not dictate the movements. Let the body find the actions. Trusting the body to find the organic truth with time, the body structure will understand. This might begin with simple walking with those animal instincts. What movements begin to surface? Play with those movements. Expand them. Allow the full body to follow through from the simple impulse.
4. Trusting the body to find the organic truth, with time, the body structure will understand. This might begin with simple walking with those animal instincts. What movements begin to surface? Play with those movements. Expand them. Allow the full body to follow through from the simple impulse.
5. Remember that the emotions will be there when the body is found. Do not be concerned with finding the emotion. Trust that the emotion will be there when the truth of the physical reality is found.

Once an animal-infused character is established, actors may pair up and use their text (or improvised text) and their newly discovered physicality to spar with each other both verbally and physically, seeing how the animal manifests itself in the tactical variety they choose.

Ultimately, it is not just the mind that creates the character but the body. When we look to traditions in acting technique, this philosophy appears again and again. Even in Asia, we find agreement with Grotowski's philosophy in the teaching of Tadashi Suzuki, who also embraces movement as a way to find the proper characterizations needed. We need to develop our imagination skills and find both discipline and creative physicalization to bring them to life. Since scientists have already proven that our emotional states impact our bodies, it is only logical that if the actor locates the body's truth in the character, it will impact the mind (Walbott 1998, 879–96).

Both Adler and Grotowski advocate for a marriage between the physical and the psychological by first finding the body of the character. For the actor to impose a physical choice without the exploration might tend to be problematic and lead to indication, rather than truthfulness. Acting is a two-way street that navigates a path between the mind, the body, and the heart, and blending them seems the best way of living a fully challenged and artistic life.

Bibliography

Adler, Stella. 1988. *The Technique of Acting*. New York: Bantam Books.
Barton, John, and Trevor Nunn. 1984. *Playing Shakespeare: An Actor's Guide*. New York: Anchor Books.
Ebert, Roger. 2004. "The Phantom of the Opera Movie Review." *RogerEbert.com*, December 14. www.rogerebert.com/reviews/great-movie-the-phantom-of-the-opera-1925.
Euripides. 1936. *Ten Plays by Euripides*. Translated by Moses Hadas and John McLean. New York: Bantam.
———. 1955. *Euripides I*. Translated by David Grene and Richmond Lattimore. Chicago: University of Chicago Press.
Grotowski, Jerzy. 1968. *Towards a Poor Theatre*. Holstebro: Odin Teatrets Forlag.
Miller, Arthur. 1959. *The Crucible: A Play in Four Acts*. New York, NY: Bantam.
Petit, Lenard. 2010. *The Michael Chekhov Handbook for Actor*. London: Routledge.
Richards, Thomas, and Jerzy Grotowski. 1995. *At Work with Grotowski on Physical Actions*. London: Routledge.
Shakespeare, William. 1939. *The Kittredge Shakespeare*. Boston: Ginn and Co.
Suzuki, Tadashi. 1985. *The Way of Acting: The Theatre Writings Of Tadashi Suzuki*. New York: Theatre Communications Group.
Walbott, H. G. 1998. "Bodily Expression of Emotion." *European Journal of Social Psychology* 28 (6): 879–96.

4
(3" × 5") × 40

A Journey to Embodiment

Louis Fantasia

In the summer of 1981, I was leading a workshop on Brecht for students at the (then) American College in Paris, and we needed a venue for a weekend visit to London. My friend and colleague Elaine Turner, of Warwick University, arranged for us to use The Museum of the Shakespearean Stage, a warehouse in South London with little in it except a large stuffed bear, a replica of the Restoration Cockpit stage, and Sam Wanamaker, the visionary American actor who was the driving force behind the rebuilding of Shakespeare's Globe.

Perched in the balcony over the Cockpit, Sam watched me work. I had no idea who the man in the balcony was until he introduced himself and invited me to join the Globe project. "This is where we're going to rebuild Shakespeare's theatre," he said. I tried not to be too skeptical. There wasn't even a hole in the ground at the time. But I found myself saying yes to Sam, as most people did. Over the next two decades, I directed two of the Globe's institutes (one for university acting and directing students; the other for high school English and drama teachers) and served on the Globe's US board, as well as being its education director in Southern California. In 1996, I was the first American to direct on the reconstructed stage, with a production of *Much Ado About Nothing* with students from Hugh Richmond's Shakespeare program at UC Berkeley. This is, I must admit, an odd list of accomplishments for someone who failed "Shakespeare" as an undergraduate at Georgetown and who avoided "Shakespeare" for most of his early career as a director. But there I was, present at the creation of Shakespeare's Globe.

Since then I have been lucky enough to travel the world – early on for the Globe; later, in my own right – directing and teaching "Shakespeare." Almost everything I used in my work was written down on two worn 3" × 5" index cards that I carried with me from the beginning. One card had two columns:

DOI: 10.4324/9781003204060-6

Nouns	I. About
Verbs	II. Tune
I/thou	III. Texture
adj./adv.	IV. End
rep. for breath	

. . . and a line of code at the bottom: "u-/u-/u-/u-/u-."

The second 3" × 5" card had simply two lines on it: first, "why, etc.??," and below that, "order/disorder/rebellion – yes? no? – 2nd order."

From those index cards, which were based on exercises I had devised in those summer programs for Sam, I could deliver a 30-minute lecture, or a weekend workshop, or a semester-long class. They served as the basis for my 2002 book, *Instant Shakespeare*, and for this chapter. As much as these notes have stayed the same over the years, they have changed, as I have, and as has "Shakespeare," along with the world we inhabit with him and his works. Over this period, my job, I felt, was not to tell you – teachers, performers, readers, educators, directors, producers, scholars – what "Shakespeare" was about or what his works meant, but to offer a set of tools that might help you in your own search for meaning in his plays and poems. I still believe that.

I

My starting point, scribbled on my 3" × 5" cards as "why, etc.??", is a question I call the "Shakespeare Paradigm": *Why does this particular character say these particular words in this particular order at this particular moment?*

What is the difference between a character who says, "So foul and fair a day I have not seen," and one who says, "So fair and foul a day I have not seen"? Perhaps one sees the glass half empty and the other half full? Or one has a propensity toward evil the other doesn't? I don't know for sure, but there is a difference, which is why I am opposed to paraphrasing, and worse, those online "translations." What drives me, in any encounter with the text, is a need to discover the "why." This leads to a contradiction that I will explore later in this chapter, and that is that *language is the least important element in Shakespeare*. Let me explain:

> If, while cooking dinner, you accidentally put your hand on a hot stove, you say "Ouch!" (or a stronger expletive) and then pull your hand away. You do not say "Ouch!" and put your hand on the stove: *impulse precedes language*. Our job, at this stage of reading, is to discover the *impulse*, or, more precisely, the possible impulses that produce and propel the language of the play. "*Why does this particular character say these particular words in this particular order at this particular moment?*" This is the microcosmic, inch-by-inch study of the script that is often

ignored by those who bring a "reading" or "concept" to the text which cannot be justified by what the words actually mean. Let me explain:

> Once, at a workshop for educators, a very experienced English/drama teacher was directing a group of peers in a scene from *A Midsummer Night's Dream*

(2.1.62–65)

Oberon: Ill met by moonlight, proud Titania.
Titania: What, jealous Oberon? Fairies, skip hence.
 I have forsworn his bed and company.
Oberon: Tarry, rash wanton. Am not I thy lord?[1]

I let the scene play out for exactly these four lines before stopping the group and asking them to repeat the scene. "What's wrong with the scene?" I asked. Again the same four lines, and again I stopped the scene and asked what was wrong. There was some outrage that I hadn't been fair to the teacher/director, hadn't let the scene "evolve," and that I was looking for some sort of "right" answer. We did the scene one more time, stopping at the fourth line, "Tarry, rash wanton. Am not I thy lord?" Finally, after an excruciatingly long silence, one teacher, not in the performing group, spoke up. "Why does Oberon say 'tarry' if Titania isn't going anywhere?" Exactly. How Titania goes, what she's wearing, who you cast in the role, and how you choose to portray (if you do) the sexual/political dynamics of their relationship are all up for discussion and debate – interpretation. What is not debatable is that she *must move* for Oberon to have the *impulse* to make her "tarry." It's all about the "why, etc."

Remembering that we want to progress from two-dimensional analysis to three-dimensional performance, then we need to physically embody the meanings of the words we are exploring. Back to my index cards:

Nouns	I.	About
Verbs	II.	Tune
I/thou	III.	Texture
adj./adv.	IV.	End
rep. for breath		

These are what I call "frog overlays." In my youth, biology books featured transparencies of dead frogs: the circulatory system, nervous system, skeletal system, and so on. Laying these transparencies on top of one another, you got a very clear picture of a dead frog. Similarly, the "overlays" that follow are analytic tools, giving you a very clear picture of a two-dimensional, *dead* text. They are tools for analysis, not interpretation.

1. *Make the nouns sound like what they mean.* Image (as well as impulse) precedes language. Characters *choose* their words at a specific moment, in a specific order, because it is the *only* way they can describe the image they see. Why does Macbeth *choose* to say, "Is this a *dagger* which I see before me," and not *hatchet*, or *stiletto*? Why does Juliet *choose* to say, "Gallop apace, ye fiery footed *steeds*," instead of *horses*, or *nags*? Characters in action have agency. They, as we bring them to life, make choices about the language they use. What exactly is Portia's idea of the "quality of mercy" (*Mer*, 4.1.190) or Isabella's four-fold cry for "justice" (*MM*, 5.1.27)? Our job is to make the audience see exactly the kind of dagger, steed, mercy, or justice that these characters see, at the specific moment they see it. This is along the lines of what T.S. Eliot meant by the "objective correlative": the object described (dagger/steed/mercy) elicits a specific image (one, and only one, kind of dagger), which evokes a specific emotional response, drawing the audience deeper into the world of the play.[2]
2. *Push the verbs.* Verbs are action words. Plays are about action. Push the verbs to move the action forward. "*Gallop* apace, ye fiery-footed steeds!" "*Is* this a dagger . . ." etc. Use the verbs to drive the line! Look at the forward energy needed here. Juliet doesn't think or act word by word. Why should we? (*R&J*, 3.2.21–27):

    > Juliet: *Come*, gentle night; *come*, loving black-browed night,
    > *Give* me my Romeo, and when I *shall die*,
    > *Take* him and *cut* him out in little stars,
    > And he *will make* the face of heaven so fine
    > That all the world *will be* in love with night
    > And *pay* no worship to the garish sun.

3. *Leave the adjectives and adverbs alone.* Look again at Juliet's speech. There's no need to gild the lily. Shakespeare is quite capable of embellishing his own images. But how many times have we heard Juliet emphasize "loving," "black-browed," "little" stars, "so fine," "all" the world, and "garish" sun, turning the speech into hyperactive, unintelligible mush? Tell the story by playing the nouns and verbs. In typing classes, a popular practice test often used the sentence, "The quick brown fox jumps over the lazy dog." What is the essence of this lengthy sentence? "Fox jumps dog." It is a headline, made up of nouns and a verb, that grabs our attention. The adverbs and adjectives (quick, brown, lazy, over, etc.) are colorful filler, but not essential. Tell the story and trust your audience.
4. *Play the "I/thou" relationships.* Who are you talking to, and what are you talking about? "I/thou" and "I/it" were the two great phrases of theologian Martin Buber (1878–1965). Buber was one of the leading philosophers of the twentieth century, and his work was influential to both modern Jewish and Christian thought. "I/thou" expresses mutuality and recognition, while

"I/it" expresses functional behavior. I use them on a much simpler level. Take Macbeth's speech (*Mac*, 2.1.42–4):

Macbeth: Is this a dagger which I see before me,
The handle toward my hand? Come, let me clutch thee.
I have thee not, and yet I see thee still . . .

Who is Macbeth talking to in the first line and a half? It might be himself. It might be the audience or even the gods, but we know it is *not* the dagger, because he shifts gears and turns his attention to the dagger on the next half line. He continues until he shifts again, turning to the "real" dagger:

Macbeth: I see thee yet, in form as palpable
As this which now I draw . . .

Notice how Shakespeare puts the iambic stress on "this." What does that tell you? (Draw the dagger!).

Who are you talking to, and what are you talking about? This "partnering" should be clear on every line and was one of the great discoveries on the Globe stage: Shakespeare's monologues are not interior, stream of consciousness musings. They are debates and discussions with and to members of a specific audience whom you are trying to convince.

5. *Repunctuate for breath.* Don't trust the editors! Modern editors, for all sorts of reasons, tend to over-punctuate Shakespeare. This is not to advocate for the primacy of the First Folio, as I think the Quarto editions deserve careful study as well, and the Folio is rife with typographical errors and compromises. It simply means you pause where you need to breathe (usually at a thought change), not where some editor tells you to. Sometimes the pause is longer (periods, colons, dashes), sometimes shorter (commas, semicolons), but it is almost always tied to a thought, which is tied to the breath. *Acting is a study of the breath.* An example of editors complicating our work can be seen in *Antony and Cleopatra*. Caesar August hears the news of Marc Antony's death, and even though the two have been at war, he says the following (*A&C*, 5.1.31–33):

Caesar: Look you sad friends,
The gods rebuke me, but it is tidings
To wash the eyes of kings.   (First Folio 1623)
Caesar: Look **you, sad** friends,
The gods rebuke me, but it is **a** tidings
To wash the eyes of kings.   (Third Folio 1663)

Caesar: Look you **sad, friends**?
　　　　　The gods rebuke me, but it is **a** tidings
　　　　　To wash the eyes of kings.　　　(Shakespeare 1954)
Caesar: Look you **sad, friends**?
　　　　　The gods rebuke me, but **it is tidings**
　　　　　To wash the eyes of kings.　　　(Folger Digital Text 2022)

Which do you play? *You* must decide, choose, and take responsibility for the words that come out of your mouth. This is why I advocate using as many different editions of a text as possible in rehearsal, so that you can see what the editors – and not Shakespeare – have done to the play. Too often we wind up *playing the punctuation* (pausing for commas, etc.) and not the play itself. (The *King Lear* scene in the next section is an example of how a single punctuation mark can change an entire characterization.)

II

We need some sort of "macro" frame on which to hang our "micro," line-by-line discoveries. How do we continue this transition from two-dimensional text to three-dimensional events and get these dead frogs up on their feet? Let's begin with a view of the world that I believe is found in the majority of Shakespeare's plays: a worldview of disorder, restored order, more rebellion, and order yet again restored:

1. *Disorder:* when the play begins, the world is in chaos;
2. *Order 1:* an inadequate solution imposed by a Duke or King, resulting in
3. *Rebellion:* against that Duke or King (successful in comedy; unsuccessful in tragedy), leading to
4. *Order 2:* the installation of a new (or renewed) Duke or King, resulting in a less satisfying resolution of the play.

Take *Macbeth*: the disorder of the opening revolt and Thane of Cawdor's treason is quickly put down by Duncan's establishment of a new order centered on Malcolm, his son. There is a rebellion against this order, as Macbeth moves to take the throne. It is not successful (if your head is on a pike, you did not succeed, even if you were a tyrant for a while). A second order is then restored as Malcolm takes the throne. It is "less satisfying" in that I have never seen a production of *Macbeth* where anyone actually wants Malcom to be king. What we want, and where the essence of the tragedy lies, is for Macbeth's better angels to have won the day and made a "good" Macbeth worthy to be king. So much potential wasted! Whether Shakespeare was conscious of this pattern or not, I don't know, but the value of this structure is that it informs you where you, the character, are in your own narrative. Knowing that a character will enter, see the glass as half empty, rebel, and ultimately fail begins to lay out a set of dots for you, as an actor, to connect in your rehearsal process. To this we add a second frame or skeleton, again from my 40-year-old file cards:

1. What's the play about?
2. What's the tune?
3. What's the texture?
4. What's the end?

Let us start with the easy ones first: *what's the end?*

The end is on the last page. *Macbeth* does not end with the death of Macbeth, nor does Hamlet end with the death of the melancholy prince. Malcolm is to be crowned at Scone, and all the Scottish thanes will now be earls. Macbeth's ambition was to be Thane-of-this and Thane-of-that, and now all of that intrigue and murder have been rendered meaningless. Only Malcolm knows the new rules. Hamlet's body (and the bodies of Claudius and Gertrude, depending on whether you follow the Folio or Quarto) is carried off, and the stage is left to conquering Fortinbras and possibly Horatio, who has already started bending the truth to his advantage. Take the vaguely creepy last page of *Midsummer*, or the awkward epilogue to *As You Like It*. What do these endings tell you about the plays? Often they undercut our comfortable assumptions of what the play might be about. Certainly you can cut these endings, change them, revise them, or comment on or with them, but do so knowing that those edits will change what the previous 95% of the play is now about.

What's the tune? Imagine you are at a musical, say, *Hello, Dolly!*, and you leave the theatre whistling "Put on Your Sunday Clothes." Obviously you had a good time, but something is wrong. The production put the emphasis on the wrong tune. They told the wrong story. They focused the play on the wrong characters. How do we apply this lesson to Shakespeare? I'm not talking about "theme" here. I am being literal: what's the *tune*, the word or image, on every page?

Macbeth is pretty straightforward: it's blood. From the pricking of the witch's thumb to the tyrant's head on a pike, every page of the play is steeped in blood. What's on every page of *Hamlet?* Rot – ghosts, graves, enseaméd beds, poisoned ears, rotting corpses, everything is rotten in Denmark. *Romeo and Juliet?* Light – stars, fires, blades of steel flashing in the night, all extinguished as quickly as young love. While knowing this might help a director or designer in staging the play, how does it help an actor embody the text? Very simply: what do you *do* with this blood, or rot, or light? How do you handle it, taste it, feel it, play with it, create it? This is you making physical, specific choices. "There's blood upon thy face," says Macbeth to one of Banquo's Murderers (*Mac.*, 3.4.14). Just imagine what you can do – physically and specifically – in that one moment to reveal (a) Macbeth's character and (b) where he is in his own narrative.

This leads us to *What's the texture?* What kind of blood, rot, light do you want on stage? What are you trying to make visible and palpable? You might think of "texture" as "style," but style is ambiguous and intellectual. Texture is physical, a real-world choice: candlelight for the Capulets' ball or disco mirror balls? Thick, mossy brownish blood for Scotland or high-tech acrylic red? How do I show the "rot" that devoured old King Hamlet from the inside out and is now devouring his country and eating up his son? What about the "nothingness" in *Lear*, or the "mercy" in *Merchant*, or the "justice" in *Measure*? What type of actor best fits physically and vocally within a given texture and so on?

Suddenly we find ourselves in the world of casting, costuming, movement – the world of interpretation! There are no longer any right answers, only choices that will work or not work. "There's blood upon thy face . . ." Do I wipe it off, taste it, terrify the poor Murderer so that he scrubs his face clean in front of me? What am I trying to show? *What's the play about?* A Macbeth who, with almost Hannibal Lecter–like glee, gets to taste his victim's blood, is in a different play and world from a Macbeth who, with a glance, can so terrify a brutal murderer that the man wipes his face clean like a guilty schoolboy. This is what I meant earlier by "possible impulses." Either choice (and plenty more) will work, but which one best fulfills your vision of *what the play is about*?

By this, I don't mean the English-class essay answer that says *Macbeth* is "about" ambition. If you ever need to write such a paper, then "love is blind" will do for all the comedies and "absolute power corrupts absolutely" will work for everything else Shakespeare wrote. What I am talking about is *interpretation in performance*. What is the specific point and purpose of your production? What are you trying to say with this specific text, at this specific moment, to this specific audience, in this specific space? What is there about a bloody tyrant, or star-crossed lovers, or a possibly mad prince, that only *you* can say at this time, that still serves and respects the text? The difficulty in forming this interpretation, comes, as I have hinted at in the Macbeth/Murderer dialogue, in the space *between* the words and not in the words themselves. Again, take the earlier workshop teacher's *Midsummer Night's Dream* scene:

Oberon: Ill met by moonlight, proud Titania.
Titania: What, jealous Oberon? Fairies, skip hence.
 I have forsworn his bed and company.
Oberon: Tarry, rash wanton. Am not I thy lord?

At what point do the Fairies "skip hence"? Immediately here or after "company"? What makes Titania turn back? What prompts Oberon's command to "tarry"? The fact that he calls her a "wanton"? Or that he still thinks he is her "lord"? Had the teacher taken the time to explore these few options, rather than trying to mount a half dozen pages of iambic pentameter, everyone involved would have had a much richer experience.

The silence between the lines, the white space on the page, is an unexplored block of potentiality and possibility waiting to be discovered, mined, and molded. It is the essence of the theatrical event, and *an event occurs every time there is a change in a relationship on stage.*

We build the forward momentum of a play by creating a series of ever-escalating events that leads to the crisis, climax, recognition, and reversal of the play. Even epic or postmodern plays turn on these events: something happens to somebody, which causes something to happen to somebody else, and so on, until a terrible reckoning is achieved. Look at this exchange from *King Lear* (1.1.94–101), which illustrates the concept of the "space between the lines":

Lear:	What can you say to draw
	A third more opulent than your sisters?
	Speak.
Cordelia:	Nothing, my Lord.
[*Lear:*	Nothing? (!)
Cordelia:	Nothing.]
Lear:	Nothing will come of nothing. Speak again,
Cordelia:	Unhappy that I am, I cannot heave
	My heart into my mouth . . .

First, let's note some details: (1) the lines in square brackets appear only in the Folio. The 1608 Quarto reads: "*Cord.* Nothing my Lord./*Lear.* How, nothing can come of nothing, speake (againe)*"*; (2) some editors (to the point I made earlier) substitute an exclamation mark (!) for the Folio's question mark (?), neither of which appears in the Quarto. What does this do to the scene? The exclamation mark (which editors justify on the grounds that the two marks were used interchangeably by Elizabethan typesetters) indicates an angry or insulted Lear, one with a short fuse. The Folio's question mark implies a kinder, gentler Lear, one who might be a little deaf or is giving his daughter a second chance. Which one do you want to play? Which Lear is your performance about? Do not let the editor dictate your interpretation. Use multiple editions (including Folio and Quarto facsimiles, if available) throughout your rehearsal process. *What's the play about?* With that in mind, let's return to the exercise:

Lear:	What can you say to draw
	A third more opulent than your sisters?
	Speak.
Cordelia:	Nothing, my Lord.

Lear: Nothing? (!)
Cordelia: Nothing.
Lear: Nothing will come of nothing. Speak again,
Cordelia: Unhappy that I am, I cannot heave
My heart into my mouth . . .

How long or short is the silence between Lear and Cordelia?

With a partner, try running this brief dialogue four times. The first time, let the lines overlap; Cordelia will be as rash and impulsive as her father (and he will be the Lear of the exclamation mark). Then, run the scene with a count of three between the lines; father and daughter will sound like reasonable people, disagreeing. Extend the silence to five beats and watch the tension grow. Stretch it to a seven count, and the silence becomes devastating, with Lear publicly humiliating his daughter and she defying him with all her might.

The scene, characters, and play have totally changed by playing the space between the lines. The space – the silence – between the lines is so powerful because it is the space for breath, and as mentioned earlier, *acting is a study of the breath*. No idea can be expressed in performance without the breath. The study of the breath is the study of impulses (remember our hot stove). The language of impulses is the language of wants and needs, the language of desire. Every character on stage wants something and needs something, and often those wants and needs conflict (Macbeth might want "power" but needs "security," etc.).[3]

Nothing in Shakespeare's language will tell you how to play the silences or even where to find them within lines of iambic pentameter (the "u-/u-/u-/u-/u-" from my cards). For this you need *inspiration* – and I mean that literally.

In Shakespeare's day "inspiration" meant "the drawing of air into the lungs." Two hundred years earlier, it meant divine influence on a person (inspiration from the Holy Ghost, for example). It wasn't until the nineteenth century that it took on the meaning of moving or influencing the intellect or emotions.[4] So for Shakespeare, you literally need to take a breath and fill your lungs in order to be inspired . . . and then what? You have to "expire" and let the breath out. Expiration is "the last emission of breath; death."[5] The only way to avoid death, on stage and off, is through "inspiration," and taking another breath in.

Acting, as a study of the breath, is the constant exercise of inspiration and expiration. We use our breath to bring to life the ephemeral, three-dimensional nature of the theatrical event, which is defined by – and subject to – venue, voice, and time, the three elements that make up the ephemeral nature of the theatrical event.

III

We manipulate the essentially fixed nature of venue through voice and time. We manipulate the essentially human nature of voice by means of venue and time. And finally, we manipulate the essentially subjective nature of time through the use of voice and venue. There can be no theatrical event without venue. Venue implies potential: this fixed space can become an infinite variety of other spaces, transporting us away from our everyday lives. No event can take place without an address. No one can create if the right to venue, free from censorship, exorbitant rents, and arbitrary exclusion, is denied. Only then can we assemble and achieve inspiration from our voices.

There can be no theatrical event without voice. Voice is the uniquely human power of utterance, making ourselves known and understood in the world. When a child is born, he or she has the potential to speak every language in the world, classical and modern, living or dead. Only our customs and fears limit our potential. Only in the theatre, I think, do we have the possibility of finding a venue in which we can raise our voices so that our own potential can overcome and transform our own customs and fears. Voice means the right and opportunity to be heard. And we can be heard only over time.

There can be no theatrical event without time. Time is a continuum in which events occur in an apparently irreversible manner. It is the interval separating two points on that continuum, such as sunrise and sunset. Each of us has our own subjective clock, evaluating and judging time as we measure it. Time is thrilling, boring, precious, wasted, and so on. While time is apparently irreversible in our lives – or at least in our memories – we are constantly playing back the tapes as we evaluate time, rewinding to some remembrance of a thing past when, we believe, we were happier, sadder, stronger, or weaker than we are now. Time, then, is the measurement of nostalgia divided by hope.

I believe theatre exists only in that intangible moment when human beings breathe the same air together, at the same time, within the same space. An actor on stage defines one side of a six-sided cube, their body forming one plane, the floor, ceiling, back, and two side walls of the venue making up the other five. That actor moving across the stage constantly redefines this cube and its volume; its sounds and its silence; its breath. It is within that block of possibilities that we create the theatrical event, an event whose essence is simple, direct, and immediate yet completely ephemeral. It is there that the magic happens and we make, as Peter Brook said, the invisible visible (1995). What a gift. What an honor. What a responsibility.

So after 40 years, you have my 3" × 5" cards and my journey. How you use them, and what you do with them, is up to you on your journey, which I hope will be even more rewarding than my own has been. Good luck!

Notes

1. All quotations from the *Folger Digital Shakespeare*. Barbara Mowat, Paul Werstine, Michael Poston, Rebecca Niles, eds., *Shakespeare's Plays, Sonnets and Poems* (Washington, DC: Folger Shakespeare Library, n.d.), accessed February 28, 2022. https://shakespeare.folger.edu.

2. A simple way to see this in action is to watch a rerun of the game show *Password*: a specific sounding "cup" will elicit the password "saucer" without fail. (See: www.youtube.com/watch?v=t5tx8ybnwK8.)
3. Knowing something of Maslow's "hierarchy of needs" can be useful here. (See: www.verywellmind.com/what-is-maslows-hierarchy-of-needs-4136760.)
4. *Merriam-Webster.com Dictionary*, s.v. "inspiration," accessed February 28, 2022, www.merriam-webster.com/dictionary/inspiration.
5. *Merriam-Webster.com Dictionary*, s.v. "expiration," accessed February 28, 2022, www.merriam-webster.com/dictionary/expiration.

Bibliography

Brook, Peter. 1995. *The Empty Space: A Book About the Theatre: Deadly, Holy, Rough, Immediate*. New York: Scribner.

Fantasia, Louis. 2002. *Instant Shakespeare: A Proven Guide for Actors, Directors, and Teachers*. Lanham, MD: Ivan R. Dee, all rights reserved.

Mowat, Barbara, Paul Paul Werstine, Michael Poston, and Rebecca Niles, eds. n.d. *Folger Digital Shakespeare: Shakespeare's Plays, Sonnets and Poems*. Washington: Folger Shakespeare Library. Accessed February 28, 2022. https://shakespeare.folger.edu.

Shakespeare, William. 1954. *The Arden Edition of the Complete Works of William Shakespeare*. London: Methuen.

5

THE WORDS

Golden Keys to the Inner Life of the Character

Baron Kelly

In everyday life, our primary method of communicating is speech. We rely on the spoken word to share information, as well as to indicate our needs and desires. Plays are primarily scripted spoken language. Spoken dialogue – through its images and meanings personal to each actor – has the power to stimulate body language and, ultimately, behavior.

When an actor begins to think more specifically about words, they realize that the wealth of each word's meaning is tied to specific memories. Words, therefore, have the power to stimulate the actor's sensorial energies through the specific memory they carry. Think of the words *house* and *love*. Instantly, your mind might flood with an image of each of these words. Emotions associated with these images are also stimulated. No two actors will find the same words evoking identical images because each actor's imagination embraces or invokes different experiences. Interpreting the playwright's intentions is not a simple matter. Characters in drama, like ordinary men and women, are all too often ambiguous. They do not often say what they mean, or mean what they say.

As a fundamental source, the image in the actor's mind is more dynamic than the actual sounds they make; the same words may express love or hate, trust or suspicion, respect or contempt. "I love you" may mean what it says, or the opposite. Indeed, ambiguity is also a condition of poetry. It is a tool of the playwright-poet, whether they are writing in verse or contemporary prose. It is the "words, words, words" given to the characters to speak that, by their logical and emotional order in the context of the scene, reveal the images and acts intended by the playwright.

Initially, there is an image, then a spoken word representing that image, then written symbols describing that word's sounds. The actor begins with the written

DOI: 10.4324/9781003204060-7

word and works back to the spoken word; from this, the actor goes back further still, to the original image. Without that image pictured clearly in the actor's mind, the word is no more than an empty sound, lifeless, and almost meaningless. When the image is clear, the ambiguity in the spoken word is clear.

Consider some symbols that are also letters of our alphabet: *o e s r*. They mean nothing in their present arrangement but can be rearranged into the word *rose*. Even this very simple word contains within it an ambiguity that becomes apparent when the word is part of a poetic utterance. It may mean a flower or a particular color, halfway between red and white. It may symbolize a feeling of love, or a person bearing the name Rose, or be an image of the Virgin Mother. It may mean something completely different, as in the past tense of the verb "to rise." Context of course will also determine the stress and inflection the actor will give the word.

Shakespeare's plays, because of their poetic construction (which extends itself even into his prose speeches) are language *experiences* that stimulate a sensorial life. Actors must not only develop an appreciation for the imagery but a taste for Shakespeare's words, as well, in a sensory experience that closely resembles taste. With Shakespeare, actors learn to experience language viscerally and sensorially and, therefore, psychologically.

Using speech discipline, the space for an emotionally imaginative release can be created for the actor in discovering different tones and attitudes of character. Additionally, learning to work through levels of word meanings can help actors learn to group their words into phrases, reinforcing their imagery in the text. In turn, these skills cultivate the control needed to give proper force and vitality to words.

In *Romeo and Juliet* (Act III, Scene 1), is Tybalt agitated, angry, cunning, or contemptuous? Each actor will speak the line "Thou art a villain" differently, depending on which image of Tybalt is to be projected. "Thou art a *villain*" may be uttered in one breath, stressing only the last word before stopping for breath. Or the actor may break the sentence into two phrases "*Thou* [pause] art a *villain*," stressing *thou* and *villain*. By breaking the line, the actor has time to suggest an insult in the first phrase with a slow and highly inflected pronunciation of *thou*. Now they have more breath, and more time, to give the word *villain* all the venom, disdain, and challenge they wish. How will the actor know the right amount of time to take? *Villain* is undoubtedly the word loaded with the greatest emotion, receiving the strongest stress regardless of whether the line is read as two phrases or one. If the stress is "Thou *art* a villain," it will sound as if the line is a response to "I am *not* a villain." There is no such preceding statement in the play, therefore, a stress on *art* sounds unnatural. Only the actor's intuition and the response to their scene partner will guide them in the moment to pack each phrase with as much or as little meaning as they think necessary.

So how do we viscerally understand that Shakespeare dictates so much of the behavior and psychological life of his characters through language? In class and rehearsal, many actors concern themselves solely with the *Denotative* (literal) definition, or the first level of meaning. In order to understand how rich the meaning of words and Shakespeare's language is, this chapter will outline a Blueprint for Analysis, based on the work of Ross Shenker, for actors to make a word chart illustrating two different levels of meaning: the Denotative (literal) and the Connotative/Associative (personal). The Connotative/Associative level is where words mean different things to different people. Therefore the same role will change when played by different actors, because they are filtering the words through their own unique experiences.

The *Oxford English Dictionary* provides the most complete etymology and list of definitions of any dictionary available. Language is constantly changing, and since the Renaissance, English has undergone many changes. Words that had a particular meaning during Shakespeare's day may have lost that meaning over the years or even gone out of our language altogether.

By understanding the formation of words, an actor has the optimum opportunity to communicate their interpretation of the ambiguities in language, which are both horizontal and vertical. Thus, the text releases its own life and imagined world, giving the performance richness of texture and nuance.

Once the Denotative and Connotative Meanings are clear, the actor can move on to charting their Paraphrase, or Translation. Paraphrasing personalizes an actor's physical responses to the text and makes the words themselves a potent stimulant for need, behavior, and emotional relationships.

There are different levels of paraphrasing:

1. Paraphrasing With the Denotative
2. Paraphrasing With the Connotative/Associative
3. Paraphrasing With the Germinal (originating) Idea

Let's examine how a Blueprint for Analysis works, by looking at a Blueprint of Cassius's monologue from act 1, scene 2 of *Julius Caesar*.

Cassius: Why, man, he doth bestride the narrow world
Like a Colossus, and we petty men
Walk under his huge legs and peep about
To find ourselves dishonourable graves.
Men at some time are masters of their fates:
The fault, dear Brutus, is not in our stars,
But in ourselves, that we are underlings.
Brutus and Caesar: what should be in that 'Caesar'?
Why should that name be sounded more than yours?
Write them together, yours is as fair a name;

Step 1: Creating a Word Chart

When looking up the individual words in the dictionary, the actor will discover multiple meanings playing underneath the surface of the text; therefore, every actor's paraphrase of a monologue or scene will be different. Actors must come up with the most comprehensive meaning that is personal to them. The subtextual layers of the performance can begin to move not only horizontally in a linear fashion but can also move with a layer of verticality. The word-experiencing functions on several levels at the same time.

Word	*Denotative Meaning (Collins)*	*Connotative Meaning*
Why	begins a question as to the reason for something	an introductory expression of surprise, indeed
man	adult human being	Brutus, Caesar, Senators
bestride	to have a leg on either side of	taking large steps/strides
narrow	limited, lacking breadth of vision	thin, narrow-minded
world	the earth and its inhabitants	oceans, land, everything under the sun
Colossus	something very large, especially a statue	Titans, who were antecedents to the Gods
petty	trivial, inessential, minor	resentful, vengeful
Walk	to travel on foot	as opposed to run; slow, methodical, careful
under	below or beneath, lower rank	subordinate, under a shadow
huge	extremely large in size	massive, wide
legs	structure in animals used for locomotion or support	beneath you, shadows
peep	to utter shrill small noises	to poke one's head out
find	to meet with or discover by chance	search out, look for desperately
ourselves	reflexive form of we	the corporeal body, a sense of shared identity
dishonor-able	showing a lack of honor or integrity; base; disgraceful; shameful	as in a soldier or statesman having done wrong
graves	burial places	older men, grave men, sadness
men	see "Man"	weak, vengeful, violent, cruel
some time	at some unspecified point in time	occasional, infrequent
masters	a person with the ability or power to use, control, or dispose of something	an expert, a teacher
fates	the end or final result	the three goddesses who control the destinies of the lives of man; destiny

(Continued)

(Continued)

Word	Denotative Meaning (Collins)	Connotative Meaning
fault	imperfection, failing, defect, flaw	cracks in the earth, an earthquake, blame
dear	beloved, precious	my dear, my love
Brutus	Marcus Junius, a Roman statesman who, with Cassius, led the conspiracy to assassinate Caesar; committed suicide after being defeated by Antony and Octavian (Augustus) at Philippi	my friend, confidante, object of attention and affection, co-conspirator
stars	any vast number of celestial objects visible in the night sky	bright, shining, twinkling, the Gods
underlings	subordinates or lackeys	animals that crawl in the dirt
Caesar	Gaius Julius, Roman general, statesman, and historian. Fear of his sovereign power led to his assassination.	any emperor, dictator, or other powerful ruler
name	a word or term by which a person or thing is commonly and distinctively known	mere outward appearance or form, as opposed to fact; word, title, phrase descriptive of character, usually abusive or derogatory
sounded	to be heard, as a sound	to have the law as its basis or foundation
write	to draw or mark on a surface, usually paper, with a pen, pencil or other instrument	to publish, create
together	in or into contact or union with another	as one, unified
fair	beautiful, lovely, pleasant	just, balanced, reasonable

Step 2: Comparing Line Paraphrases

Now that we've mapped out Denotative and Connotative meanings for these words, we can layer in subtext, personal correlations, and associations through paraphrasing that considers not only text and plot but the poetic devices that arise when these words are used in larger phrases. The sound of rhetorical devices, repetitions, and patterns of imagery can yield a more thorough understanding of the play than standard imagery studies or plot analyses.

Shakespeare's Text	Denotative Paraphrase	Connotative Paraphrase
Why, man, he doth bestride the narrow world	Indeed, this adult male human puts his legs on either side of this limited earth	Here is an expression of surprise! Caesar takes giant strides through this thin, narrow-minded land under the sun,

The Words

Shakespeare's Text	Denotative Paraphrase	Connotative Paraphrase
Like a Colossus, and we petty men **Walk under his huge legs and peep about**	like an enormous statue. And we trivial men travel on foot below his extremely large structures for locomotion and utter shrill small noises	like a father to the Gods. And we resentful people, slowly and methodically move under the shadow of his massiveness, and poke our heads out desperately looking for a sense of a shared identity,
To find ourselves dishonorable graves.	only to be met with shameful burial places.	to only find that we are soldiers and statesmen who have done wrong and therefore are old men, grave and sad.
Men at sometimes are masters of their fates	Men, at certain unspecified points in time, have the ability to control the final results of things.	Weak though we are, occasionally or infrequently we are the experts and teachers over our destinies.
The fault, dear Brutus, is not in our stars,	The imperfection, my beloved Marcus Junius, is not to do with any number of vast celestial objects in the night sky.	The cracks and blame my love, my friend, my confidante, are not within the bright shining, twinkling, Gods above but in us.
But in ourselves that we are underlings.	But in us.	These animals that crawl around lamely in the dirt.
Brutus and Caesar: what should be in that 'Caesar'?	Marcus Junius Brutus, Roman statesman, and Gaius Julius Caesar, Emperor, what meaning should we impart on Gaius Julius Caesar?	Let's create something with your name and his name as one unified force and we'll see that your name is just as balanced and reasonable to befit the tongue, teeth, and lips.
Why should that name be sounded more than yours?	Make someone hear them, your name comes to be in the opening through which we issue vocal sounds just the same as Caesar's.	If we put both of you on the scale of justice, you have the same gravitas.
Write them together, yours is as fair a name;	Draw both names on paper in union with each other, yours is just as beautiful, lovely, and pleasant.	If we put both of you on the scale of justice, you have the same gravitas.

Step 3: Germinal Idea Paraphrase

Taking this work a step further, the germinal idea paraphrases in the table are different from those in the previous section to further help the actor discover what is happening, moment by moment, in the play. The power of language, particularly verse, can affect an actor the way music affects listeners and musicians. The sounds and rhythm are capable of evoking an experiential knowledge of the character's state of mind. The germinal is another level of paraphrase to help the actor with the "feel" of the language, as part of the analytical process. The actor must make the character's imagery come out of a sense of what they are saying, helping the actor experience that moment in the play fully. To find and trust the basic idea of the language to help give the actor keys to character and action.

Shakespeare's Text	*Germinal Idea Paraphrase*
Why, man, he doth bestride the narrow world	Caesar struts about
Like a Colossus, and we petty men	like a giant, and we
Walk under his huge legs and peep about	are shamefully
To find ourselves dishonorable graves.	subservient to him.
Men at sometimes are masters of their fates	Let's take charge.
The fault, dear Brutus, is not in our stars,	This is not the fault of the Gods.
But in ourselves that we are underlings.	We allowed this.
Brutus and Caesar: what should be in that "Caesar"?	Why Caesar?
Why should that name be sounded more than yours?	Compare your names.
Write them together, yours is as fair a name;	Yours possesses all the worth too.

Step 4: The Fly Back

Read each paraphrase aloud to hear how the work that's been done is reflected in the feel of the language. This will help bring the character's imagery to life out of a sense of what they are saying, realized at the moment of speaking. In turn, the actor may find character and frame of mind exposed on different levels.

1. Paraphrasing With the Denotative Meaning

    Indeed, this adult male human puts his legs on either side of this limited earth like an enormous statue. And we trivial men travel on foot below his extremely large structures for locomotion and utter shrill small noises only to be met with shameful burial places. Men, at certain unspecified points in time, have the ability to control the final results of things. The imperfection, my beloved Marcus Junius, is not to do with any number of vast celestial objects in the night sky but in us, because we are subordinate lackeys. Marcus Junius Brutus, Roman statesman, and Gaius Julius

Caesar, Emperor, what meaning should we impart on Gaius Julius Caesar? Why should that word or term be heard more often than yours? Draw both names on paper in union with each other, yours is just as beautiful, lovely, and pleasant.

2. Paraphrasing With the Connotative/Emotional Attitudes

   Here is an expression of surprise! Caesar takes giant strides through this thin, narrow-minded land under the sun like a father to the Gods. And we resentful people, slowly and methodically move under the shadow of his massiveness and poke our heads out desperately looking for a sense of a shared identity, and only find that we are soldiers and statesmen who have done wrong and therefore are old men, grave and sad. Weak though we are, occasionally or infrequently we are the experts and teachers over our destinies. The cracks and blame my love, my friend, my confidante, are not within the bright shining, twinkling, Gods above but in us, these animals that crawl around lamely in the dirt. If we compare a good statesman to any popular dictator, we will find that there is nothing underneath that dictator's outward appearance to suggest that he should be ruler, especially when we consider the rule of law. Let's publish or create something with your name and his name as one unified force and we'll see that your name is just as balanced and reasonable to befit the tongue, teeth, and lips. If we put both of you on the scale of justice, you have the same gravitas.

3. Paraphrasing With the Germinal Idea

   Caesar struts about like a giant and we are shamefully subservient to him. Sometimes, men must take charge of their own destinies. What has come to pass is no fault of Caesar or the Gods, but our own because we have allowed it to happen. Let's look at you and look at Caesar side by side. You possess all the same gravitas and worth. I do not understand what Caesar has done to deserve all this praise and adoration.

The Blueprint for Analysis can help create signposts for the character's inner goals or problems, their manner of experiencing different circumstances and events, their positive or negative mindset, and their personal experience of moments as they differ from how other types of characters would experience the same things. Shakespeare appeals to the total person. To both the intellect and the emotional understanding of the actor. The Blueprint for Analysis can help direct the actor directly to the impulse for the word; they will learn to appreciate how the language of body and action may teach them a simpler way to do things and reveal impulses they had within but had not suspected. They will grow an awareness and sensation of how language can flow throughout the body and between self and others.

Bibliography

Shakespeare, William. 1974. *Riverside Shakespeare*. Edited by G. Blakemore Evans. Boston: Houghton Mifflin Co.

6
EMBODIMENT THROUGH BREATH AND THE VOICE

Josephine Hall

The rich language that forms the plays from the Restoration period and comedy of manners is truly a gift for an actor. In an interview on *Inside the Actor's Studio*, James Lipton asked Colin Firth what language meant to him. He replied, "It informs your body. It's an amazing effect . . . actors as creatures are utterly dependent on the language. There is nothing more beautiful than taking phrasing, syntax, poetic ideas, concepts, which would naturally be out of your intellectual reach, and owning them" (Inside the Actor's Studio 2018). That is the goal: to truly own the language.

To an actor, a script is like a recipe for a cake. A baker combines ingredients in the most advantageous way possible in order to create something that did not exist before: the cake. A script is the skeleton of an impending creation; the actor's job is to discover and embody the life that transforms itself into the full-bodied human that ultimately and inevitably expresses itself through the words that were listed in the original recipe. Actors do that by discovering all the facets that make up the life of the character. The most important and essential element of all life, including the life of the character in the play, is breath. Yet when faced with heightened text, it is common for actors to tense up out of fear and fail to fully engage the breath. The most basic movement, the movement of breath, becomes stilted and shallow, leading to stiff physicality that bears little relation to the goals and intentions pursued by the character. Therefore, before actors can discover any kind of physicality and embodiment of character, they must first embrace the movement and embodiment of the breath as dictated by the words of the original recipe, the script.

Characters in Restoration plays and within the genre comedy of manners use words not only to communicate but also to express themselves. Theatre is an aural medium; an audience *listens* to a play. However, actors today are often inspired to take up the craft after watching movies, a visual medium; viewers *watch* a movie. They (and we) are not accustomed to expressing themselves through precise and complex language. In heightened text, *how* characters choose to express themselves is just as important as the basic information given by the script. Clues for characterization lie in the words chosen by the playwright, and even in the vowels and consonants that comprise those words. The dexterity required for clear articulation and facility with the sheer volume of words a playwright chooses to express character's needs can be challenging. Given the length of phrases and individual sentences in classical texts, it is imperative that the actor maps out where to breathe. This mapping ensures that breath will be part of the equation. Young actors tend to resist this work because they feel it is too prescriptive; they hope, instead, to merely apply their instinct. However, instinct is unreliable and will fail when needed most. The only reliable tool is technique, and this involves making conscious choices about where to breathe and how much breath is needed to support the thought being expressed. As actors discover the volume of breath necessary to speak the text, they will consequently discover the natural breath patterns of the character. Marking the breaths in the script will help actors ensure they have enough air for each phrase or part of a phrase; if an extra breath is needed, take it. Be sure not to push the voice from the chest or throat, a common result of not having adequate breath to complete a thought or phrase. The breath must be supported and anchored deep in the lower abdomen. Once the breath is fully engaged and truly supported, as Colin Firth says, it affects the whole body. The actor expresses the thoughts and needs of the character through the words spoken. This, in turn, helps the actor discover the natural physical movement for a character. Breath is where it all starts; it is the literal life of the character. If the actor does not employ adequate breath to speak the text, the body will naturally tense up in order to force the words out of the body. Once force is employed, everything becomes stilted, restricting the actor's, and therefore the character's, whole physicality.

The actor must also discover the operative words that tell the story of the play – scene by scene and, ultimately, moment by moment. Many of these plays include language that is alien to most modern readers. In *The School for Scandal*, Richard Brinsley Sheridan uses words such as *traduce, extempore,* and *cicisbeo* – words that are, at the very least, unfamiliar to most people today. Identifying and defining every word not readily understood and working up strong paraphrases of the narrative ensures a clearer understanding of the text. Sometimes archaic definitions of words are slightly different to modern definitions, so use of a quality dictionary such as Merriam-Webster is imperative. Once words are clarified, they must also be practiced aloud, to develop the muscle memory required to speak them fluently.

Once an actor has a clear sense of the overall story and the meanings of individual words, they must then clarify which words in each sentence actually illuminate the story: the *operative* words. In any sentence, there are words that are basically just connectors. In the previous sentence, the following words might serve as connectors: *in, there, are, that, are,* and *just,* though *just* is arguably a little more important than the others. In contrast, the words that hold the clues to the story of that sentence – the operative words – are *sentence, words, basically, connectors.* Highlighting these four words, the reader can understand the gist of what is being said. To make a story clear to an audience, the actor would highlight these operative words and allow the other words to connect them without pulling focus. The key to making these words pop out clearly in the speaking of a sentence is its musicality.

Start from a physical state of ease so that the voice is grounded within the body allowing for utilization of full vocal resonance. To find a useful baseline for the voice work to begin, explore how low in pitch you can speak without pushing the sound down and forcing it into the chest; maintain a sense of ease. Then, from that lowest, comfortable pitch, work up about three musical steps so you are not sitting on the bass note. This establishes a pitch level to work from and is where most of the words live when no emphasis is needed. In contrast, operative words – those words that need to be highlighted to make the story clear – usually need to be musically higher in pitch. Of course, pitch is not the only tool available to an actor. English speakers have many other options to emphasize key words, such as timing or volume. However, these other tools are at their most effective when used in conjunction with pitch. The pitches explored in spoken text differ from singing, which generally has predetermined pitches for each word or syllable. The basic tune of a sentence needed for clarity of story is relatively consistent. For example, let's begin by examining a sentence spoken by Lydia Languish in Sheridan's *The Rivals* (act I, scene ii):

"Then before we are interrupted, let me impart to you some of my distress!"

To make this sentence clear to an audience, the actor must select the words that communicate the story:

"before . . . interrupted . . . impart . . . distress"

The energy of this line builds throughout, with the highest point being on the second syllable of the final word. The emphasis of any word is always based on its stressed syllable; the music of the four-syllable word "interrupted" is based on the emphasized "rup" with the rest of the word tagging along for the ride:

                              rup-
in-   ter-   ted

Within the whole sentence, the actor must then rank the words in importance. In this particular sentence, without any information gathered from other characters, it is most likely to be a straightforward build:

"Then *before* we are *interrupted*, let me **impart** to you some of my **DISTRESS**."

In order to stress these words without tension, the actor may use imagery that reflects the musicality of a phrase, such as the shallow waves of a sea ebbing and flowing, with the emphasized words flowing further onto the beach; the further inland the words flow, the higher the pitch of the vocal tone. The resulting musicality of the line would look roughly like this:

```
                                                                    distress
          before                          impart
                       interrupted                   to you some of my
Then             we are             let me
```

The connecting words ("we are . . . let me . . . to you some of my") will not all be spoken on the same note, but the actor should aim to keep these words grounded in the lower part of the voice while, at the same time, allowing them to be influenced by the emphasized words around them. If the actor fails to root these connecting words, there is the danger of the whole phrase becoming trapped in the upper ranges of the voice, losing emotional connection to the words as well as the grounding that gives the voice authority.

It is worth noting here that the first word, *Then*, is a great opportunity for the actor to establish an immediacy to the moment. The simplest way to do that is to completely finish the "n" before moving on to the next word. The result is a separation of *Then* from the next word, *before*. It is not exactly a pause, but it allows the actor to establish the moment without losing the urgency of the rest of the line.

The specific words emphasized in a sentence may change depending on what other characters have said. If Lydia's cousin Julia had just said that an interruption was imminent, Lydia's emphasis might change thus:

```
                                                                    distress
          before                          impart
                       interrupted                   to you some of my
Then             we are             let me
```

Distress is still the most important word, but now *before* becomes more important than in the previous example. It is this musicality that reflects an actor's understanding of the text. While an instinctual approach to the text can serve the actor up to a point, the language of these period plays is, for the most part, more complicated than most modern actors use in everyday life. Consequently, relying solely on instinct is not only unreliable but often restrictive too. How the character speaks the words of the text is as revealing as what the specific words convey.

Musical intervals between words will likely vary with each performance; they are dictated by the energy of the scene, the interchange between the actors, and even the response of an audience. Most importantly, as you work on the text, do not limit the upper upper vocal range of the line. It can often feel strange to an actor when the voice frees so much, they feel they have lost control; the actor may restrict themselves by a need to feel "real." However, trying to limit the musicality will certainly limit the energy and spontaneity of the scene.

It is *so **important*** to make good **CHOICES** regarding *word emphasis*. Young actors, especially, have a tendency to hit connector words and adjectives; for example, it is *so* important to make *good* choices *regarding* word emphasis. In that case, the audience hears "so," "good," and maybe "regarding." They understand something is extreme because of the "so," that something else is "good," and it's in relation to something, but they have little idea of what the character is trying to communicate because the actor is not emphasizing the words that express the specifics of the story.

In the next section is Celimene's speech from act III of Molière's *The Misanthrope* with some suggestions to help with the text. This is not set in stone and will change as the actor becomes more familiar with the text, the character, and the given circumstances. However, it offers a place to start. The "/" between phrases indicates breath marks, or at least a break in the flow of the text. Sometimes that break can be achieved simply by completing a word fully instead of running on into the next part of the sentence. The operative words are ranked in importance thus: *one*, *two*, ***three***, **FOUR**. This is just a starting point from which to play with the text. These suggestions are not set in stone. The choices of which words to emphasize and how much to do so may well change. Be flexible during the rehearsal process and remain open to new discoveries. However, since this language is different from the way we speak today, it is helpful to make some decisions before entering the rehearsal space. This exercise helps you discover where to breathe, how much breath you need for each phrase, and which words are important to the clarity of the story. A bit of context: this speech is in reaction to Celimene's friend Arsinoe informing her that "virtuous" people are gossiping about her and her "coquettish ways." These details inform some of the choices here:

Embodiment Through Breath and the Voice

Madam, /	The salutation should stand alone. Completely finish the final "m" before continuing.
I have *many thanks* in *return* to *you,*/and *such advice* lays me under *great* **OBLIGATION**.	The sentence is driving toward the high point of "obligation."
Far from taking it *unkindly,*/I am only too *anxious* at *once* to *prove* my *gratitude*/by giving *you* on *my part*/a certain piece of *advice,*/which, **wonderful** to *say,*/closely concerns **YOUR** *honor,* /	Normally, pronouns would not be emphasized, but here Celimene is directly reflecting what was just said to her and turning the tables to question Arsinoe's honor.
and as I see you *prove* yourself my *friend* by *informing* me of the *reports* that people *spread* about *me,*/I wish, in *my turn,*/to follow so *pleasing* an *example*/by *acquainting you* with what is said of **YOU**.	There is a lot of fun to be had here setting *me/my* against *you*.
In a *certain house*, where I was **visiting** the other day,/I *met* with people of the most *striking merit;*/and **they**, speaking of the **duties** of a person who leads a *virtuous life,*/turned the **conversation**,/*madam,*/upon **YOU**.	Notice that although the adjectives give a lot of flavor, they should not be emphasized more than the noun, the word that tells the story: *certain* **house**; *striking* **merit**; *virtuous* **life**
THERE,/your *prudishness* and the *vehemence* of your *zeal*/were by no means quoted as a *good* **example**. /	This time the first word is the most important as it emphasizes where the conversation took place.
That *affectation* of a *grave demeanour;*/your *everlasting speeches* on **discretion** and **HONOUR**;/your *simpering,*/and your *outcries* at the *shadow* of any *impropriety* which an *innocent* though *ambiguous word* may **PRESENT**;/the *high esteem* in which you **hold** *yourself,*/and the *looks* of *pity* you *cast* upon *others;*/your *frequent lectures*/and your *sharp censures* on *things* which are **harmless** and **pure**;/all **THIS**,/*madam,*/if I may speak the *plain truth,*/was *blamed* by *common* **ACCORD**. /	This passage contains a list of Arsinoe's behaviors. Lists are tricky. They need to build, step by step, but each item must stand alone, as if you could finish the sentence after any of the semi-colons. "This, madam, if . . ." – to make the "madam" really stand out, finish the "s" of "This" and the second "m" of "madam" before moving on.
"*What* **signify**," said they,/"that *modest mien* and that *grave manner,*/which are **belied** by all the **REST**?/She is most *exact* at all her *prayers,*/but she *beats* her *servants*/and **pays** them no **WAGES**. She makes the *greatest* **display** of *fervor* in *all* places of *worship,*/but she *paints* and wishes to appear **beautiful**./ She has all *nudities* covered in her *pictures,*/but she **delights** in the **REALITY**." /	Be sure to establish the quotation by dropping "said they" into a lower vocal register, then pick the pitch back up to connect back to the quotation. Make it clear that she mistreats her servants in two ways (beating them and not paying them) by separating the phrases, not necessarily with a breath, but by completing the "s" of "servants."

64 Josephine Hall

For *my part,*/I undertook your *defense* against every *one*,/and *assured* them it was all **CALUMNY**; /
but the *general opinion* went *against* me,/ and the *conclusion* was that you would do *well* to be *less solicitous* about *other people's actions*/and take *more pains* about your *own*;/ that we should *examine ourselves* a great deal/before *thinking* of *condemning others*;/ that we *ought* to add the *weight* of an *exemplary life*/to the *corrections* we **PRETEND** to *make* in our *neighbors*;/and that, after all,/ it would be *better still* to **leave** that *care*/to those who were *ordained* by **Heaven** for it. /
Madam, /

Use the comma by finishing the "t" of "part" before continuing. You may not need to take a breath.
Remember that these emphases are just suggestions to use as a starting point. Things may change in rehearsal when there is a live person reacting to what you say.

Notice the repeated salutation from the opening. Treat it with the same musicality as the opening and separate the sounds from the words around it, but be careful not to change the comma to a period; the energy of the salutation continues into the next sentence.

I believe that **you** *ALSO* are too *sensible* not to take in *good part* this **KINDLY**-*meant advice*,/and not to *attribute* it to the *earnestness* of an *affection*/which makes *me anxious* for **YOUR** *welfare.*

An option here is to echo the treatment of the pronouns from earlier in the speech, justified because Celimene is echoing what her friend preached to her earlier. However, be sure not to lose the items referred to: anxious and welfare. Complete the sentence with full voice using adequate breath support.

The previous suggestions are not the only options for musicality. What is important is that you start with something and remember that not all words are created equal. Some tell the story and others connect those storytelling elements. It is through the musicality of the spoken word that the important words stand out from the rest.

To physically feel this musicality and truly embody the breath required, the actor can play with different exercises:

- Physicalize the spoken line with a gesture, placing the biggest movement on the most emphasized word: distress. If you choose upward gestures to emphasize the operative words and therefore the musical high points of the sentence, remember to anchor the base tones of the voice so that the upward inflection is grounded even while a word is emphasized.

- Have fun with the line by singing it — an impromptu recitative. The added advantage of singing is that it requires full engagement of breath. I strongly suggest that female-identifying actors avoid exclusively using their chest register as that often encourages more tension in less-experienced performers.
  - Singing also encourages the elongation of vowels. The tense actor often rushes the spoken word, clipping short the vowel and consequently shortchanging the emotion that accompanies it. Once the breath travels throughout a word, you discover many more opportunities to play with expression.
- Bending the knees while speaking the emphasized words helps with the sensation of grounding, even as you rise higher in pitch.
- A tennis ball is a great tool for playing with emphasis. On each operative word, toss the ball into the air and do not continue talking until you catch it. The more important the word, the higher the ball is thrown. On the most important word of the sentence, in this case "distress," toss the ball to a scene partner.

The tension caused by the stress of speaking unfamiliar words and linguistic rhythms may lead you to emphasize words through force, stabbing at important words instead of supporting the voice throughout the whole phrase. This results in an unevenness of vocal line that is difficult for an audience to follow. To counter this, stand at one side of a room and speak the line as if all individual words are traveling to and hitting the opposite wall. If you stab at the sentence, you will find that some of the words feel as if they are dropping onto the floor before reaching the wall. Do this first while speaking in a continuous monotone, ensuring that all the words are spoken on the train of the breath. It may also help to think of printed music with phrasing lines gliding over the notes. That phrasing line represents the constant flow of breath throughout the sentence. No stabbing needed.

Tension can also lead to placing the baseline of a sentence two to three tones higher than a particular actor's ideal, grounded placement. When this happens, the actor tends to drop down onto operative words using downward inflections, which sends the sound into the stage floor, rather than out toward a scene partner and into the theatre to the ears of the audience. Once breath and sound are moving consistently across the room, envision a ladder on the far wall. There needs to be enough breath for all the words to reach the ladder, but the more important the word is, the higher up the ladder it must land, while connector words remain huddled toward the bottom of the ladder.

Now that the sentence is moving in a constant, fluid motion, it is important to check for other areas of unnecessary bodily tension. Add flowing movement in the arms and legs by engaging the core and letting the movement radiate outward, from the center of the body and the spine. The movements should be fluid, snaking constantly with no jerking motions, moving the weight from one foot to the other. These physical movements may even prompt some genuine interaction not previously discovered. While this movement is certainly not a choice for the final physicalization of the character, the freedom encouraged through random, fluid movement can help you find the same freedom while moving in a more traditional way in the scene, teaching the body to move and speak with ease instead of tension.

Employed during personal preparation and in early stages of rehearsal, these exercises help the actor find ways to make the text clear for their fellow cast members and the audience. Through rehearsal, the basic work of an actor is incorporated through relationships with others: listening, responding, exploring objectives and obstacles in the way, finding tactics to achieve those objectives. This work helps the actors discover all the different vocal tactics they can access to achieve their goals. Most importantly, they will tell the story clearly and articulately. In performance, actors should no longer need to think about when to take the breath or which words to hit. Their preparation, plus the process of rehearsal, should integrate the elements that result in only one possible outcome: an accurate interpretation of the original recipe, the script.

Reference

Inside the Actor's Studio. 2018. "Colin Firth on Mr. Darcy, Language, Mark Darcy, Shakespeare and How Much of Him is in a Character." *YouTube Video*, 22:02. August 18, 2018. www.youtube.com/watch?v=Hel1FJHxEMc.

7
PLAYING THE PERSIAN QUEEN

Stratos E. Constantinidis

Introduction

Aeschylus' *Persians* was first staged at the Theatre of Dionysus in 472 BCE during the annual competitive drama festival in Athens where it was awarded the top prize. *Persians* is the world's oldest anti-imperialist play that has survived almost intact from antiquity. It dramatizes the defeat of a world power by a negligible adversary. In *Persians*, 14 Athenian performers impersonate members of the Persian elite on the day they receive bad news from the battlefront. The Athenian performers act out the suffering of the vanquished Persians without denigrating them or minimizing their pain. At the same time, they show how the imperialist ideology comes apart at the seams by dividing a family, a nation, and an empire. Aeschylus is the first known playwright who dared to present the anatomy of imperialism and the viewpoint of an enemy people. And he did so with impunity even though he asked his fellow citizens (who had lost relatives and friends when the imperial troops destroyed Athens eight years earlier) not only to control their fear of the enemy that had wreaked havoc upon their city but also to feel mercy toward the Persians whom they had killed, captured, or driven away. So the play is not only about 12 Persian councilmen who (1) avoid interpreting the dream of the emperor's mother, (2) listen to a messenger describe the naval battle that sank their hopes for world dominance, (3) seek advice from the ghost of their former emperor (Darius I) about the future of the dynasty and the empire, and (4) give their current defeated emperor (Xerxes I) a thankless homecoming. It is also about the queen (who is the widow of Darius and the mother of Xerxes). She is a central character because the dramatic action on the stage is shaped by her relationship

DOI: 10.4324/9781003204060-9

and interaction with the other characters. Contemporary performers who are interested in learning how to play tragic female roles in Greek drama can begin by studying the foundational role of the queen in Aeschylus' *Persians*. The exercises below will help them take the first step.

The best preserved, handwritten medieval copy of *Persians* (M) is like a libretto without its musical score, choreographic notations, and stage directions. M has a total of 1,077 lines distributed among five characters: Xerxes (69 lines), the ghost of Darius (94 lines), the queen (172 lines), the messenger (206 lines), and the 12 councilmen, a choir of dancers acting as one collective character, who sing the remaining lines. The first three characters belong to the same family and embody the imperialist ideology of the hereditary monarchy. Aeschylus and his generation defended Athenian democracy and autonomy against the imperialist agenda of these two Persian monarchs – Darius and Xerxes. His play reckons the response of the queen and the 12 councilmen to the breaking news about the debacle of the Persian invasion of Greece in 480 BCE. According to Aeschylus and Herodotus, the great armada of the Persian Empire consisted of 1,207 battleships. After the Persians captured and destroyed Athens, their armada cornered the Greek fleet in the straits between Attica and the island of Salamis on September 26. According to Aeschylus, who fought the Persians at Salamis, the Greek fleet had 310 battleships (200 of them were Athenian). The Persians suffered a momentous defeat and sustained heavy losses in men and ships.

The following exercises will help prospective performers (1) learn the queen's body language; (2) assign cause to her movements and vocalizations, using one scene of the play as a case study (lines 155-248); and (3) inhabit the role and embody the text from moment to moment. The moments build one upon the other, so what applies to this scene will help performers understand what applies to the rest of the scenes in the play. The exercises will analyze four moments: the queen's silent entrance, which is framed by the comments of the head councilman (lines 150–59); the queen's conversation with the head councilman and the repetitions of the conjunctive particle "because" (lines 160–75); the queen's dream, which she shares with the 12 councilmen before she asks them to interpret it (lines 176–225); and the queen's verbal trap, which captures the head councilman right before they are interrupted by a messenger who arrives from the battlefront (lines 226–48).

Moment 1: The Queen Enters Silently

Questions for consideration: First impressions (whether true or false) are important. The queen's silent entrance requires that you consider how she might be perceived by the audience. What is her physical appearance? What is her personality type? How might these reflect her public – and private – history, as well as her ethos? Does the head councilman's description of the way she enters and approaches them support or contradict the way she enters?

Head Councilman:
But here comes the mother of the king; even so she is still my queen.   150
She is rushing ahead with eyes as shiny as those of the gods.
I will just bow down, but I will greet her in a manner that is not mean.
By using *all* the titles and labels due to her, I'll mend our odds.
    [Bows slightly]
Hello, supreme queen of the Persian women, who are famous for their
    slim waist,   155
wife of Darius and elderly mother of Xerxes, whom all of us here have
    embraced,
bedmate of a godlike Persian and mother of a godlike son born to you and
    Darius.
Unless some ancient demon changed camps now, Xerxes would still be
    gregarious.

Clues from history: The queen (550–475 BCE) was the daughter of Cyrus I and the widow of three Persian Emperors (Cambyses II, Smerdis, and Darius I), as well as the mother of four sons fathered by Darius. In 480 BCE, she was an elegant and magnificent 70-year-old grandmother at the height of her influence in the affairs of the empire. She is never identified by name in the play, but in his *Histories* (3.88), Herodotus identified her as Atossa (1998, 211). In Avestan and Farsi, Atossa (also transliterated as Atusa, Atousa, and Atoosa) means "magnificent and/or munificent." Atossa was educated, refined, ambitious, and politically astute, so she gained great sociopolitical influence (not necessarily power) as Darius' second wife. At age 70, she still has an agile mind and body. When Darius consulted her before his invasion of Greece in 490 BCE, she gave him three reasons why he should wage war against the Greeks: (a) to show his strength to his own subjects, (b) to detract his subjects from plotting against him at home, and (c) to send captive Greek girls from Argos, Athens, Corinth, and Sparta to wait upon her at Susa. The latter ambition was never fulfilled because the Athenians defeated Darius' imperial troops at Marathon. In the play, the queen is a master of understatement; she carefully selects topics and words, and when she is silent, she is an expert of overstatement through her body language and use of dress code. She is a tragic, not a comic, character.

Cues found in the text: Persian protocol dictated that Darius' successor should be his firstborn son from his first wife. However, Atossa persuaded him to make Xerxes (*their* firstborn son) the crown prince, even though Xerxes showed little interest and aptitude for public office and received little administrative training compared to his half-brother and rival. Xerxes is described in the play as an impetuous young leader who tries to prove himself by emulating his father but ruins the lives, prosperity, and prospects of the Persians and their allies in the process. His defeat jeopardizes everything his father has built. As a result, the ghost of Darius cares less about the survival of his son and more about the survival of the dynasty. The queen remains loyal to Xerxes and manages the crisis by having difficult conversations with 12 powerful politicians, trying to call the shots in this high-stakes war saga. Within the hour, these conversations will determine whether her son will be deposed or continue to reign.

Contextualizing the moment: The head councilman is displeased to see the queen approaching. He tells the other Persian men (and, at the same time, the Athenian audience) that he will not prostrate himself at her feet, as Persian custom requires. The Greeks deemed prostration degrading, so they refused to do it (Herodotus, *Histories* 7.136). For the Persians, however, the absence of prostration was a sign of disrespect or insubordination. For example, in Aeschylus' *Agamemnon,* Clytemnestra prostrates herself at the feet of King Agamemnon, who is her husband, but only because she wants to make him look like a non-Greek despot in the eyes of the democratic Athenian audience. She does this to predispose the audience to condone his assassination, which she plans to carry out later in the play (Aeschylus, *Agamemnon* 918–22). In *Persians*, the head councilman states that he will only bow down and will address her with all the titles she expects to hear because he wants to mitigate with words any negative visual impact of disrespect that the absence of prostration will indicate. The queen enters from the street in a carriage drawn by four slaves and is followed by six handmaids on foot. The first handmaid carries Xerxes' mask, the second handmaid carries Darius' mask, the third handmaid is wearing a Doric dress, the fourth handmaid carries a yoke, the fifth handmaid carries a folding stool for the queen, and the sixth handmaid helps the queen step down from the carriage. The queen is wearing an elegant, colorful dress and expensive, tasteful jewelry. Her feet never touch the ground because the slaves unroll crimson runners one after the other before her feet and roll them back up after she passes.

Exercises for rehearsal: Read aloud the verses above and note any words that relate to the queen's physical appearance. Examine the text above for clues about (1) how the queen enters the stage, (2) how the queen makes eye contact with the 12 councilmen (especially when she notices the absence of prostration), and (3) how the queen's facial expression and the rest of her body language reveal her thoughts and demeanor.

Moment 2: The Queen Talks to the Head Councilman

Questions for consideration: Does the queen rehearse her speech before seeking the councilmen's advice in the street outside the audience hall? Why does she refrain from greeting the head councilman back, focusing her response on his usage of the conjunction "unless"? When does she gesture to the councilmen to quit bowing down? Why does she repeat the conjunctive particle "because" (gar) three times within five lines (168–72)? Why does the head councilman use the same conjunctive particle "because" (175) when he replies to the queen?

Queen:
This is *exactly* why I've come here! My decision to talk with you didn't seem barmy
when I left the gold-trimmed house and the bedroom that I once shared with Darius. 160
My heart is torn with grave concerns, too. I will now tell you all a story without bias.
    [Catches her breath]
My friends, I am not free of fear myself. I am scared that our great wealth,
that Darius has amassed with help from some god who was kind,
might be turned to dust like trampled topsoil that quickly loses its health.
These then are the two unspoken concerns that trouble my mind: 165
    [Pauses]
A rich nation cannot command respect abroad when its armed forces are broken.
Nor can a mighty force outshine its foes overseas when its treasury goes broke.
Just *because* our treasury is unscathed, my fearful eyes don't see this as a token,
because I regard my son's presence at home as an amulet against ill-wishing folk.
    [Pauses]
So, men of Persia, trusty elders, your sharp thinking on this matter is key 170
when you consider the things that make me seek your sound advice
because everything will rest on the wise counsel that you will give to me.

Head Councilman:
You can *count* on us, queen of this land; you do not need to ask *twice*
for anything that is in our power to *guide* you with words or action,
because we're *willing* to advise you on any matter when you call on us. 175

Clues from the grammar: The conjunctive particle "because" is repeated to mark the vacillating attitudes of the queen and the councilmen as they are treading on the quicksand of dramatic action (Constantinidis 2018, 395–96). In line 168, "because" reveals how the queen reasons by introducing a syllogism about protecting the imperial wealth and her son's well-being. The second "because" (line 169) stresses how important her son's presence is for defending the welfare and wealth of her dynastic house (oikos) against ill-wishers. The third "because" (line 172) pins *everything* related to Persia's imperial future on the 12 councilmen's ability to give her sound advice. The fourth "because" (175) is spoken by the head councilman;

in his guarded diplomatic reply, he parodies the queen's repetitive use of it but also chooses his words carefully, as if the councilmen had failed to give her son wise advice in the past. He assures her of their willingness to give her sound advice *because* he knows that this Persian queen has influence and is willing to use it.

Cues found in the text: The queen worries about two interdependent things: the welfare of her family (Xerxes) and the welfare of the state (the imperial dynasty). She speaks as a queen mother whose primary duty is to show concern for the well-being of her son. She is afraid that Persian wealth is vulnerable and cannot be protected from either internal enemies (insurrection) or external ones (invaders) because the Persian men have left to invade Greece. If the empire is bankrupted or its military force is broken, the dynasty will lose control of domestic and foreign foes.

Contextualizing the moment: The councilmen know that the Achaemenid Dynasty is a centrally run family business. The heart of the imperialist enterprise is the emperor's inner court that consists of men, women, eunuchs, servants, and the councilmen. The emperor's power rests on close association with those courtiers (like the councilmen) whom he had raised to positions of power and prestige. The queen hopes that Xerxes will return home to affirm his control of the throne, the treasury, and the inner court by killing rivals and dissenters. His father (Darius) ascended to the throne by killing Smerdis (who had killed Cambyses) and legitimized his reign by taking control of their inner court. He married the wives or sisters of his predecessors, incorporated them into his own harem, fathered children (like Xerxes) with them, and raised them to high status (as he did with Atossa).

Exercises for rehearsal: Read aloud the verses in the previous section and consider (1) how the queen interacts with the councilmen through eye contact, (2) why mentioning Darius will help her get support for Xerxes, (3) how any perceived weakness in either the economy or the army might break the fortunes of the imperial house, and (4) why Xerxes' return would affirm the safety of her household and the security of the regime.

Moment 3: The Queen Shares Her Dream

Questions for consideration: The Persians adopted the eagle as the official emblem of their empire, so why do the Greeks think that the true emblem of the Persian Empire is the yoke? What emotions drive Xerxes to tear up his clothes in the queen's dream? How did the queen rehearse her handmaids to mime the dream? How does the queen focus attention more squarely on the action by sitting down? How do the councilmen respond to this display?

Queen:
Many dreams have come to me, always at night to my satisfaction,
ever since my child raised an army and left home without much fuss,
    [Sits down on the folding stool]

wanting to plunder the land owned by the European Greeks.
But I've never seen a dream as vivid as the one I saw last night.
I will tell you all about it; but please hold off on your critiques.   180
I saw two well-dressed women. They were both quite a sight!
    [HANDMAIDS 3 & 6 mime the dream]
They looked like two sisters to me who had the same roots.
Except one had a Persian dress on, while the other a Doric.
In size and looks they were superior to other women recruits.
Their beauty was impeccable; to look at them was euphoric.   185
    [HANDMAID 1 puts on the mask of Xerxes]
The one in the Doric dress called Greece her home.
The other's home was the land of one of our allophone allies.
They were squabbling like bees on a honeycomb
when at long last my son Xerxes heard their cries.
    [HANDMAID 1 quiets HANDMAIDS 3 & 6]
He grabbed them by the neck and pushed their faces deep down   190
to force them to be quiet. Then he yoked them to his chariot apace.
Our Asian allophone ally wore the gear proudly like a royal gown,
especially the bit in her mouth that kept her submissive with grace.
    [HANDMAID 3 bucks]
But the European Greek fought back with both hands. She did not fiddle.
She tore apart the chariot's harness, and, freeing herself from the bridle,   195
she pulled the chariot so violently that she broke the yoke in the middle.
My Xerxes fell hard onto the ground while Darius, his father and his idol,
    [HANDMAID 2 puts on the mask of Darius]
was watching him. Darius shook his head at Xerxes, vastly disappointed.
Xerxes felt ashamed and tore up his robe as his nerves grew tauter.
You can tell that what I dreamed about last night was a bit disjointed!   200
I got out of bed, and I splashed the fresh and soothing running water
    [The QUEEN stands up]
from the spring on my hands and face. Then I went out to the altar
because I wanted to make a peace offering for the sake of my son
to appease the demon with all the due rites that no one can alter.
Then I saw an eagle that flew past me heading for the blazing sun.   205
    [The HANDMAIDS follow the queen's gaze]
I stood speechless, my friends, because I was utterly petrified.
Next, I saw a hawk flapping its wings to gain speed and altitude,
before it swooped onto the eagle's head; its talons tore off the hide.
All that the eagle did was cower, showing a total lack of fortitude,
giving up his body to the hawk. This fight was as scary for me to see   210
as perhaps it is for you to hear. Because, as all of you know full well,
if my son wins the war, he will be much admired. Don't you agree?

But if he loses, he'll not be answerable to the state. Isn't that swell?
He is still the master of this land, provided that he survives the war.

Head Councilman:
Queen mother, we do not want our words to shock you to the core   215
or to make you overconfident. But if you think that what you saw is bad,
then approach the gods with a petition. Ask them to avert any disaster
for you, your son, and all the people in the state who are lonely and sad,
especially those who are your friends and loyally serve the royal master.
Secondly, make sure that you pour libations on the ground and the dead.   220
Respectfully ask your husband Darius, whom you saw in your bad dream,
to send good fortune to you and to your son from the dark world we dread
and to keep bad fortune underground and underfoot to aid our self-esteem.
   [Points to the other councilmen]
We respectfully urge you to do all this because we share a premonition.
We hope everything will work out well for you and yours in every way.   225

Clues from the culture: For the Persians, the emblem of the Persian Empire was the eagle. For the Greeks, the emblem of the Persian Empire was the yoke. In the first part of the queen's dream, a European Greek breaks the Persian yoke, causing Xerxes to lose his balance and fall. Xerxes is so distressed and ashamed in his mother's dream that he tears up his robe. In the Hebrew Bible, people tear up their robes when they feel deep grief, extreme distress, great shame, or genuine repentance. For instance, Mordecai, an eminent Jew, tore up his clothes when he found out that Xerxes had issued orders for genocidal pogroms to be carried out against the Jews who were living in the Persian Empire (*Esther* 4:1). When the queen awakens, she goes to the altar in the yard to make a tithing (a "peace offering"), and an eagle, pursued by a hawk, flies past her heading east. Her "peace offering" was a porridge-like soup (pelanos) that was made with honey, oil, and meal; it could either be burned up as an offering to the gods in the sky or could be poured down as an offering to the gods of the underworld.

Cues found in the text: The queen describes the violent conflict between the conquering Persians and the resisting Greeks in the simple terms of a dream. The European Greeks in continental Greece and the Asian Greeks (a.k.a. "Ionians") in Asia Minor were blood relatives, a connection emphasized in several Athenian tragedies (Aristotle, *Poetics* 1453b15–26). The Persians had already conquered the Asian Greeks. The first woman in the queen's dream is wearing a Persian dress, but she is a foreigner. Her land was subjugated and became one of Persia's allophone allies. The second woman in her dream is wearing a Doric dress (peplos, line 183), which was a one-piece, close-fitting, ankle-long dress made of patterned wool and fastened with a pin at the shoulder and a belt at the waist. Doric fashion was prevalent among the Greeks on the European continent (from Sparta to Athens) and was evident in clothing, hairstyles, makeup, footwear, accessories, and architecture, but also in body posture and lifestyle. See, for example, the 46 outer Doric pillars of the Parthenon.

Contextualizing the moment: The queen says that she is seeking the councilmen's advice because she had a bad dream and saw a bad omen. In her dream, two beautiful and well-dressed women who looked like sisters – an Asian Greek and a European Greek – were squabbling. Xerxes grabbed them by the neck to silence them, and he yoked them to his Persian chariot. First, he harnessed the Asian Greek, who was submissive, but the European Greek resisted him. She fought back, tore the harness apart, spat out the bit, and pulled so hard she broke the yoke, causing Xerxes to fall. Darius shook his head in disappointment, and Xerxes, overwhelmed by shame and distress, tore up his robe. The handmaids stop miming the dream when the queen stands up and says that she got out of bed, washed her face to calm herself, and went to the yard to make a peace offering at the altar to appease a demon for the sake of her son. At the altar, she was surprised when an eagle flew past her, pursued by a hawk. If the dream and the omen are prophetic signs of bad things to come, the queen reminds everyone that Xerxes will not be answerable to the Persian people and their allies because he is still their master. In the democratic city-state of Athens (Aeschylus' *polis*), all leaders were accountable for their decisions and actions, and they answered to a state board of review. Her assertion about Xerxes' unaccountability shows the rift between Athenian democratic leadership and Persian autocratic leadership in terms of both principles and practices. The queen asks the councilmen to interpret the dream and the omen in hopes of reading their minds, but they avoid interpreting either. Instead, they advise her to summon her dead husband from the underworld because only Darius could advise her about the future of the empire under Xerxes.

Exercises for rehearsal: Read aloud the verses above, paying close attention to (1) the details she uses to describe her dream; (2) how she has orchestrated a depiction of the dream through her handmaids; (3) what physical actions might best reveal the response of Asian and European Greeks to Persian dominance; (4) what Xerxes' reaction tells us about his relationship with his father; and (5) how the queen tries to uncover what the councilmen think about the future of Xerxes and the monarchy, especially when they are diplomatically shielding their thoughts.

Moment 4: Head Councilman Saved by the Bell

Questions for consideration: Why is the queen gracious toward the councilmen? Why does she ask for the location of Athens, though she already knows? How does she try to entrap them with questions? Does the head councilman's description of how the messenger runs to meet them support or contradict the way the messenger runs? What might be the queen's reaction to the messenger?

Queen:
At any rate you are the first kindly judge of these signs of intuition.
Your hopes confirm mine. My son and my house will see a better day.
    [Gets closer to read their faces]
May these kindnesses come about! I will go home per your advice
to get ready and to bring here everything we will need to conjure up
the spirits of my dead dear ones from the underworld at any price.   230
Oh, dear ones, teach me this well. Where on earth is Athens set up?

Head Councilman:
Where they say it is – far away to the west where the regal sun sets!

Queen:
But why did my son really crave to hunt down the citizens of that state?

Head Councilman:
Because, when Athens is taken, all Greece will fall into the king's nets.

Queen:
Has the Athenian army ever had more men or ships than ours to date?   235

Head Councilman:
Never, and yet it inflicted much harm to warriors from Persian lands.

Queen:
Is it because they are better archers with more arrows in their hands?

Head Councilman:
No, not at all! They use strap shields and thrust their spears standing erect.

Queen:
What else besides polearms? Have they enough cash in their houses?

Head Councilman:
They have some silver from the silver mines, a treasure of their land.   240

Queen:
Who is the shepherd whose rule every Athenian soldier espouses?

Head Councilman:
No one! They aren't slaves or subjects. They obey no one's command.

Queen:
Then how do they ever manage to withstand any invading troops?

Head Councilman:
    [Falls into the queen's verbal trap]
They manage. They destroyed Darius' great and splendid marines.

Queen:
> *[Shakes her head disapprovingly]*
You speak of terrors the parents of the departed must heed! Oops!   245

Head Councilman:
> *[Draws her attention away from himself]*
I think you will soon receive full and accurate news saved for queens because the way that man runs to get here shows that he is a Persian. He is bringing some official news that we will call either good or bad.
> *[The bronze bell of Susa sounds the death knell]*

Clues from the rhetoric: The bad dream and the bad omen were two complementary stories that mirrored, on a tiny scale, the bigger narrative of the entire play. The practice of placing a minuscule copy of a story (or image) within the larger story (or image) is called *mise en abyme* in French. The dream and the omen abridge and illustrate (in a nutshell) the main theme of the play – the defeat of the giant eagle (the Persian armada) by a small hawk (the Greek fleet) and the humiliation of Xerxes (the imperial scion) by an untamed teenage woman (a European Greek) who breaks the Persian yoke. The queen knows that the councilmen are avoiding interpreting the dream and the omen, but she is gracious toward them since she plans to catch them in a verbal trap. She addresses them as a group by using the noun "judge" (critēs) in the singular, instead of "judges" (crites) in the plural, which may also mean that she is talking just to the head councilman and that he is speaking on behalf of the collective.

Cues found in the text: Aeschylus wrote that, in close combat, the Athenians thrust their "spears standing upright" (line 238). His pun is based on two words (egche stadaia) and can mean that, in hand-to-hand combat, the Athenians either thrust their spears standing upright (literal meaning), or they thrust their penises standing erect (figurative meaning) (Constantinidis 2021, 88). The queen disregards the figurative meaning by refocusing everyone's attention on what profit-making prospects the invasion will create for the Persians. They know about the silver mines at Laureion in Attica and expect that their troops will loot the silver coins stored in each Athenian household. But they do not know that, in 483 BCE, the Athenians took the advice of politician and general Themistocles, and instead of dividing the surplus from the mines into ten drachma bonuses for each male citizen and household, they used the surplus to build a fleet of 200 battleships (triremes). This decision illustrates how the Athenians sacrificed personal gains for the sake of public safety. The Persian queen cannot appreciate the way the democratic state of Athens manages its affairs. She also cannot fathom how Athens can rely on an army of citizens who voluntarily fight and die in defense of their homeland and its democratic institutions. To drive this point home, the queen uses the term "shepherd" (poimanoor, line 241), which was used by monarchs in both Europe and Asia as far back as the Trojan War. Homer used it to describe King Nestor (*Iliad* 2.104) and, later, King Agamemnon as "shepherd of the army" (*Iliad* 2.288; 7.367; 19.63; *Odyssey* 5.533). In a monarchy, the "shepherd" is both the chief-of-state and commander-in-chief responsible for leading his people to war like a herd of sheep to slaughter. The queen seems baffled. If the Athenians are not ruled and led around by a "shepherd," then how did they manage to repel the invasion spearheaded by Darius? The head councilman's answer is clear – the Athenians are nobody's slaves or subjects because they submit to no one's command (line 242).

Contextualizing the moment: The verbal exchange between the queen and the head councilman shows that they have conflicting opinions about Xerxes' invasion of Greece. Like a wily lawyer, the queen knows the answers to her own questions. She asks the councilmen to explain to her why they let Xerxes disregard the hard lesson of Darius' defeat at Marathon near Athens and advised him to "hunt down" the Athenians into their lair. They fall in her verbal trap when they admit that the Athenians had defeated Darius' marines, and in doing so, they reveal that they misadvised Xerxes. The queen is afraid that if Xerxes' invasion fails, he might be turned into a scapegoat by his rivals if he returns to Susa (lines 213–14, 226–27). Her fear is valid because, in the next scene, she learns that Xerxes, the hunter, and his soldiers are now on the run hunted down by the Greeks. Later in the play, the necromancy scene reveals that the ghost of Darius condones the assassination of inept emperors, but the queen is unwilling to betray her son and remains loyal to him (Constantinidis 2012, 6). She hopes that he will survive and will keep the wealth (ploutos) and prosperity (olbos) of their house as a means of wielding imperial power. Her "dead dear ones" (line 229) are her three husbands. Her living "dear ones" (line 231) are the councilmen whose loyalty she doubts. They are as old as Darius, who, in the necromancy scene, conceals the fact that the Athenians had defeated his naval infantry at the Battle of Marathon. What the Athenians had done to Darius' soldiers then is now a scary reminder for both the queen mother and the parents of the departed soldiers (line 245). This reminder proves that the councilmen had misadvised Xerxes to attack Athens. The queen's line of questioning is interrupted by a messenger who brings bad news from the battlefront. The head councilman realizes that he is metaphorically and literally saved by the bell – the bronze bell of Susa – so he diverts the queen's attention from the memory of Darius' demise to the news about Xerxes' defeat.

Exercises for rehearsal: Read the verses in the previous section aloud several times on your feet, thinking about (1) how the queen interacts with the councilmen by remaining agreeable; (2) how the queen disregards the bawdy pun and stays focused on her line of questioning; (3) whether the queen knows the answers to the questions that she asks and keeps the pressure on the head councilman until he inadvertently admits that he and the other councilmen had misadvised Xerxes; (4) the queen's displeasure with the head councilman's callousness; (5) his attempt to divert her attention away from himself and toward the messenger; and (6) how the conversation is abruptly interrupted by the messenger and the sonorous knell of the bronze bell of Susa. As you grow more familiar with the text, begin to make well-thought-out choices about how movement will enhance each of these details.

Conclusion

In this scene, the queen is belatedly responding to everything the councilmen have said or done in the past. The focus must be on her present thoughts and circumstances because although her thoughts will progress in the next scene, her circumstances will regress. Keep track of the emotional roller coaster she is on and pace yourself by controlling your pauses (meaningful silences) and your utterances (speech acts). Do not needlessly crowd each moment with body language that communicates only what has already been made available to the audience in words. It is not known at this point what will happen if the councilmen opt out of their fiduciary duty of loyalty to her son or give her more bad advice. Will they lose their heads or just their jobs? Mark this scene with each character's overt or covert intent by highlighting verbs (to indicate actions or reactions), adverbs (to indicate manner or degree), adjectives (to indicate quality or quantity), and nouns (to indicate objects or dispositions). Then read through them to understand what ties them all together. Consider how these will influence your stage behavior (verbal, paraverbal, and body language) in the role of the queen. In the queen's dream, for example, the submissive gestures of the Asian Greek and the defiant gestures of the European Greek can be precise and decisive, rather than large and extravagant. The Persian queen is a clever woman who is both articulate and subtle.

The role of the queen is perfect for every performer who needs to learn how to control his verbal language in relation to his body language and paralanguage. The illocutionary and perlocutionary force of each character's speech acts are used to influence the thoughts, emotions, and behaviors of the others (Austin 1976, 99–103). The exercises in this chapter will help performers learn a bigger lesson, namely, that performing a Greek tragedy in a translation is a more profound, exacting, and exciting endeavor than performing a Greek tragedy in an adaptation. By completing the exercises above, actors will understand that *Persians* is not a play about loud characters with conspicuous motives and extravagant behaviors, but a subtle commentary on imperialism. This will help audiences experience and understand the anti-imperialist, anti-slavery culture of Aeschylus' play in a meaningful way by highlighting the thinking and lifestyle of the imperialist, proslavery Persian elite – beginning with the queen.

References

Austin, J. L. 1976. *How to Do Things with Words*, 2nd ed. Edited by J. O. Urmson and Marina Sbisà. Oxford: Oxford University Press.

Constantinidis, Stratos E. 2012. "The Aristophanes-Chaeris Hypothesis: Did Aristophanes See an Adaptation of Aeschylus' *Persians* During the Peloponnesian War?" In *Text & Presentation 2011: The Comparative Drama Conference Series*, 5–15. Jefferson, NC and London: McFarland & Co., Inc. Publishers.

Constantinidis, Stratos E. 2018. "The Broadhead Hypothesis: Did Aeschylus Perform Word Repetition in Persians?" In *Brill's Companion to the Reception of Aeschylus*, edited by Rebecca Futo Kennedy, 381–407. Leiden and Boston: Brill.

Constantinidis, Stratos E. 2021. "The Didymus-Herodicus Hypothesis: Did Aeschylus Choreograph and Perform the Puns in *Persians?*" *Revista do Laboratorio de Dramaturgia* 17: 87–110.

Herodotus. 1998. *The Histories*. Translated by Robin Waterfield. Oxford and New York: Oxford University Press.

PART 2
Teaching

As teachers, we use pedagogy in creative ways to help students think critically and examine the world, and themselves, with curiosity. In stretching them, and ourselves, beyond everyday habits, ideas, opinions, choices, and expressions, we open up a wide range of artistic possibilities for the field as a whole. In our own classrooms, we have noticed that when our students learn how to embody poetic text – of any kind – their acting skills tend to improve tremendously. They become more alive to the formation and meanings of words and more aware of how their whole body can express an idea. The contributors in this collection of essays write on developmental classwork approaches aimed at expanding actors' access to their own physical, vocal, emotional, and intellectual resources. As in the previous section, the chapters are organized from broader exercises to more detailed explorations and should be consulted in whatever order is most useful to you and your teaching at any given moment. We hope the book will be a valuable, exciting resource for you as you write syllabi, construct a rehearsal process, or solve problems as they arise. We also hope you will discover launching pads for innovation that will take this work even further.

We kick off with Peter Zazzali's "Sculpting and Imaging the Text: An Equitable and Inclusive Approach to Speaking Heightened Language," a chapter that discusses how we can consider culture and identity while working on poetic text. His work invites the body and voice to physically respond to language, creating a new sense of ownership over imagery and words, especially for students whose first language is not English.

Next, we move on to "The Sound in the Silence; the Movement in the Stillness: Discovering Embodiment in Presence," by Karen Kopryanski and Peter Balkwill, which features exercises inspired by the work of Robyn Hunt and Steve

Pearson. This chapter centers on grounding, silence, and stillness so that actors can observe and recognize impulses as they arise in each moment, empowering them to make choices about how to use those impulses, physically and vocally, on stage.

The third chapter in this section, "Grace, Gravitas, and Grounding – Approaching Greek Tragedy Through a New Translation of Hecuba," outlines Tamara Meneghini's approach to staging the premiere of a new translation of Euripides' play and takes us through exercises she used during rehearsals, infusing voice and movement work into every level of the production process.

Doreen Bechtol's "Animating the Ancients: A Scaffolded Approach to Physicalizing Greek Theatre" focuses on the body as a primary location for story in Greek tragedy, analyzing sculptural imagery to inform the practice of working in a mask. She interrogates gesture as a pathway for illuminating character, especially when, as in ancient Greek tragedy, the actor's face is concealed.

Candice Brown also uses artwork as part of the inspiration for her chapter, "Naughty, Bawdy Characters and Comedy of Manners," in which she invites us into the world of bawdy language and explores how to balance voice, movement, imagery, and language with playfulness and nuance in both the classroom and the rehearsal process.

The chapter that follows, Matt Davies' " 'O, Villain, Villain, Smiling, Damned Villain': *Hamlet* and the Rhetoric of Repetition," is a fascinating inquiry into whether a single rhetorical device in *Hamlet* has the potential to uncover multiple layers of meaning for the actor. His examination demonstrates both the relevance and importance of rhetoric and inspires exploration in both actor training and the rehearsal hall.

We conclude with "Agamemnon's Homecoming: Using Active Analysis to Explore Ancient Theatre," which features Sharon Marie Carnicke's groundbreaking work on Stanislavski's etudes and considers how these exercises in guided improvisation can reveal important details about Greek tragedy, even for those who are not actors.

We encourage you to use the exercises, rather than simply going through them in a mechanical way. Respond to the process. The best actors use both verbal and nonverbal communication to make the playwright's words come to life. We teach actors to externalize thoughts and feelings by finding a bridge between voice, movement, and script work in one continual arc of experience. This is what we mean by building embodiment.

8

SCULPTING AND IMAGING THE TEXT

An Equitable and Inclusive Approach to Speaking Heightened Language

Peter Zazzali

Introduction: A Contextual Overview

As I began teaching a course titled Classical Acting Techniques at Singapore's LASALLE College of the Arts, I was confronted with a humbling moment of racial and cultural difference when one of my students declared himself "inadequate" at performing Shakespeare.[1] A young man of Malaysian descent, he was reduced to tears while attempting to understand and speak Lysander's passage in act 1, scene 1, wherein the character decries "the course of true love never did run smooth" (132). The student, sobbing, exclaimed, "I have always felt inferior with Shakespeare and was led to think that I couldn't do it because English is not my first language. I want so badly to be able to speak it, to be a legitimate actor, but it is too much for me."[2] I was heartbroken to hear such a young and proud performer erroneously discredit himself. I counseled him with as much reassurance – and reality – as I could muster, but he was having none of it; the wounds from his past experience with Shakespeare ran deep. He had been traumatized, which is not an overstatement.

My student's courageous confession was – and is – both poignant and informative. It prompts teachers to account for identity and power when approaching heightened-language plays penned in English, especially the oeuvre of Shakespeare. The idea that one's ability to handle Shakespeare "legitimizes" an actor is shortsighted and patently false. The professional theatre and on-camera mediums are lined with thousands of accomplished people who never played the likes of Hamlet or Cleopatra. Furthermore, the notion of being "classically trained" is a limiting proposition. While working on poetic verse and elevated prose develops important skills, mastering them is not a prerequisite for proficiency and success. Telling

DOI: 10.4324/9781003204060-11

students their path to sublimity depends on being able to speak, experience, and deliver Shakespeare's roles is inaccurate and reductive. This myth becomes especially damaging to students like mine, whose second language is English, who identifies racially and culturally as non-Western, and who have been directly or implicitly told they must master the Bard. I contend that we should demystify the *process* of acting Shakespeare as we guide our students in the exploration of his texts. In doing so, we must be sensitive to how each actor's racial and cultural identity frames their engagement of the work, thereby helping us instruct with empathy and care.

I have been developing a systemic approach for embodying and activating heightened language texts toward performing them with precision, power, clarity, and grace. Titled *sculpting and imaging* (or S&I), the technique locates consonants and imagery in conjunction with specific parts of the actor's body. The fricative "f," as in "first," for example, is launched from the forehead, thereby providing a catalyst for embodying the syllable and, by extension, the word in which it sits. Additionally, actors undergo a process by which they allow associative imagery to drop into their bodies to connect to the language and activate it through *intentional* speaking.[3] This chapter presents S&I as a physical praxis that yields tangible results toward providing confidence and skill in speaking poetic prose/verse. In learning this technique, actors do not surrender their personal and cultural identity. Rather than learning an indoctrinated system of speech sounds (e.g., Received Pronunciation), they are emboldened to make discoveries and engage the language on their own terms. The approach can be likened to other strategies addressing personal, cultural, racial, gender, and national identity in the subfield of actor training.[4] The pedagogy invites actors to claim ownership of their speaking in ways that account for who they are, how they sound, and where they are from. A cross-cultural balance is suggested to achieve this outcome. Shakespeare and Eliot, for example, might be taught alongside Kalidasa and Tagore – two poet/playwrights in India's rich dramatic tradition. The key is to unlock one's identity while engaging the text toward a performance full of psychophysical nuance. It is thus an equitable and inclusive approach to speaking heightened language.

This chapter is divided into three parts. First, I will examine the cross-cultural essence of the research investigating the complexities and responsibilities of delivering curricula in an intersectional training environment. Second and third, I will describe and unpack the two components of the pedagogy – sculpting and imaging the text – by explaining it in practice. My goal is for the reader to find the technique useful when speaking heightened language while also appreciating it as an equitable and inclusive approach to teaching and learning.

Teaching in a Cross-Cultural Learning Community

LASALLE is part of Singapore's national university of the arts and one of the leading institutions of its kind in Australasia. The acting program is especially distinguished and a member of the Asia Pacific Bond of Theatre Schools, an elite consortium created under the auspices of UNESCO in 2008.[5] In many ways, the program reflects the racial and national diversity of Singapore, insofar as its student population roughly echoes the city-state's demographic of Chinese (74%), Malay (14.5%), Indian (9%), and "other" (6%) (Ong 2021). The course's pedagogy integrates Western and Asian approaches within a European-styled conservatoire adhering to British standards of assessment and accreditation.[6] This is in part because it was founded by a Catholic brother (Joseph McNally) in a nation that – unlike many of its regional counterparts – has embraced colonialism and foreign investment throughout its young history.[7] Indeed, the so-called Singaporean miracle of the 1960s and 1970s resulted in the backwater and breakaway republic developing into one of the wealthiest countries in the world. The country's first prime minister – Lee Kuan Yew – designed a scheme for inviting "foreign talent" across numerous sectors of the professional sphere, a practice that has continued ever since (Hussain 2015).[8]

LASALLE is an extension of its sociocultural environment.[9] Many of the school's full-time instructors and administrators have been imported from countries such as the UK, US, and Australia. This strategy frequently results in a cultural disconnect because expats bring their Western perspectives to the institution yet have minimal experience working in Southeast Asia. The practice of hiring foreigners occurs throughout the city-state's business and educational sectors, thereby affecting Singapore's national identity, the nebulousness of which has been a subject of recent debate (Tan Kwan Wei 2021). In the spirit of Linda Tuhiwai Smith's recommendations for researchers undertaking a decolonizing methodology, I acknowledge my position as a white male from an economically privileged country. Moreover, I recognize the conscious and unconscious biases that come with such status. I am committed to conducting my work as a trainer and researcher with humility and care, especially when engaging students whose race and culture is different from my own. As Smith so aptly states,

> The imaginary line between "East" and "West" . . . allowed for the political division of the struggle by competing Western states to establish what Said has referred to as a "flexible positional superiority" over the known and yet to become known world.
>
> *(Tuhiwai Smith 1999, 59–60; Said 1978, 12–13)*

The power dynamics of a Westerner teaching a predominantly Asian group of students how to perform Shakespeare must be responsibly understood to avoid privileging Western texts and practices while exoticizing, excluding, or minimizing indigenous ones.

Sculpting and Imaging the Text

The goal of S&I is twofold. On one hand, it provides a systemic approach to speaking and performing plays written in heightened language. From Shakespeare and Stoppard to Soyinka and Kalidasa, the technique empowers actors to take ownership of their performance toward achieving presence and truth onstage. Equally as important, it invites actors to unlock their literal and figurative voices while expressing their personal and artistic identities. It is an inherently equitable and inclusive engagement of the actor's work.

S&I is a process of embodying phonemes to activate speech and communicate effectively. It draws, in part, on Rudolf Steiner's work with eurythmy. Eurythmy can be of great significance [to] the actor because it invites physicalizing vowels and consonants as a way of absorbing the substance of each word and its function in a phrase. Eurythmy is primal in practice and, by Steiner's estimation, inherently spiritual:

> The actor must be able to experience for himself how the word, the artistically formed and spoken word, can reveal the whole being of man. This penetrating insight that can behold the word as a revelation of man cannot fail to give him a more spiritual conception of his calling.
>
> *(2007, 227)*[10]

Eurythmy likewise contributed to Michael Chekhov's process of psychophysical gesture in which archetypal imagery and movement create a mind/body connection infused with action. Just as Chekhov's system deploys specific and repeatable gestures to access a character's emotional life, eurythmy is a movement-based process that causes a fluid continuum between the performer's mind and body (Chekhov 2002, 63–76). The result in both cases is a theatricalized expressivity commensurate with the craft of stage acting.

Heightened language is distinct from everyday conversation in both form and content. Packed with rhetorical devices (e.g., metaphor) and vivid imagery, poetic writing eclipses the prosaic while attempting to access sublimity. This is evident through the grand and decidedly human themes and ideas woven throughout such texts. To borrow from Shakespeare, it engenders "such stuff as dreams" and lifts listeners beyond a pedestrian worldview while arcing toward that which is sublime (Shakespeare 1974, 4.1.156–57). Though nature is often the muse of its authors, poetry ought not be confused with the ordinariness of the natural world. Indeed, Steiner makes this point in decrying the "greyness of speech" and its functional, if uninspired, use in our daily lives (Steiner 2007, 175). From Romeo's and Dushyanta's depictions of their love interests (Juliet and Shakuntala) to Derek Walcott's elegant renderings of Trinidadian folklore, poetic writing enriches the human condition by transcending it.

The notion of "Shakespeare" and heightened language connotes elitism and – for many people – causes fear and resistance. The eminent voice teacher Cicely Berry in fact acknowledges that "educated speech" and "class overtones" can be "alienating" to people given how they self-identify (Berry 2011, 33). Similar issues have been raised in response to a "standard" way to "speak classical plays," a system founded by Edith Skinner, whose relevance has been justifiably questioned.[11] The recent practice-based research of Daron Oram offers a more equitable engagement of voice and speech training. Oram is committed to each student discovering and expressing their individual voice – both literally and figuratively – alongside developing skills that are indispensable to speaking effectively. Connecting to breath, fully engaging one's articulators, and finding ease in releasing sound are as relevant today as they have always been in commanding the audience's listening. Oram's aim is to address these principles in the context of an accessible and inclusive space that accounts for cultural differences.

> I haven't rejected the practical skills associated with the free voice in my practice; what I try to do with my students is to make the cultural embeddedness of those skills more conscious.
>
> *(Oram 2020, 305)*[12]

There is not a "correct" way to sound but, instead, a prioritization of communication. The text incites a given thought and impulse that jointly become manifest in the actor's intention to affect someone else. That is the very basis of the transaction.

S&I is consistent with Berry's method of embodying language, and speaking is understood as psychophysical action that is jointly nuanced and palpable. While sculpting explores consonants, imaging invites the actor to relish a word's vowel and diphthongs by delving into its meaning and associative images. The cadence, rhythms, and sounds of a word stem from the need to communicate "to another living being" and change what they think, feel, or do (Berry 2008, 3). The stakes for such an exchange are extraordinarily high, oftentimes the difference between life and death, thereby distinguishing the heightened reality of a theatrical world from its pedestrian muse. Characters like Lady Percy and King Lear are compelled to speak under the most dramatic of circumstances. Operating as a dialectic of sorts, they simultaneously reflect upon and transcend the human condition. Themes such as love and loss are omnipresent and realized through poetry, thereby requiring actors to take ownership of what they say by going beyond a pedestrian performance and entering the realm of that which is larger than life.

Step 1: Sculpting

Sculpting begins the process. The actor engages each syllable of a particular word through its consonants, all of which are connected to a particular body part. Plosives such as /p/ and /b/ generate from the stomach, whereas nasal consonants like /m/ and /n/ are placed at the feet. Sibilant fricatives /s/ for /z/ are in the groin, as are affricates /tʃ/ in chin and /dʒ/ in joy. For consonant blends like the /tɹ/ in Troy or /kɹ/ for "crack," the corresponding body parts coalesce: the hard /t/ springs from the heart, the /k/ the thighs, and the /ɹ/ from the top of the head. Thus, the actor sculpts a consonant blend by physicalizing each component through its corporeal correlative. The sounds and corresponding body parts are not randomly associated but tethered, insofar as the former lends to being placed in a given body part. A word like *track* would therefore start from the heart and skull before concluding with the hard /k/ off the thigh. The formation of the consonants /t/ and /ɹ/, for instance, occur at the gum ridge and hard palate, thereby *suggesting* a connection to the heart that then travels to the crown of the head; it is a process facilitated by the actor's imagination and should not be seen as a hard-and-fast directive. Indeed, the latter results in a buzzing sound at the roof of the mouth that especially vibrates from the top of the head, whereas the plosive /t/ easily draws attention to the chest and – by extension – the heart. Please note that the consonant/corporeal connection is an approximation that is intended to be *evocative*, not literal. Students may ask something like, "How do I make a /t/ from my heart?" to which I invariably respond, "I invite you not to become preoccupied with forming consonants from *suggestive* body parts at the expense of freeing yourselves into fully embodying the word. Try *associating* the /t/ with the heart as a departure point for physically engaging its correlative vowel/diphthong sound(s)." While sculpting associates /t/ with the heart, as we plainly know, the tip of the tongue and gum ridge literally produce the phoneme. Sculpting is designed to cause syllables to resonate and "drop into" the actor's entire body by expanding beyond their initial points of formation, just as the soundboard of an upright piano amplifies strokes from a keyboard. The essential thing is for the actor to work the text into their instrument. Doing so marks the difference between someone merely reciting lines and an artist who takes ownership of their text, their speaking, and ultimately their performance.

It is also important to note silent and variable pronunciations of spoken English. Both phonemes are pronounced in the blend /tɹ/, for instance, but the "ck" ending the word makes only a single /k/ sound. When sculpting, it is necessary to distinguish the sounds of a given phoneme. The letter "c," for instance, has two different pronunciations in the word "circus." This chart indicates each consonant sound with the body part where it is formed.

SCULPTING THE TEXT
Consonant Sounds and Corresponding Body Parts

v	forehead
ɹ	top of the skull
m/n	feet
l	knees
f	lungs
d/t	heart
k/g	legs
h	shoulders
tʃ	heart to shoulders
s/z	center of the body
dʒ	center of the body
j	center of the body
ʃ	center of the body
w/ʍ	center of the body
p/b	stomach

Again, it is necessary to *imagine* consonants being generated from their corresponding body parts without becoming rigidly beholden to the sculpting process. It is not a literal practice but an imagistic one. Just as singers are taught to use their mind's eye to achieve a vocal output, sculpting offers a way to embody heightened text by using the quintessential element of the actor's craft: their imagination.[13] Absorbing a word's consonants allows one to release into its vowel and diphthongs.[14] The location of each sound is based on the body part most favored by its formation. A name like "Vince" involves the fricative /v/, nasal /n/, and sibilant /s/, and lends to the respective launching points of the forehead, feet, and groin. The consonants form the word's skeletal framework supporting the expression of vowel and diphthong sounds toward activating one's speaking in the playing space.

When first exploring this technique, it is common for students to become unnecessarily fixated in their association of a sound with an associative body part. On many occasions students will ask, "How do I find 'v' in my forehead . . . and why that location?"[15] My response is twofold: (1) sculpting is designed to invite actors to physicalize the phonemes toward activating their speaking. It is a way to psychophysically unlock the performer and cause them to embody each word; (2) we *imagine* the sound coming from the forehead because it is a voiced fricative that is formed with the upper front teeth and lower lip, the vibration of which lends to resonating from the forehead. Essentially, sculpting deploys organic imagery to cause the actor to physicalize their speaking through a process of repetition that results in the activation of heightened text. The result is psychophysically engaged action realized through the performer's speaking. As I often remind my students, "If you take care of your text, it will take care of your acting." Though this chiasmic maxim might seem pithy, it is nonetheless accurate. If actors take the time to vigorously engage the heightened language through sculpting, they will transform their relationship with their speaking and render characters that are jointly palpable and present.

Sculpting is a detailed process that can take upwards of three minutes for a multisyllabic word that has an operative function in a phrase.[16] If one were sculpting Titania's "forgeries of jealousy" speech, for instance, they might spend five minutes sculpting just the opening line (Shakespeare 1974, 2.1.81). Embodying the entire passage could easily take an hour and a half. As with every facet of the actor's work, it necessitates being specific. It is essential to account for each individual sound, just as one would detail their character's score of actions, a practice that echoes Shakespearean trainers ranging from Berry to Barton.

To investigate the system of sounds and experiment with sculpting them, we explore a few simple words while being mindful of healthy vocal habits: dropping in the breath, opening the channel for sound, releasing one's speaking, etc. First, we apply the approach to "Shakespearean Insults," choosing three words from a list of terms that Shakespeare coined, two adjectives followed by a noun, each as onomatopoeic as it is degrading to its would-be recipient. Sculpt the three words (and their constitutive phonemes) while fully exploring their potential as action and include the second-person pronoun "you" in what ultimately becomes a saucy phrase intended to demean an interlocutor. Choose a partner and engage in a verbal joust fueled by the newly fashioned insult (e.g., "You yeasty, onion-eyed rabbit-sucker"). In my own classroom, the actors have great fun with the "insult" exercise, forming two teams that playfully cheer on their mate who exchanges jibes with an opponent.

After the technique has been introduced, choose a piece of verse drama, which must be fully sculpted before undertaking the "imaging" part of the process. Let us consider one of Helena's speeches in act 1, scene 1 from *A Midsummer Night's Dream*:

> Call you me fair? that fair again unsay.
> Demetrius loves your fair: O happy fair!
> Your eyes are lode-stars; and your tongue's sweet air
> More tuneable than lark to shepherd's ear,
> When wheat is green, when hawthorn buds appear.
> Sickness is catching: O, were favor so,
> Yours would I catch, fair Hermia, ere I go;
> My ear should catch your voice, my eye your eye,
> My tongue should catch your tongue's sweet melody.
> Were the world mine, Demetrius being bated,

The rest I'd give to be to you translated.
O, teach me how you look, and with what art
You sway the motion of Demetrius' heart.

Helena's speech spans 13 lines of iambic pentameter. It would take an actor roughly 30 minutes to sculpt this passage. S&I unlocks the emotional size of Shakespeare's verse in all its linguistic nuance. To succinctly illustrate how it works, refer to the first line of the speech, where she responds to Hermia, who has called her "fair": "Call you me fair? That fair again unsay" (1.1.181). In sculpting the first word of Helena's text, we can imagine the /k/ sound generating from the thighs, before releasing into the long /ɔ/ vowel and consonant /l/, which comes from the knees. Working on your feet and using the chart of consonant sounds, sculpt each sound before stringing them together to embody the entire word. When confident with the exploration, proceed to the next word, which in this instance is the pronoun "you." Engage your center to sculpt the /j/ sound and long /u/ vowel before moving onto the third and final word of the phrase, "fair," shaped by envisioning the /f/ emanating from the lungs and releasing into the diphthong /ɛɚ/.

Step 2: Imaging

Whereas sculpting is a rigorous engagement of a word's consonants, "imaging" savors its vowels and diphthongs while absorbing their associative meaning(s). In some ways, the approach can be compared to Linklater's directive to "indulge" the sensorial and emotional elements of a word for the purpose of "resurrecting the life of language" (Linklater 1992, 13).

Lie on your backs while slowly and gently allowing each part of a word to "drop into" the solar plexus. Through deep breathing, enter a state of calm and vulnerability, if not repose and meditation. In releasing unnecessary tension, you become available to a word's sounds and images, thereby investigating its multiple properties and layers. In Helena's passage, she repeatedly utters Demetrius' name, which signals her deep affection for him. Imagine who Demetrius is, what he looks like, how he sounds, and what he means to Helena. Soak up the phonemes constituting the name "Demetrius" by tasting the pair of crisp vowels and lone diphthong, anchored by three voiceless and one voiced consonant.[17] The purpose of "imaging" is to avail one's tactile and emotional experience to a word's corresponding images. Repeatedly utter the word while luxuriating in its sounds, its imagery, and its meaning. Feel your ownership of its features, which when combined with sculpting empowers actors to string together phrases with eloquence and intention.

It may be helpful to listen to instrumental music while absorbing the language. Depending on its length and complexity, imaging can take multiple sessions to complete. Once speeches have been fully worked through, actors can form a circle and take turns entering to deliver their speech. Music can serve as underscoring and invite a deeper attachment to the speaking. The actors' connection to the text – and by extension, their character – is oftentimes remarkable as they take command of their speaking through an interconnection of mind and body to achieve exceptional presence.

Results

In teaching S&I to my students in Singapore, we cover four selections of text in a pair of units, one dedicated to Shakespeare and the other Kalidasa. Because LASALLE's acting program is a balance of Asian and Western content, it is important to choose material that reflects the diversity of our student population. In addition to Shakespearean text, we applied S&I to a passage of King Dushyanta's from *Shakuntala*, a Sanskrit drama based on an Indian myth. In keeping with our commitment to an accessible and inclusive learning environment, we take a nonbinary approach to casting, inviting the actors to play characters across gender identities, which many of them choose to do. Several students shared their experience with S&I:

> The sculpting exercise was very beneficial because it allowed me to physically embody the text I was speaking. Working with classical plays (Shakespeare to be precise) can be challenging in the sense that the actor must meet the grandeur of their language. Sculpting taught me to add color and invigorate my speaking, enabling me to paint the metaphors and images in Shakespeare's writing through my speaking.
>
> *(Hirah Tejas)*[18]

> Accessing Shakespeare's language through sculpting and imaging freed me to taste and savor the letters and syllables of every word. It empowered my body to release the energy lying within the text.
>
> *(Miza Syazwina)*[19]

> Sculpting and imaging work, while at first extremely exhausting both physically and emotionally, has proven helpful for me to start exploring the muscularity of language and is a useful tool for embodying heightened text.
>
> *(Teh En Matthias)*[20]

Perhaps the most telling testimonial came from the student mentioned at the chapter's outset, the one who was resistant about performing Shakespeare. After learning S&I, he discovered a new relationship with heightened-language texts. He states the following:

As someone who has had previous reservations approaching Shakespeare, sculpting enabled me to embody and understand the text in a non-cognitive way. It allowed me to tap into my strengths as a physically inclined actor and overcome my self-perceived weakness in handling heightened language.

(Anonymous)[21]

Sculpting and imaging gives actors a way to take ownership of heightened language without surrendering their personal identity. It invites the interconnection of one's mind and body through absorbing the sounds and meanings of a word with its function within a phrase. Because we all experience the world in our own way, how we physically and mentally respond to text is as varied as our personhood and that which constitutes our lived experience: culture, society, family, history, etc. This approach is inherently diverse, equitable, and inclusive. Informed by the works of Steiner and Berry, it offers a practical way for students to overcome whatever misgivings they might have with poetic texts and perform them with clarity, intention, and detail. Ultimately, sculpting and imaging empowers actors to deploy their speaking as action, textured by the renderer's singular identity.

Notes

1. Anonymous student from BA acting program, interview with author, October 2021.
2. Anonymous student from BA acting program, interview with author, October 14, 2021.
3. The parlance "dropping into the body" is commonly used among actor trainers to signify the performer's physical engagement of words and their corresponding phonemes.
4. Since Philip B. Zarrilli's groundbreaking anthology, *Acting (Re)Considered*, in 1995, several important works have addressed intercultural approaches to actor training. For insightful research into this area, see Cláudia Tatinge Nascimento, *Cross Cultural Borders Through the Actor's Work: Foreign Bodies of Knowledge* (London: Routledge, 2010); Stefan Aquilina, "Cultural Transmission of Actor Training Techniques: A Research Project," *Theatre, Dance, and Performance Training* 10, no. 1 (May 2019): 4–20; and Phillip B. Zarrilli, *Psychophysical Acting: An Intercultural Approach After Stanislavski* (London: Routledge, 2009). Also, see Zarrilli's co-edited volume with T. Sasitharan and Anuradha Kapur, *Intercultural Acting and Performer Training* (London: Routledge, 2019).
5. For more on LASALLE's involvement with the Asia Pacific Bond of Theatre Schools, see, accessed October 15, 2021, www.lasalle.edu.sg/industry-collaborations/asia-pacific-bond-theatre-schools.
6. Please note that the word "course" is synonymous with "program" in the UK and its former colonies.
7. Singapore was founded in 1965 when it separated from Malaysia to become a sovereign state.
8. For a thorough documentation of Singapore's modern history and Lee's 30-year rule as prime minister, see Lee Kuan Yew, *The Singapore Story: Memoirs of Lee Kuan Yew* (Singapore: Marshall Cavendish, 2015).
9. For a sociocultural investigation of acting programs throughout the world, see Peter Zazzali, *Actor Training in Anglophone Countries: Past, Present, and Future* (London: Routledge, 2021).

10. See also Poplawski 1998.
11. For more on Edith Skinner's approach, see Edith Skinner, *Speak with Distinction* (New York: Applause, 1990).
12. Andrea Caban, Julie Foh, and Jeffrey Parker, *Experiencing Speech: A Skills-Based, Panlingual Approach to Actor Training* (New York: Routledge, 2021) See also Dudley Knight and Phil Thompson, *Speaking with Skill: An Introduction to Knight-Thompson Speechwork* (London: Bloomsbury, 2012).
13. Voice and singing teachers have been using an imagistic approach to training for centuries. For a pair of informative texts, one academic the other practical, see also Jon F. Clements, "The Use of Imagery in Teaching Voice to the Twenty-first Century Student" (Phd diss., Florida State University, 2008); William D. Leyerle, *Vocal Development through Organic Imagery* (Geneseo, NY: Leyerle Publications, 1977).
14. I acknowledge that not all non-consonant sounds in English are either a vowel or diphthong. Indeed, triphthongs such as the "ire" sound in a word like "fire" are also part of the language. Given that triphthongs are comparably rare, and in the interest of readability and flow, I am choosing to limit my comments to vowels/diphthongs when discussing the acoustic guts – as it were – of a word.
15. Anonymous LASALLE acting student, interview with author, October 12, 2021.
16. According to Webster's Dictionary, an "operative" word "has the most relevance or significance in a phrase or sentence." Quoted from Merriam Webster Online Dictionary, accessed August 18, 2022, www.merriam-webster.com/dictionary/operative.
17. I take a nonbinary approach to gendered casting for this exercise. In addition to Helena's speech, I assign Lysander's "For aught that I could ever read . . ." lament from the same scene. I then let the students choose between the two and highly recommend exploring such an approach. In addition to demonstrating the value of an inclusive training space, a nonbinary engagement of the actor's work invites rewarding learning outcomes.
18. Hirah Tejas, email correspondence with author, October 14, 2021.
19. Miza Syazwina, email correspondence with author, October 13, 2021.
20. Teh En Matthias, email correspondence with author, October 13, 2021.
21. Anonymous student from BA acting program, email correspondence with author, October 14, 2021.

References

Berry, Cicely. 2008. *From Word to Play*. London: Oberon Books. 3.
———. 2011. *The Actor & The Text*. London: Virgin Books.
Chekhov, Michael. 2002. *To the Actor: On the Technique of Acting*. London: Routledge.
Hussain, Zarina. 2015. "How Lee Kuan Yew Engineered Singapore's Economic Miracle." *BBC News.com*, March 24. www.bbc.com/news/business-32028693.
Linklater, Kristen. 1992. *Freeing Shakespeare's Voice: An Actor's Guide to Talking Text*. New York: Routledge.
Ong, Justin. 2021. "Race-based Data in Population Census Needed for S'pore to Help Ethnic Groups Meaningfully: Indranee." *The Strait Times*, June 16. www.straitstimes.com/singapore/politics/race-based-data-in-population-census-needed-for-spore-to-help-ethnic-groups.
Oram, Daren. 2020. "The Heuristic Pedagogue: Navigating Myths and Truths in Pursuit of an Equitable Approach to Voice Training." *Theatre, Dance, and Performance Training* 11 (3) (September): 300–9.
Poplawski, Thomas. 1998. *Eurythmy: Rhythm, Dance, and Soul*. Edinburgh: Floris Books.

Said, Edward W. 1978. *Orientalism*. London: Routledge.
Shakespeare, William. 1974. *Riverside Shakespeare*. Edited by G. Blakemore Evans. Boston: Houghton Mifflin Co.
Skinner, Edith. 1990. *Speak with Distinction*. New York: Applause.
Steiner, Rudolf. 2007. *Speech and Drama*. Hudson, NY: Anthroposophic Press.
Tan Kwan Wei, Kevin. 2021. "In Singapore, Backlash against Foreign Workers Is Becoming a Hot Political Issue." *The Print*, July 30. https://theprint.in/world/in-singapore-backlash-against-foreign-workers-is-becoming-a-hot-political-issue/705946/.
Tuhiwai Smith, Linda. 1999. *Decolonizing Methodologies: Research and Indigenous Peoples*. London: Zed Books.

9

THE SOUND IN THE SILENCE; THE MOVEMENT IN THE STILLNESS

Discovering Embodiment in Presence

Karen Kopryanski and Peter Balkwill

In *Freeing Shakespeare's Voice*, Kristin Linklater writes,

> Great art lasts, and when the theatre wants to re-produce its past, performers are confronted by artistic demands very different from those posed by contemporary fare. Classical music is played on instruments that bear a distinct resemblance to their ancestors, but classical drama has to be played on a human instrument that experiences and expresses life in a manner radically altered even from a hundred years ago.
>
> *(Linklater 1993, 3)*

We could further argue that the pace of these changes has increased drastically over the past 50 years and that innovations in technology generally move more quickly than the human ability to adapt, resulting in changes to our everyday tempo that powerfully affect our sensory experience of the world. Ancient Greek theatre audiences relied on the spoken word more than the written word and were accustomed to listening to oral histories and storytelling, which would have informed how they engaged with and received dramatic performance. Play festivals often lasted 10 to 12 hours with only short intervals between offerings, and audiences would have been familiar with the stories being told, enthralled by inventive reinterpretations.

Today, our relationship to hearing – and to theatre – is wildly different. North American culture, and many others, are primarily visual, instead of aural. Screens figure prominently in our lives, and actors can find the answer to almost any question at the click of a button. While the accessibility of information is, no doubt, an asset, our phones, tablets, and computers also activate the reward center of the brain, and studies have shown that the mere presence of smartphones can reduce attention and memory (Mendoza 2018, 53). This challenges the work of the actor (and the audience) in new and unexpected ways because the screens we use to connect to the world also detach us from our emotional impulses, our experiences, *and* from others (Cummins 2020). They spark an expectation for instant knowledge and gratification, keeping us mentally busy, but at an emotional remove.

To move forward, we may need to stand still; to reconnect to our internal impulses, we may need to rediscover silence. Consider Penelope, who waited ten years for the return of Odysseus. In order to embody such a character, we must slow ourselves down and allow the body to recalibrate. Without taking the time to cultivate *presence*, essence is supplanted by effort, an energetic shift that is both misguided and ineffective on stage.

The challenges and complexities of classical text demand a deeper understanding than is possible with the click of a button. Greek tragedy, in particular, calls on the actor to generate an expansive, expressive (even *epic*) physical and emotional life, conveyed with appropriate vocal energy. What might be required to help an actor embody and give voice to a character within an epic circumstance – one that feels and appears larger than life? We believe the actor must master a firm point of presence, breath, and weight on stage. All three are directly and inextricably linked to being in the moment, and while they can be discovered in a classroom, cultivating any possible mastery requires an investment that extends past a student's training and into a lifetime of practice. We assert that one pathway to vocal and physical embodiment is to discover – in conjunction with full engagement of the imagination – how the sound in the silence and the movement in the stillness may open up a universe of possibilities for self-expression, inviting fully embodied characterizations to rise to the surface and finding "logic with the body and the voice, not with the mind" (Porter 2022, 51).

This chapter outlines several exercises in silent narrative designed to slow actors down so they may be present to their work. Doing so creates a "conceptual space where new ways of being can be contemplated" (Bissell and Fuller 2011, 15) and reforges the connection between mind, body, and inner life. It quiets the overstimulated mind and eases the need for immediate gratification so the actor can rediscover impulse and increased emotional responsiveness, generating greater expansiveness and a deeper relationship to words and character. At first, these approaches may appear abstract, redundant, or even irrelevant toward the task at hand. We suggest that by investing in exercises that – on the surface – do not present themselves as speedy conduits toward a polished performance, a valuable deconstruction of prescriptive, pedestrian expression might occur, along with a reawakening of the artist's unique creative perspective.

98 Karen Kopryanski and Peter Balkwill

KI

Robyn Hunt and Steve Pearson's decade of training with Tadashi Suzuki, and later with his contemporary, director Shogo Ohta, led the pair to investigate something that is central to all Japanese art and training: the idea of *ki*. Hunt explained in an interview:

> The challenge for the Westerner is that *ki* (in Japanese, *chi* in Chinese) cannot adequately be translated. Japanese dictionaries define the word in many ways (care, concern; intention, inclination; ambience, atmosphere; mood, temper, disposition; and perhaps most comprehensively, one's *senses, consciousness, spirit, mind, heart*). It might be thought of as our vital energy, something we experience when we come into full coordination, as the Alexander Technique masters say; something, like our breath, which is part of daily life but which, without training specifically to awaken us to its presence, often escapes our conscious awareness. We might say it is a way of being in the world, a core idea about our essential energy.[1]

In a company of actors who train together with regularity, dedication, and discipline, *ki* training can foster deeper concentration, stamina, "fighting spirit," and a much greater, more united sense of the ensemble. Ki encourages a broader sense of self and the ability to expand beyond the confines of our everyday human experience.

We will first explore an exercise for discovering the relationship between our physical balance and Ki, and then present two practical, impactful exercises developed by Hunt and Pearson – springing from their work with Suzuki – each followed by our own variations. Each exercise will be described as pragmatically as possible, followed by a bit of deeper analysis and an unpacking of the subtle components within the action.

Exercise 1: Balancing

Before approaching either Soaring or Slow Ten, it is helpful to introduce Ki, establishing balance and postures that offer strength within ease, rather than through muscle tension. This exercise involves receiving a series of gentle pushing tests from a partner, inviting the actor to sense shifts in energetic flow, stability, engagement, and presence.

Preparation

Pair actors up.

Part A: Inefficient Balancing

1. Actor A stands: feet hip width apart, knees locked, weight centered back in the heels and attention in the head.
2. Actor B gently nudges A's upper body forward, back, and side to side to see where stillness and balance can (or cannot) be maintained.
3. Actor A should resist being pushed off balance, and may articulate the unique muscular tensions required to maintain their position.

Part B: Connecting to Ki

1. Pause the testing, and ask Actor A to change their posture in the following ways:
   a. Soften the backs of the knees (without fully bending).
   b. Shift weight slightly forward over the balls of the feet.
   c. Draw attention to the body's low center, a few inches below the navel, and imagine that this center is drawing energy up from the floor through the soles of the feet and down from above through the length of the spine.
   d. Imagine a stream of energy extending from this low-center, in all directions.
   e. Have a sense of the weight on the underside of the body, working with gravity to allow the top side of the body to release.
   f. Note any shifts within the breath.

Part C: Balancing With Ki

1. Repeat the series of nudges from Part A while maintaining this connection to Ki.

Mark how the shift in physicality grounds the actor with a sense of ease and simplicity in presence and invokes the ability to send and receive energy. At this point, it is possible to repeat the inefficient balancing to note the difference. Once a common understanding of Ki and ease in balance are introduced, the group can begin further artistic explorations.

Testing Balance

The object is not to push the actors off balance but rather to invite them to find an efficient balanced position allowing them to experience Ki. In aikido training, one might engage in this test every day with varying results. The strength and flexibility of our training can enable us to navigate the intersection of our complex lives and our artistic activities.

Far Focus

Just as an actor must balance their character's intentions with the needs of the ensemble and the play as a whole, all of the exercises shared here require deep concentration and an awareness of attention and points in space where the gaze is directed. The actor must be aware of what is happening onstage, using all of their senses to connect to others in the space and gauge their connection to the whole. An image may spring to the actor's mind or they may become more aware of how their feet contact the floor, or their breath, or the sounds in the room. Awareness and observation encourage stability. Patsy Rodenburg might describe this as consciously connecting to Second Circle energy:

> In Second Circle, your energy is focused. It moves out toward the object of your attention, touches it, and then receives energy back from it. You are living in a two-way street – you give to and are responsive with that energy, reacting and communicating freely. . . . You influence [others] by allowing them to influence you. You hear others and take in what they are really saying.
>
> *(2008, 20)*

Soaring

Set to music, Soaring is a powerful exercise that aligns body and mind and increases the collective sensibility and strength of the ensemble. The activity also is meditative – it calms the mind/body and encourages a present-moment awareness of breath, ease, and stability. It strives for a collective alignment in the choreography and asks the artist to navigate their own imbalances and distractions, offering an opportunity to value process over product and accept imperfection. Soaring can be done in large group circles or in scattered spacing, either facing the same direction or with participants choosing their own focus.

Exercise 2: Soaring

Wendy Mortimer defines the activity as follows:

> Soaring is an exercise . . . in which actors stand with a far focus, and based on cues from a selected piece of music, go through a series of simple motions that require concentration, balance, and ease – all movement is choreographed to cues in the music.
>
> *(2005, 321)*

The series of movements is completed only once, in slow tempo, with the goal of spreading the movement out across the entire piece of music. Here, we will describe the exercise in more detail and offer a partnered variation.

Preparation

a. Stand with your feet hip-width apart, arms relaxed at your sides.
b. Close your eyes for a moment and sense your breath and that of the ensemble.
c. Breathe and feel your physical connection with the ground.
d. Listen and look far into the distance.

Prologue

1. When music begins,[2] breathe and see what arises (this might be an image, a sensation, or even a sound).

Soaring (additional thoughts to follow)

1. As lyrics or instrumentals begin, observe your right arm as it slowly begins to raise forward to shoulder height. Pause. In the next musical phrase, watch the arm return to its original position.
2. Now shift your attention to your left arm and repeat the sequence.
3. Shift your weight to allow the right leg to extend behind you, lengthening from the hip through the toe, rather than bending at the knee, and watch some part of your body (perhaps the standing leg) as balance allows.
4. Repeat with your left leg.
5. As the cue or musical phrase changes, slowly shift your visual focus from your body to something far in the distance.
6. Shift your weight and allow your left arm to raise forward and your right leg to extend back (in opposition, as if walking).
7. Repeat with your right arm and left leg. The entire group should complete this movement before Step 8.
8. Lift both arms outward to shoulder height, continuing to breathe as you feel the length in your neck and torso and your weight into the floor.
9. As the arms lower, gently come to stillness.
10. Remain present, still, and focused until the music ends and the director releases you out of the exercise via a cue or clap.

> **Music**
>
> Music is a framework that gives an arc to the journey and provides a sense of tempo for the ensemble, but rather than counting beats as one might within traditional choreography, we search for a more intuitive relationship between movement and the duration of themes within the music, while moving together in the same way.

Additional Thoughts for the Actor

Within the basic structure, we can begin to investigate Ki in each moment of the exercise. Attention is offered to our arm, we begin to extend energy out the tips of the fingers, and in the same way a garden hose will begin to move in response to the flow of water, the arm raises. Balance improves by sensing the weight *under* the arm, as opposed to over it.[3] Care should be taken to ensure that the limbs do not overextend – doing so requires more muscle tension than is necessary. Soaring is a simple sequence warming up the collective energy in the room.

Additional Thoughts for the Ensemble

The ensemble will naturally begin to explore what it means to *be* together, as opposed to simply moving in choreographed unison. The tempo and duration of each phrase might vary slightly from person to person, but if the actors *receive* each member of the ensemble, and extend themselves *to* each member of the ensemble, they will begin to work toward a collective connection. As they breathe through the movement, they will begin to breathe together and envision their movement as the movement of the ensemble.

Wobbling

When we are standing on one foot, we may experience a wobble in our balance. This poses a lovely foundational challenge for the artistic journey. Do we allow this moment to distract us, or is the wobble an invitation to recognize the inevitability of imperfection and let go, knowing that true art is not despite our imperfections but because of them? What happens when another member of the ensemble cannot maintain their balance? Do we extend frustrated energy at the person, or can we open ourselves up and offer our own energy to support them?

Another type of wobble occurs when we realize we have deviated significantly from the timing of the group. As we work to bring ourselves back to the ensemble, it is not necessary to abruptly shift gears, or even indicate that we are off track. If the level of investment and focus is the same as it would be on an imagined opening night, we can explore what it means to wobble, check in, and reconnect with the group, committing to an intended shape and allowing the audience to interpret it as they will. Jazz musician Chet Atkins reportedly said, "Do it again on the next verse and people think you meant it." This sentiment is not offered as an excuse but to help the artist maintain a fluid relationship with the pursuit of excellence and emphasize the value of process over product.

Exercise 3: Soaring With Enhancement

Expanding upon Soaring, the exercise can also be performed in pairs to layer a sense of energetic connection between members of the ensemble. Actors may pair up as scene partners, compatible characters, or even those working on the same character. One partner will soar at a time (Group A, then Group B), and then the whole ensemble will complete one final soar together; it is suggested to plan this timing carefully so that the entire process can occur in a single session.

Preparation

a. Group A spreads out across the playing space, facing the same direction and ensuring they have access to a clear line of vision to establish far focus.
b. Group B stands on the sidelines while A prepares.
c. A grounds their feet and closes their eyes for a moment to connect to their breathing.
d. B gently steps into the space and stands closely behind A.

The director should give the actors a moment to settle into each other's presence before officially starting the exercise.

Prologue

1. When music begins, A breathes and notices what arises (again, this might be an image, a sensation, or even a sound).

Soaring With Enhancement

A will soar as previously described. The following instructions are for *Actor B*:[4]

1. As A begins to lift their right arm, B places a hand several inches BELOW and follows the progress of the limb as it raises and lowers.
2. As the right arm returns to rest, B repeats the process for the left arm.
3. To follow the progress of the legs, B takes a step back and hovers both hands several inches away from the calf.
4. B repeats this process with the left leg.
5. When A moves opposing limbs, B mirrors the movement with one hand under the arm and one hand behind the leg.
6. B repeats on the opposite side.
7. As both of A's arms raise and lower, B hovers their hands several inches below.
8. Stay in place until the music is completed.
9. Both partners close their eyes and share a breath.
10. B steps gently away.

The director should give Group A a moment to assimilate the experience before clapping them out of the exercise. Switch partners and repeat the process. After both actors have soared individually, the entire group should scatter themselves across the space. Partners should stay connected with each other, even if they have no visual contact. The entire group will soar one final time, to and with their partners.

Soaring with enhancement highlights the ways in which energy is shared across space. No matter where an individual actor is placed, they are extending their support in all directions: forward to those in front of them, helping to channel and direct the power that comes to them from behind, or even sharing that energy on either side, in any direction. When the group returns to the original Soaring exercise, this shared energy can be recalled, no matter which direction each member of the ensemble is facing.

Ki and the Voice

In discovering the wellspring of Ki, we also identify the center of our breathing, from which we create and support sound. Kristin Linklater used the image of an internal forest pool from which vibration arises (McCance and Linklater 2011, 36), and Catherine Fitzmaurice, in *Structured Breathing*, describes how the transverse abdominis, or deep layer of belly muscle, is used to send sound up and out via an imagined focus line, which centers our attention on the person (or image) we are in relationship with (Fitzmaurice 2003). Just as extraneous muscle tension inhibits the flow of Ki, it also inhibits breath and vocal vibration. When we work with Ki, we open our bodies to a sense of ease and expansiveness which allows the body to access an efficient connection to breath. This freedom can translate into more balanced vocal resonance and a richer overall timbre. Just as an amplifier uses a tweeter and a woofer in concert to create a full, rich sound, our head and body resonance work together as well.

As an actor experiences an expansive sense of physical self, they can engage those bodily sensations toward vocal expression without habitual tension. Anytime the body is moving, the breath should be moving, and the voice can be sounding.

As noted later, vocal expression does not imply shouting, and volume does not necessarily equal power.

Slow Ten

While the Soaring exercise is a strong vehicle for the exchange of energy, Tadashi Suzuki's Slow Ten connects both impulse and imagination and asks the actor to work in a different tempo. Hunt tells us that in Slow Ten, Suzuki is asking the actor to move continuously without a pulse or a launch, making it appear that "the scenery upstage is moving while the actor is standing still."

As in Soaring, music plays an important role and creates a parameter around the length and tempo of the exercise, while also offering cues for determined points of action.[5] It is helpful to listen to the chosen music together and designate clear cues for

(1) completing the first cross,
(2) any moments of stillness,
(3) turning downstage (in the direction of the audience) to face the opposite direction, and
(4) the moment when the exercise should be complete.

Exercise 4: Slow Ten

Hunt describes Slow Ten as follows:

> Actors form two lines facing each other on either side of the stage, staggering their positions so that they will be able to pass through each other as they cross. At the cue, everyone begins to travel toward the center of the stage. Moving very slowly, the weight is carefully transferred to the heel of the foot and rolls on through to give that foot the whole weight as the other foot comes through. The tempo and sensation should be continuous – no pause, no pulse in the hips, no launching onto the other foot. When the movement is smooth and the actor finds the exact length of the stride required, the effect creates the impression that the actor is floating across the stage. The walk should be natural; what appears extraordinary is the perfect continuity of the locomotion. When they reach the other side of the stage, on a shift in the music, they will slowly make a downstage turn in the same tempo as the cross. Then they will continue back to their original place on stage, passing through the other group on their way home.[6]

As actors progress, gestures or shapes with arms may be added.

Exercise 5: Hamlet and Ophelia

Another variation, created by Robyn Hunt, is called *Hamlet and Ophelia*, or *Lady M and Mac*. Actors are split into two groups, assigned without regard to gender, and are prompted to cross the room in Slow Ten and in character.

1. Begin a slow, sustained walk across the space as outlined previously.
2. As you pass your partner, there is a spark in your journey, as though you've seen something out of the corner of your eye or sensed something new.

3. When you reach the other side of the stage, allow an impulse to turn to interrupt the importance of going forward. Pause, caught between the pull of these two energies.
4. On the next music cue, begin a downstage turn and see your counterpart for the first time, continue breathing.
5. Once you've made eye contact, begin to cross the space back to your original starting place, toward the other character.
6. As you pass the other character, explore a possible slowing of tempo as you navigate the pass and the decision to stay or continue.
7. When you reach the edge of the stage, pause, continue to keep the connection with the other character alive.
8. Either turn back and face your partner, or continue your journey forward; stay open to the possibility of a change of mind.
9. Pause in stillness.

Exercise 6: The Moment of Discovery (additional thoughts to follow)

Our final exercise is a variation on Slow Ten that zooms in on Step 4 as a vehicle for discovery when working on Greek tragedy, in particular. The formalized style of Greek plays can be difficult for contemporary actors – Shakespeare at least affords us the familiarity of a heartbeat rhythm, but Greek epic poems were originally written in dactylic hexameter, a rhythm that doesn't always lend itself well to the English language. And even when we are working with a good translation of the story, the epic quality of events in these plays (war, slavery, homicide, patricide, all of the -cides, maiming, the appearance of and intervention by the Gods, being stuck at sea for ten years, visiting the underworld) can be difficult to relate to. By slowing down and listening to one's impulses, "it is possible for the actor's inner life to evolve from choices that the body makes" (Porter 2022, 28).

For this variation on Slow Ten, each actor should focus on a Greek tragic character they are exploring; it is not necessary for the audience to know what choice the actor has made, but it is essential for the actor to have text memorized to speak at the culmination of the exercise. There should be no investment in facial expressions or attempts to try to make the moment interesting – do not try to show the story.

Divide the group in two, with half of the group working on their feet and the other half offering observant energy. This serves two functions: those working are able to examine active, shared power, and the observers are invited to witness and learn with their whole body.

Preparation

a. Before beginning, center your thoughts around the character you are going to embody – their given circumstances, obstacles, and desires.

b. Adjust your feet so that you are mid-stride, as if you are already in motion in the world of the play.
c. Try not to anticipate what will happen.

Prologue

1. As music begins, breathe and notice what arises.
2. Follow the initial steps for Hamlet and Ophelia, as previously noted, crossing the space with a slow, sustained walk, allowing an impulse to turn to interrupt the forward motion, and being caught in the pull of energy from your passing partner.
3. On the chosen music cue, begin your downstage turn and *allow yourself to be surprised by who shows up in your story* (spontaneously attribute another character to your counterpart).
4. Observe your response to their presence, and any impulses that arise.
5. Once you've made eye contact, begin to cross back to your original starting place.
6. As you pass the other character, and you observe a slowing of tempo and a heightened connection, allow yourself to follow your impulses. This may mean you stop and watch the person for a moment, or that you begin to walk backward, or follow them across the stage.
7. As you follow these impulses, notice where they serve you and the story.
8. By the final music cue, you should end up on one side of the stage or the other, even as you stay open to the possibility that you might change your mind.
9. Pause in stillness.
10. At this point, actors should speak their text; this can happen as an entire group or one actor at a time. The director should remind actors that speaking the text is not a competition. Actors should employ what they discovered, but it is not necessary to shout to be heard over one another. Full embodiment is paramount.

In this variation of the exercise, the goal is not a finished product but a clarification of your own connection to and perspective on the story. You may discover a new point of view, a clearer understanding of the character's motivation, or even a new plot element that you would like to develop further.

Additional Thoughts for the Actor

Just as the character in the story doesn't know what's going to happen next, the actor is learning to respond to new stimuli instead of what they anticipate or expect. For example, someone who has chosen to play the Sentry from *Antigone* might turn to discover Antigone herself, or King Creon, or the ghost of Polynices, and each one of these discoveries invites the actor to interrogate their unique internal responses to the story.

Additional Thoughts for the Director

Before beginning the exercise, as the actors meditate on their chosen character, it is possible to bring up other principles important to the work you are teaching: given circumstances, Michael Chekhov's Four Brothers, chakra focus, Leading Centers, the elements, rasas, or even a touch of sound. Remind the performers to breathe.

It is also possible to coach from the side and gently remind actors about shape, form, and other components; make sure the actors know that the sound of your voice should not break their focus, nor should they indicate receipt of the note. If they don't understand, they should continue, and you can clarify after the exercise is complete.

The Lifelong Journey

As mentioned earlier, these exercises are excellent tools for sparking a compelling artistic journey through imagination, vitality, and process, especially as they relate to the embodiment of character and text. Developing a relationship with one's personal energy, examining the impulses that arise in moments of silence and stillness, and cultivating a vast wealth of imagery all enhance the actor's ability to own their character's words and expand their presence to epic proportions.

Notes

1. Hunt, Robyn, interview by authors via Zoom, May 4, 2022.
2. Music we use for Soaring:

    "New World," Spotify, track 7 on Bjork, Selmasongs: Music From the Motion Picture Soundtrack 'Dancer in the Dark.' One Little Indian Records, 2000.
    "Creep," Spotify, track 2 on Radiohead, *Pablo Honey*. Parlophone, 1993.

3. Additionally, as each limb returns, we can imagine its lingering imprint in space and gain a sense of the residual energy that is left behind. This helps the actor develop a stronger relationship with soft focus by reminding us that the whole body is engaged, regardless of the directed focus on a single area.
4. B provides support for A and must remain equally focused and grounded so they disturb the air as little as possible. Managing the enhancing movements can feel physically complicated; B may need to step slightly to the side to see the arm raise and lower clearly but must also minimize contact that would disrupt the focus.
5. Music we use for Slow Ten:

    "Todo Sobre Mi Madre," Spotify, track 7 on Alberto Iglesias, *Todo Sobre Mi Madre Original Soundtrack*, Quartet Records, 1999.
    "Thursday," Spotify, track 8 on Morphine, *Cure for Pain*, Rykodisc, 1993.
    Suggested by Robyn Hunt: "Fever," Spotify, track 14 on Peggy Lee, *Things Are Swingin'*, Capitol Records, 1959.

6. Hunt, Robyn, interview by authors via Zoom, May 4, 2022.

Bibliography

Allain, Paul. 2003. *The Art of Stillness: The Theatre Practice of Tadashi Suzuki*. New York, NY: Palgrave Macmillan.

Bissell, David, and Gillian Fuller. 2011. *Stillness in a Mobile World*. New York: Routledge.
Bogart, Anne, and Tina Landau. 2005. *The Viewpoints Book*. New York: Theatre Communications Group.
Cummins, Eleanor. 2020. "Our Screens Are Making Us Dissociate." *Medium*. OneZero, March 4, 2020. https://onezero.medium.com/our-digital-devices-have-sparked-a-dissociation-pandemic-46cc18ae0b5b.
Dunbar, Zachary, and Stephe Harrop. 2019. *Greek Tragedy and the Contemporary Actor*. London, UK: Palgrave Macmillan.
Fitzmaurice, Catherine. 2003. "Structured Breathing." *VASTA Newsletter* 17 (1).
Iyer, Pico. 2014. *The Art of Stillness*. New York: TED Books.
Linklater, Kristin. 1993. *Freeing Shakespeare's Voice*. New York: Theatre Communications Group.
Loth, Jo, and Rob Pensalfini. 2021. "Body. Breath. Text. Freedom: An Investigation of Concurrent Training in Linklater Voice and the Suzuki Actor Training Method." *Theatre, Dance and Performance Training* 12 (1): 80–94. doi:10.1080/19443927.2020.1725616.
McCance, Dawne, and Kristin Linklater. 2011. "Crossings: An Interview with Kristin Linklater." *Mosaic: An Interdisciplinary Critical Journal* 44 (1): 1–45. www.jstor.org/stable/44030303.
Mendoza, Jessica S., et. al. 2018. "The Effect of Cellphones on Attention and Learning: The Influences of Time, Distraction, and Nomophobia." *Computers in Human Behavior* 86: 52–60.
Mortimer, Wendy. 2005. "Researching the Potential of Merging Suzuki's Method of Actor Training with Western Vocal Pedagogy: An Interview with Robyn Hunt and Steve Pearson." *The Voice and Speech Review* 4 (1): 319–26.
Porter, Maria. 2022. *Re-Purposing Suzuki: A Hybrid Approach to Actor Training*. New York: Taylor and Francis.
Rodenburg, Patsy. 2008. *The Second Circle: How to Use Positive Energy for Success in Every Situation*. New York: W. W. Norton.
Suzuki, Tadashi. 1986. *The Way of Acting*. New York: Theatre Communications Group.
———. 2015. *Culture is the Body*. New York: Theatre Communications Group.

10

GRACE, GRAVITAS, AND GROUNDING – APPROACHING GREEK TRAGEDY

Through a New Translation of *Hecuba*

Tamara Meneghini

Introduction

A common question when approaching a Greek tragedy can often be distilled down to one word: *Why?* Specifically, why this story now and – most importantly – *how* do we successfully communicate the sensibilities, rhythm, language, and style from a world so far removed to an audience of today? Using a 2018 University of Colorado Boulder production of Euripides' *Hecuba* as an example, this chapter will outline a process for uncovering the connective tissue between the audience and the setting of the play. Through the evolution of a new translation by Diane Rayor, the physical technique of working in a mask, and gaining an understanding of the rhythm, texture, tone, and movement of an unfamiliar style of acting, actors were allowed to fully embody the story and, thus, share it with an audience. This chapter aims to provide a map of the process that allowed the company of actors to more fully experience the world of Greek tragedy set in the original time period and share their experience with audiences in Boulder, Colorado. This chapter will share some of our process and discoveries to help enhance your own approach to performing heightened Greek texts that require a full commitment to an embodied style by the actor.

We proposed a production as close to the originally performed play as possible, but what we arrived at was informed by experiences in the rehearsal process, along with our careful study and consideration of Euripides' intent as a poet. Our dramaturg, John Gibert, wrote in his notes for the production (2018):

> To some, Hecuba feels almost like a staged experiment: subject a human being to unbearable strain and observe the effects on her character. But when we

see what she is capable of, are we meant to approve, disapprove, or shudder in horror without judgment? Is there a stable foundation of justice in this world? There are no easy answers, but Greek tragedy's ability to turn such a spectacle into art somehow depends on protecting human conflict onto a distant age of mythical heroes. At the same time, historical context inevitably shapes one's experience of the play.

Hecuba was the most widely read tragedy by Euripides when it was first produced. The play was admired for its stirring pathos, dazzling rhetoric, and plot of ultimate revenge. This makes it a perfect project to work with actors on the physical embodiment of text. The poetry bids the actor to explore how they might experience expanded vibration of sound and far-reaching gestures. Even the simplicity of sitting at a table and reading the text out loud for the first time requires full breath support and intention given toward a specific moment of heightened emotion and circumstance. There are many moments identified in the play where actors are not necessarily moving across the stage, but must, in stillness, discover a feeling of physical expansion so their voice can be fully resonant. When the body is engaged, the actor can use their dynamic voice to ignite an empathetic physical response in the audience.

Themes and Beginnings

Hecuba's themes are powerfully relevant, even today. It is a play about a community recovering from war, struggling to process the complete decimation of their culture, and the unbearable separation of families. These themes directly relate to the separation of modern-day families: at the border, in the courtroom, in communities close to home and far away. Actors can imagine the weight of the circumstances of the play and transform the story, becoming a community by virtue of speaking the poetic text aloud together.

We start with a profound story, poetic words, breath, and the bodies of the characters, the actors, and the chorus or ensemble. We identify what demands the world of the play and script entails:

a. *Working with a living, breathing translation.* Whether you have a translator present or not, create space to explore and experience the origin story so that it is clear and can be felt and understood by the audience.
b. *Essential and expressive breath* as a unifying pathway to presence in the process and as the required partner in vocal and physical expansive discovery.
c. *Experience the expansive body through the mask.* The physical instrument, the actors' body, is the main conduit of this tragic story.
d. *Embodied musicality.* Through the learning of studied ancient Greek sounds, rhythm, dance, tone, and quality, there is the open invitation to participate fully in sustained, resonant, and clear communication of the visceral text.

Discovery of Heightened Text

From the first reading, be aware of the visceral connection to the formation of sounds in Euripides' poetry. Notice moments when the poetry demands emphasis on the physical properties of the language. Since we start with words, remember that words are carefully structured sound compositions; they are carefully chosen sounds, shapes, and rhythms that communicate meaning, feeling, and story. Actors should listen, take notes, and field questions regarding feeling, imagery, and meaning, paying close attention to these first sounds, rhythms, and structures. This is mindful entry into the feeling of the text and a necessary foundation for the process.

The foundation of all language is in sound and vibration as it is generated in the body. Language conveys meaning first through the body and then travels out to the audience. In initial sounding work, rehearsals should explore the emotions contained in specific vowel shapes and tones as well as the energetic qualities of consonants, particularly those present in the more dramatic and intense moments of the story. This intersection of the intellectual consideration of the text with the physical embodiment of sound will evoke the vital next component in the rehearsal process and progression toward movement.

Here are two short passages from Rayor's translation of Hecuba (forthcoming). Speak them aloud and practice creating more space in your mouth on the vowels and more distinct consonant energy. What do you notice and feel? In the second short passage, Euripides indicates singing; what happens when you sing this text? What shapes do you feel happening in your vocal apparatus as you speak and sing these lines (and is there a difference between the two)?

Hecuba: *[speaks]*
          O burning light of Zeus, O dark Night, why was I wakened by such a terrible dream?
          Hallowed Earth, mother of dark-winged dreams, I banish the visions of last night!
Hecuba: *[sings]*
          How unhappy I am! What can I possibly say? What cry, what lament?
          Misery of miserable old age and slavery impossible to endure, impossible to bear. Oimoi, moi!

In its most authentic sounds, shape, and energy, the simplicity of this poetic text evokes dynamic shifts in movement. It calls the actor away from the horizontality of reading at a table and prompts the words to move through the body, supported by breath, up and out, into the vertical rising and falling shape of the tragedy. The line between humans and gods, both above and below and the vertical axis, prevails in Greek tragedy.

Activating the Body for Acting

Next, we transition from the formation of words and articulation of speech, to the ways in which these sounds elicit sensations in the body and shape a characters' relationships and experiences. We ask the question: what happens when you allow the quality and meaning of sounds – as you first experience them – to inspire ascending and descending, opening and enclosing, and pushing and pulling in the physicality of your body? The first three-dimensional expansion is experienced in an awareness of the phenomenon of breath and the natural rising and falling occurring in the body. After a first reading, give yourself permission to place your script aside so that the body can take center stage and become the focus of your work.

At the heart of all I practice as a teacher, actor, and director are the Williamson Technique, a physical training method for actors created by Loyd Williamson, and Fitzmaurice Voicework, created by Catherine Fitzmaurice. The Williamson Technique is concerned with the physical process of communication and, in our case, the storytelling of the play, specifically the interaction between an actor's body and the imaginary world of the play. An essential component of the work is in the awakening of the five senses through the breath and an intimate connection to the imaginary world of the play through contact with those senses. Fitzmaurice Voicework begins with a process called *Destructuring*. In her article "Breathing is Meaning," Fitzmaurice writes, "The Destructuring work consists of a deep exploration into the autonomic nervous system functions: the spontaneous, organic impulses which every actor aspires to incorporate into the acting process" (Fitzmaurice 1997). My examination of the synthesis of these two techniques, specifically while working on Greek tragedy, illuminates new strategies for heighted connection to the world of the play and provides actors with ways to enter that world and continue to make discoveries about themselves and the characters throughout the process.

Breathing Body and Behavior (Motion and Sound)

Let's begin with Williamson's exercise "Ten Minutes to Do Nothing." Set a timer for ten minutes. Lie down on the floor, in a comfortable position. This is a moment of awareness and acceptance, with no judgment or expectations, as you transition from the pedestrian world to the world of the artist, and even further into the imaginary world of the play. Become aware of your body in the floor, of the air in the room around you, and of your interaction with that air as you breathe. Without deliberately changing anything, notice the very first impulse for movement that arises in the body but focus on the fundamental movement of the torso as you connect with your organic breath.

As you continue to allow yourself to fully connect to what is happening in your body as a result of your own expansion and release of the torso in the breathing process, allow movement to emerge on the exhale. Breathing in and connecting to that in-breath and exhaling with movement. We will call this a stretching preparation. Flowing from one movement to the next, following your own impulses on the breath. In our rehearsal process, we utilized a Fitzmaurice Destructuring sequence of dynamic efforts designed to produce tremors in the body for the purpose of allowing the muscles to release and the breath to experience greater capacity and ease in the body. If you know a sequence such as a sun salutation or have your own version of a stretching sequence that feels good to you, integrate it into this transition to movement from the ten-minute exercise. The process will become part of your warm-up later on.

After your timer goes off, begin to flow into a series of dimensional stretches that arise out of a visceral connection to the shapes of the breathing body. An example of this progression might look something like this:

- Direct your focus and describe what is happening in your body. Do you notice the expanding and releasing of your torso? As you take a breath in, the torso expands, and as you allow breath to leave your body, your body releases. Allow for time to connect to this sensation.
- The next time you take a breath in and expand, allow yourself to translate the breath into any kind of motion on the exhalation? This can be whatever feels good to you: rolling, rocking, crawling, walking, dancing. Continue this process, connecting with the air by taking it into your body and then sending it out on both an exhale and a movement or gesture. What emerges? How does it feel to move in this way, allowing the breath to directly inspire you to move?
- Begin to give specific shape and dimension to the movements. On the exhale, experiment with the following three-dimensional movements: rising/falling (vertical), expanding/ releasing (horizontal), and pushing/pulling (sagittal). Allow the inhale to inspire you to move, to shape, to discover.

As you explore the potential power and expanded size of the breathing body, two things begin to happen:

- The essential shape of the breathing body, in contact with the imagination and sensual elements of the story, gives way to the expansive vocal vibrance required for heightened text. This happens gradually as the actors begin to integrate the structured sound of the specific text.
- Through this process, each actor discovers their own unique way through authentic breath, voice, and movement. This may shed light on their unique,

pivotal perspective on the story (of the play) and lead them to a more autonomous expression of character, even within the tangled community of the play.

Polarity Play – A Greek Tragedy Physical and Vocal Etude

An integrated part of the process is a three-dimensional polarity physical etude composed of a specifically charted flow of movements from one side of a dimension to the other, accompanied by inspired text of shared values of the tragedy. It was inspired by Susan Dibble's series of balance and opposition work with Shakespeare (2002, 130–43), an integrated part of the process is articulating shape, flow, and energy through a three-dimensional physical etude. It begins by exploring polar opposites of movement, gradually working toward experiencing a more expansive body and voice through establishing the flow from one dimension to the next. This movement series became part of our daily rehearsal process and, eventually, a way of warming up and connecting to the ensemble before performances and was used at specific moments for desired articulation of shape, flow, and energy.

Actors begin by standing in a neutral position. Flowing from one shape to another and speaking as each dimensional shape is experienced in the body.

1. Movement: spreading wide the arms and legs in an **OPENING** position
   Text: "Oh Gods, help me find the god in me."
2. Movement: reaching on the high or low diagonal, **TEARING** across the space to the opposite corner
   Text: "Drive me to my destiny."
3. Movement: closing the body into itself, **EMBRACING** the physical space
   Text: "Nothing in excess."
4. Movement: **PUSHING** or **REACHING** body toward the front sagittal space
   Text: "Give me power."
5. Movement: the **PULLING** body toward the space behind the body
   Text: "Give me courage."
6. Movement: the **RISING** body, extending the arms and body up to vertical
   Text: "All you Gods, fill me with your fire."
7. Movement: the **WRINGING** body, muscular spiraling initiating from the torso, limbs in concert
   Text: "Drive me to wonder."
8. Movement: return to **BALANCED EQUILIBRIUM**, claiming a more expansive sense of space
   Text: "I know who I am."

"I know who I have been."
"I know who I am destined to be."
"And my name is (insert character name here)."

Rasa-Play

In these phases of continued physical exploration, Rasaboxes™ are introduced. Rasaboxes™ is a physical theatre training technique developed by Richard Schechner; it is designed to support the actor in the process of becoming an athlete of their emotions, a concept that can be traced to the theoretical writings of Vsevolod Meyerhold and Antonin Artaud. Meyerhold articulated that the actor's body must become like a musical instrument in the hands of the very actor themselves. "The actor must perfect the culture of physical expression and must develop the sensation of their body in space" (Rudinitsky 1981, 295). Like an athlete, the actor needs an astute sense of gravity, equilibrium, stability, coordination of bodily movements, and an awareness of space. Rasaboxes™ provides a primary example of this theory in practice. In tackling the physical and vocal demands of Greek tragedy poetry and performance, the work invites the actor to fully experience and develop unique ways to embody physically and vocally each of the eight rasas as outlined in the next section.

Map out a grid of nine squares on the floor with each one labeled clearly according to the Natyasastra, a Sanskrit treatise on the dramatic arts: raudra (rage), bhayanaka (fear), vira (courage), sringara (desire/love), bibhatsa (disgust), hasya (laughter), karuna (grief), and adbhuta (wonder). We used the entire stage to make a grid that was 12" by 12", but you can adjust the size to your working space. You can also explore a single scene of the play by restricting the exercise to a specific section of the grid. Each divided area devoted to the identified emotion (or rasa) has its own unique qualities and is its own area of play.

Arriving on the grid inside a rasa, imagine the flavor and qualities of that particular aesthetic. Rather than playing at, or mimicking the emotion, experience how it feels through the breath and five senses – its texture, sound, aroma, and colors. For example, the texture of a grief-inspired breath might result in a sound that is gravelly or creaky. Assume the role of both player and instrument, allowing distinct physical shapes and sound vibrations of the rasa to emerge from the imagination on expansive breath as it travels in and out of the body. By filling up completely with this quality, you begin to understand the required size of the heightened style and become comfortable with how it feels in your body.

Through the rasas, our discoveries included identifying a shared sensation of the place of the play; in the case of Hecuba, this is the encampment of women awaiting news of identified lots drawn, which affects the way in which the chorus of women sing, chant, and dance at any given moment. Use the rasa-inspired breath to return to this line of text, noting how the breath may become the amplified heartbeat of the scene:

> Because the subject matter of Greek tragedy can seem far-fetched, at best, to most contemporary audiences, and completely out of range for younger actors, the pathway we created by using the Rasas provides a direct conduit between the authentic breath and imagination through sensually connected and expansive motion and sound. The performer, in any style, needs an astute sense of gravity, equilibrium, stability, coordination of gesture and movement, and a keen awareness of space. In a heightened style such as Greek tragedy, the actor needs an opportunity to embody the required range of sensations, vibration, resonance, and movement of the play. With the Rasaboxes™ sequence, the actors' experiential journey continues to be connected to the relationship between the breath, body, and voice and may become something the audience can experience in their bodies, as well. This work can inform any continued exploration of scene and character, performance composition, analysis, and ongoing performance preparation.

The Mask

In Greek tragedy, the mask provides the form that allows the actor to express specific qualities, movement, and tone of a character. While a mask is fixed in form (it always remains the same), the design allows the actor a deeper way into the authentic character. In one of my own training experiences with a set of expressive masks made by the renowned mask artist Amleto Sartori, the leader of the workshop, Giovanni Fusetti, provided an explanation to creating character that has since influenced my work every time I approach a mask. He offered the idea of creating character as a verb meaning *to engrave or imprint*. The mask is the first impression, and the body and voice provide the follow-through for that impression as it is shared with the audience. The audience first notices the mask and then forgets about it because the body and voice assume the role of communicating the totality of the story.

For example, in our set of character masks, each of the speaking roles' masks were inspired by a specific rasa or passion. Hecuba's mask was a combination of Vira (pride) and Karuna (despair). Even if you are not working with a mask, you might consider Fusetti's definition and choose images (portraits, photographs) that engrave or imprint a core impression onto your being and allow you to work from the image, inward.

Our masks were designed by Jonathan Becker,[1] an exquisite actor and master of the physical technique practices of Jacques Lecoq, and his creations invited connections between the rasas and Lecoq's passions. Other modalities that might be helpful include Laban Movement Analysis, Michael Chekhov's Psychological Gesture, or Meyerhold's Biomechanics; all of these layering approaches can lead to greater specificity in embodiment, space, shape, and rhythm.

Conclusion

The themes in *Hecuba* resemble most other tragedies of the time: an examination of an interaction between the powerful and the powerless in time of extreme conflict. The world of the play is unstable and is characterized by sudden changes and abundant violence. Justice comes at the price of dehumanizing one side of the conflict, and emotional responses can shift dynamically from moment to moment, from one extreme (rasa or emotion) to another (rasa or emotion). If we can understand the energy required and accompanying sensation of those sudden shifts in the body through exploration of the dynamic tension between rising and falling, opening and closing, pushing and pulling, then we can begin to embody the authenticity of the tragedy.

By approaching *Hecuba* through a direct translation, we were able to integrate the sensibilities, styles, and sounds of our collected voices. Our process evolved as the actors discovered they needed more space to accommodate their expanding breath, bodies, and profound resonance, moving from a single dimension of the words on a page to the embodied dimensions of motion and sound. While we guided the process of transformation, it was the actors who ultimately made themselves fully available to the process, journeying from text to breath to body, to the spoken and sung lines, to mask, to music, and ultimately, to our audience.

We know that the Greeks were masterful storytellers and the experience of approaching Greek tragedy is largely about how, and why, the story is shared. What does the audience hear and see, and how can these mythic tales be shared more fully with audiences? We had the unique opportunity of having Euripides in the room with us by way of a Greek translator, but even without one, the impulses of breath and body can connect us to the past and help us bring the story to life today.

Note

1. Becker's work can be found at https://theater-masks.com.

References

Dibble, Susan. 2002. *Movement for the Actor*. New York: Allworth Press.
Fitzmaurice, Catherine. 1997. "Breathing is Meaning." In *The Vocal Vision*, edited by Marian Hampton. New York: Applause Books.
Gibert, John. 2018. *Dramaturg Note for Hecuba*. Translated by Diane J. Rayor and Directed by Tamara Meneghini. Boulder, CO: University of Colorado.
Rayor, Diane J., trans. and ed. Forthcoming. *Antigone, Medea, Hecuba, and Helen: New Translations of Dangerous Women of Greek Tragedy*. London: Cambridge University Press.
Rudinitsky, Konstanin. 1981. *Meyerhold the Director*. Ann Arbor: Ardis.

11
ANIMATING THE ANCIENTS

A Scaffolded Approach to Physicalizing Greek Theatre

Doreen Bechtol

For the modern actor exploring ancient Greek tragedy, one of the most noteworthy and integral components of Greek theatre is the mask. Worn over the entire face, with an opening around the mouth and eyes, the static Greek mask demanded physical eloquence to render heightened action and emotion visible to thousands of spectators. In Herbert Golder's essay, "Making a Scene: Gesture, Tableau, and the Tragic Chorus," he suggests that in ancient Greek performance, "The masked actor literally becomes a work of art, a piece of sculpture, since acting with masks requires the extensive use of gestures in order to emphasize the primary emotion" (1996, 4). Golder's research reveals how the presence of the mask instigated a stylized physical form of storytelling; however, hundreds of years later, as Western drama dispensed with the mask and actors found their face, so to speak, the body was no longer the locus for emotional expressivity. Considering that Greek theatre relied upon the legibility of the body to convey story – not the face – a modern approach to the Greek plays that relies on realistic acting methods runs askew to the form embedded in ancient Greek tragic drama.

With this in mind, as a theatre-maker and educator exploring Greek tragedy in modern classrooms and rehearsal halls without the use of original Greek masks, I am curious how we might harness the physical forms inspired by the past to resonate through our present-day bodies, voices, and identities. After all, the performance conditions that necessitated the use of the mask in ancient Greece are radically different from today's classroom and studio spaces, and yet, we have much to learn from the physicality required to animate the body whose face was

DOI: 10.4324/9781003204060-14

hidden from view. As indicated in her essay, "Divine Fire: The Myth Origin," Caridad Svich suggests,

> Theatre, ancient already and called "dead" many times over, has been finding ways to speak to its past for many years. Each generation "kills" what has come before it, and resurrects it at the same time. Art is made through active renewal and reinterpretation.
>
> *(2005, 11)*

Similarly, our present-day theatre breathes life into the past as it reimagines it. Therefore, to "resurrect" the ancient Greek is not to replicate it exactly, but through an active exploration of physicality and expressive gestures – even without a mask – we might awaken hidden parts of ourselves that fuel a "reinterpretation" of Greek tragedy. The exercises that follow offer a practical approach for students to discover how nonrealistic movement, inspired by forms associated with Greek masks, releases the imagination to experience the relationship between physical expressivity, emotion, and text.

Part I. Creating Tableaux: Embodying the Past

According to Golder, ancient Greek culture was saturated with iconography; therefore, our entryway into the Greek form begins with examining images of artifacts for clues to physical expression. Golder posits that dramatists turned to pictorial images, such as vase painting, statues, friezes, and temple paintings to capture a range of human experience. For example, a terracotta funerary plaque depicting men with raised hands to the dead and women beating their chests might inspire dramatists to metaphorically portray grief from the loss of a loved one. Similarly, we begin our exploration of the body's expressive potential using still postures, or *tableaux*, taken directly from ancient Greek iconography. Students will investigate how physical elements, such as the contours of the body, the breath, eye focus, and stillness, can create a rich emotional world.

Waking Up Ancient Greece

To immerse students in the ancient Greek culture, arrange the space like a museum with three to five images per student of vases, sculptures, friezes, paintings, or any other objects that inspire the Greek physical form. Start with music playing softly in the background to usher students out of their daily routine and into their subterranean senses that give breath to the imagination. French pianist and centenarian Colette Maze reflects, "Music is an affective language, a poetic language. In music there is everything – nature, emotion, love, revolt, dreams; it's like a spiritual food" (Beardsley 2021). Suggestions for music can be found at the end of the chapter.

As students quietly examine the material in the room, ask them to take note of images that stand out in their memory and select three images that resonate with them and, furthermore, will serve as inspiration to build their tableaux. Once they have images in hand, they can find a space in the room to work solo for the duration of the exercise detailed in the next section.

Creating the Literal Piece of Art

While sitting in their own space, encourage students to reflect on the following criteria. Ask these questions to spark the student's physical analysis, which will help them visualize the form they will soon inhabit.

- Consider the contours of the form. What shapes do you observe? Where does the body occupy curves and where angles?
- Is the spine upright at attention or gracefully bent in supplication?
- Are hands and fingers tightly bound in a fist or elegantly cupped and touching the ground?
- Are limbs symmetrical or asymmetrical?
- Are legs lunging, torsos twisting, head and shoulders angled, eyes and mouth opened or closed?
- What parts of the body meet the ground? What parts touch other points on the body?
- Where does the body seem to place weight: in heels, hands, elbows, back, head?
- Does the shape of the body extend outward into space or seem to fold inward on itself?
- Is the heart open to view or closed off?

After analyzing the images, students are ready to embody their Greek counterparts in space. To begin, students should stand in a neutral position and visualize one of their three images either with their eyes closed or open with an internal focus. To encourage wakefulness in their body, ask students to first notice their breath without any expectation or desire to change it. From this place of stillness and listening, students can start to craft their Greek form.

As students occupy their new shape, consider the same prompts from the previous section as reminders to incorporate elements of shape, weight, eyes, and finally, the breath. Once students have found their form, continue asking questions to reinforce a deeper physical connection. For instance, how does breath operate inside the form? Are lungs open or constricted? Is breathing easy or labored, shallow or full? What emotions come to the surface? What feelings, textures, or memories? Most importantly, emphasize that inside of stillness, the breath fuels and invigorates emotions within the intricate architecture of bones, sinews, and muscles tasked with resurrecting an ancient Greek form.

Once the tableaux are constructed, ask students to slowly return to their neutral position, taking care to isolate specific body parts on the return journey. If leading the exercise, call out instructions to bring their head back to neutral, then arms, hands, and torso, followed by their legs, and finally, their feet. Isolating body parts reminds students of the multiplicity of shapes and stories contained in one static form. Once students return to neutral, ask them to connect to their breath and note any shifts in their body. Do they feel different, and if so, how? Did they notice any emotions or images rise to the surface? Do some muscles feel more awake or more tense? What did they learn about their own limitations inside of the tableaux? Conclude the work on *Creating the Literal Piece of Art* exercise by constructing the remaining two images using the same process.

Wrapping Up Shape and Stillness

Once all three images are constructed, divide the room in half and allow students to observe each other's work. Return to the idea of a museum environment with half of the students set up as if they are *living sculptures*. Observers can walk around the sculptures, at a respectful distance, to examine their form from all angles. Observation is crucial for both the performer and the audience as it puts pressure on the legibility of the work and the quality of attention in witnessing work. In her essay "Theatrical Stillness," Mary Fleischer describes the power that stillness has on an audience, "Stillness exposes the body to close scrutiny, and its lack of action, of forward movement, allows the audience to 'read' the static image at its own pace and follow its own train of thought" (2016, 36–39). Encourage students to engage with stillness by connecting to their breath, as if their form is expanding and radiating to their audience on a molecular level to achieve an unshakeable permanence.

After switching groups, be sure to take time to debrief through the following questions:

- What stood out or was memorable when looking at the tableaux?
- Did you observe emotion, character, or story?
- What did you learn about the Greek silhouette while embodying the form?
- What surprised you? Were shapes uncomfortable, familiar, powerful, beautiful?
- Did anything come to the surface that you want to share with the group?

Part II. Moving Tableaux: Embodying Time and Space

British dancer and choreographer Jonathan Burrows suggests that, for practitioners, "Form is something against which to push your imagination free" (2010, 28).

Given that our work thus far focused on embodying a still form from the past, our work now, as Burrows suggests, is to find freedom inside of that form through movement. Students will explore how physical choices that affect time and space can spark the imagination and cause an emotional response. Building upon the tableaux images from the previous exercise, students will link their images to create a physical score of movement to explore elements of time and space. Slowing down an action to a deliberate speed might spark a different emotional response than that same action performed at a quickened pace. Defining the pathway an action takes across the floor can also sharpen the performer's intentions, thereby enlivening their emotional expression. Does the action publicly expand across the entire space, shrink backward into the shadows, leap or crawl to an imagined finish line? By awakening the physical instrument to the dynamic effect that time and space[1] have on performance, students deepen their practice of crafting a story from moment to moment.

Returning to Greece

To begin this exercise, students must link their three tableaux images in any order they choose. The goal is to create a fluid string of movement (physical score of material), by erasing the neutral positions between each still posture. Students might think of this material as a piece of choreography that will be repeated until it is refined and their muscles have memorized each movement. Anne Bogart, theatre director and co-creator of the Viewpoints technique, offers that "intense and conscious practice generates physical heat, thereby changing the actual makeup of the body. What happens to the body, the changes brought about by practice and heat, are real and lasting" (2013). In our practice, repetition brings about this *heat*, which cultivates a deeper listening to and connection with the chosen physical form. In addition, repetition makes it possible to layer more physical skills onto the original form, allowing students to conscientiously mark their individual transformation. With this in mind, ask students to demonstrate their linked images to reinforce repetition as well as to remind them that the pressure of an audience is another sort of useful *heat* that transforms our work.

Moving in Time

After students share their sequence, generate a bank of descriptive terms that characterize how we describe time (slow, quick, shifting, fleeting, halting). Then, choose one descriptive term and ask a student to show how their string of material might take on that quality. For instance, if the quality is *lingering*, the student might apply a slow tempo to their movement sequence to reveal time's creative potential. As with the previous exercises, prompt exploration of the breath, eyes, shifts in weight, and notice what emotions rise to the surface. To reinforce a slower tempo, suggest active visual metaphors ("move through peanut butter") or physical cues ("actively resist forward momentum by tensing leg muscles"). Before inviting the whole group to apply a slow tempo to their own string of material, ask for feedback from observers about whether working in this time signature creates story, elicits emotion, or builds character.

After the group practices moving at a slow tempo, then invite them to work in an opposing time signature such as an urgent pace. To execute a faster tempo, it is helpful to add speed incrementally over the course of three repetitions. Also, remind the group that everyone's "fastest" tempo will look different given their lived experience, and there is no judgment on how an individual occupies time. Above all, no matter their pace, do not sacrifice the integrity of form for speed. Without losing too much momentum, ask the group for a few words describing what they notice happening to their breath, eye focus, shape, and emotions when they move through their material at different tempos.

Explore time by using different combinations of slow and fast tempos across their physical score. Suggest more nuanced changes from one tempo to the next – for example, accelerating or decelerating as they work across their physical score. Or insert ten seconds of stillness to heighten the movement that came before the stillness, or one that will happen next. Make sure there is ample time to explore a range of qualities and encourage new pathways through time whenever they repeat their sequence. Music can focus the attention needed to stay inside of the movement even when it is uncomfortable or boring. Reconnect to the work by reminding them to stay curious about the skills they are learning.

Moving Through Space

Returning to the three tableaux images that students first created, they will now explore the ways in which space shapes a physical story. Students will continue to work solo; thereby, reinforcing the importance of cultivating individual choices, tastes, and imagination.

Students choose a specific location in the room where they will place one of their original tableaux forms, considering how the architecture in the space might bring attention to, frame, or wake up their tableaux in an interesting way. To further cultivate imagination, tableaux images can be altered slightly to be in conversation with the architecture. For instance, an image that began on the floor might now drape across a chair, or a lunging image might press into a wall, or a kneeling image might take up residence next to an object in the room. Once settled, students will find different locations for their other two images. Work quickly and make bold choices.

Once the three locations are chosen and repeated, explore how their physical shape moves through space by paying particular attention to the path taken across the floor to get to each position. Imagining the floor as a canvas, investigate the difference between moving in straight lines or serpentine curves, taking short or long strides, crawling on the floor or leaping off it, moving backward or sideways. Afterward, ask students to create a specific floor pattern that travels between each of their three positions. Once they create a pathway that is repeatable, then apply the principles of time that they explored earlier. For instance, a gliding pathway transformed by a slower tempo might reveal action that is labored, that strives against time. Or a crawling pathway might be quickened to convey an urgent scramble away from danger. If treated with specificity, then every movement holds the potential for fuller expression and invites new stories to blossom.

In the final exploration of time and space, while using the images and pathway they just created, students should choose and set a specific time signature for the complete physical score. Incorporate clear shifts in time, stillness, moments of acceleration and deceleration. Imagine that this physical score of material represents a whole play with a clear beginning, middle, and end. While students craft this piece, play background music to maintain focus and inspire an emotional connection to their material. Be alert to the tendency to drop a shape in order to move to the next position and encourage a fluid transformation across time and space. For instance, as they travel, choose how the arms, head, or spine transforms from one position to the next. Crafting this level of physical specificity is exacting and difficult to achieve, yet it trains the performer to stay awake and connected to subtle shifts and nuanced movements that carry meaning and express story. Everyone should demonstrate their work, with observations from the audience.

Wrapping Up Time and Space

Two students will create a physical "dialogue" with one another while using the score of material they just created. From their beginning positions, they should start their sequence of material at the same time, taking note of the other person's use of space to avoid collisions. Notice the distance between bodies, what parts of the room each person occupies, the shapes in the room, and the time signatures. Then explore shifts in time that are inspired *by* and in relation *to* their scene partner's material. Through active connection with their scene partner, they begin to play, react, and respond to one another, finding freedom in pushing against their form, as Burrows suggested. Possibilities to suggest:

- Might someone's shift in time cause you to shift your tempo or bring you to stillness?
- Might you look for ways to repeat a scene partner's tempo or work in opposition to them?
- Might you make eye contact as you travel from position to position? What discoveries do you make? What happens if you slow down your movement as you come closer to your scene partner?

- What does the audience notice happen between bodies? What moments arrest their attention?

Part III. Creating Expressive Gestures: Embodying Metaphor

In *Tragedy and Dramatic Theatre*, scholar and critic Hans-Thies Lehmann states that "tragedy offers no 'picture' of the world; it does not represent reality. It is radical in every respect: it takes exception to what is real and concretely given; it invokes the world rather than portraying it" (2016, 137). Our work with expressive or poetic gestures invites students to access an interior landscape and introduces an elegant physical vocabulary with which to embody poetic language. Rather than representing the characters and situations through realistic storytelling, expressive gestural work "invokes the world" of emotion and breathes life into performance. More specifically, expressive gestures[2] do not look like ordinary movements that you might see as you walk down the street, rather these actions are *extra*ordinary. As opposed to portraying daily behavior that is, as Lehmann terms it, "concretely given," expressive gestures give form to emotional states, such as joy, fear, rapture, envy, betrayal, or desire. With an emphasis on exploring non-naturalistic movement, the following exercises delve into emotions ripe inside of Sophocles' *Antigone*, namely, rage, grief, and passion. Finally, while *Antigone* is the chosen play for the following exercises, any Greek tragedy will work well in its place.

Waking Up Emotion

Like the initial tableaux exercise, students work individually in their own space, with music to focus the process. The group begins by considering the shape their bodies might take to reflect *rage*. Consider how the contour of their body, the pathway along the floor, tempo, stillness, weight, eye focus, and breath all reflect *rage*. Allow a few minutes to freely explore each emotion and use similar prompts to inspire students to explore movement.

- Do actions that express *rage* have sharp edges, or curves? Is *rage* inwardly focused, or does it reach outward? What part of your body holds *rage*?
- Do actions that express *grief* move swiftly or slow? If *grief* stays still, how long is it still? Is *grief* grounded on two feet, does it live in the toes, or does it recline through the spine? What part of your body remembers *grief*?
- Do actions that express *passion* take up space across the room, or is *passion* confined? Is *passion* focused upward or downward? Are eyes at an angle, open, or closed? Does *passion* move in straight lines or serpentine curves? What part of your body holds *passion*?

Invoking Antigone

Now that the physical imagination is primed, the next exercise invites students to craft a repeatable expressive gesture that is inspired by language from the selected play, in this case, *Antigone*. Before introducing lines of text, assign students to small groups, ideally trios. Each person in the group will receive a line that contains an element of *rage, grief,* or *passion,* such as, "madness breathed hatred most bitter." With their text in hand, students take time to individually reflect on their text (in the same way they connected to their images for the tableaux exercise) to discover the potential for expression. Prompt students to breathe and silently read the text, not to understand its meaning, but to imagine the shape of the images contained within the poetry.

Once students connect their imagination to the text, individually create a gesture that reveals an emotional landscape inspired by the language. It is important to emphasize that the expressive gesture must be repeatable and able to be taught to others. The gesture is not meant to reflect a realistic interpretation of the text but should invoke the emotion through their limbs, their breath, and their imagination. Rejoining their group, students silently teach each other their gesture, adjusting their material so that all bodies can execute the gesture together. Let the body demonstrate. The group will learn all three gestures and be able to perform them in unison, linking gestures, so there is no need to return to neutral.

Here are examples of phrases taken from *Antigone* (Sophocles 2014) that demonstrate expressive language:

- "Your blood runs hot"
- "Madness breathed hatred most bitter"
- "Reveals her savage heart"
- "A passion to drive a man mad"
- "Their eyes cried out for revenge"
- "A cry as sharp in bitterness as that of any bird"
- "A passionate fit of madness"
- "My soul was long since dead"
- "Sorrow heaped on each successive age"
- "No longer can I restrain my wellsprings of tears"
- "My heart takes wing"
- "Her soul is still beset with the same emotional storm"

Wrapping Up Expressive Gesture

Once the group has learned each other's gestures, they will perform their new string of gestural material and receive feedback from the group. Adjust the movement to include elements of time and space, as with the previous exercises. Invite groups to alter tempo while staying in unison, or begin the string of material at the back of the room and allow it to travel toward the front of the room, or stand in a new configuration (a line, a circle, at a distance, in close proximity, etc.). Take time to debrief, asking what images resonated with them and what new information they observed or experienced. What discoveries did they make about Greek tragedy and what emotions did they evoke through this style of exploration?

Part IV. Moving Into Text: Embodying Imagination

In his essay, *The Culture Writes Us*, Charles L. Mee explores the tensions that exist when art is fully aware of the cultural DNA from which it originates. He states,

> This tension between what has been made and what can be re-made lives in the very essence of the work – so that our common human project of making life on earth, making a society, making a bearable or wonderful civilization, is alive in every particle of the work.
>
> *(2005, 10)*

Armed with a bank of physical material, students explore ways to infuse their textual language inside of a chosen monologue with their richly crafted physical language. In doing so, they embody this collision, or tension, between the ancient Greek culture that endures and the ephemeral moment of our current theatrical exploration.

Waking Up Language

To begin, provide several monologues from which actors are free to choose a speech that resonates with them most. For the purpose of this exercise, there is an assumption that students will have read the play and be familiar with characters, themes, and plot points. Once text is chosen, everyone reads through it at least twice, analyzing features of the text that might inspire movement: punctuation points, repetitive words, imagistic language, language that suggests an action. Ask a volunteer to work on the first full sentence of their text to demonstrate how students might edit or select pieces of their tableaux, moving tableaux, or expressive gestural material to embody the text. The exploration might feel as if they are choreographing their movement within and around the boundaries of language, rather than trying to add movement to language to realistically tell a story. At this point the work becomes subjective and adheres to the tastes of students, who are not to invent new movements, but to craft their monologue from the gestures they created earlier.

Invoking Imagination

To begin curating material quickly, provide an ingredient list of elements that must be included in their monologue. Institute a time limit that encourages them to make bold decisions. After decisions are made, actions can be refined as they integrate their physical and textual language. An example of an ingredient list:

- Include all three tableaux forms.
- Include each gesture for *grief, rage,* and *passion*.
- Repeat one gesture three times.
- Include one moment of utter stillness, *that is, ten seconds*.
- Include extreme shifts in tempo: *for example, slow to fast, acceleration, deceleration*.
- Include a pathway that takes you to the floor.
- Include a pathway that travels through the space at a distance.
- Include a moment when you turn your back to the audience.
- Include a moment when your eyes look heavenward and another look to the underworld.
- Include a moment with an audible breath: *for example, a gasp, a slow exhale*.
- Include a moment where your weight is only in the toes.
- A bonus: create a unique gesture that gives reverence to a god or goddess, if mentioned in your monologue.
- Another bonus: include a gesture from someone else's material that you love.

Given the physical emphasis of this exploration, invite students to notice how their movement affects their vocal choices. For instance, does a fast tempo imply speaking quickly or slowly in opposition? If moving slowly, does volume drop to a whisper, or increase to a roar? If movement expands across space, does language likewise expand? If inhabiting a gesture of *grief*, what does *grief* sound like? Above all, the emphasis is noticing how an embodied form conveys story and, in turn, fuels an emotional connection to the text.

Wrapping Up Text

Invite the group to demonstrate the first draft of their monologue by reassuring them that they need only present what they have rehearsed with a commitment to their choices. If the monologue is not memorized, then one person may perform while another reads the monologue, or they could just perform one section of the monologue that they memorized. The goal is to reinforce the process by which they created their work, by sharing discoveries made, supporting moments of unique expression, identifying personal transformations, and pinpointing moments that will remain lodged in their memories over time.

In conclusion, by emphasizing an approach to Greek tragedy that refocuses the body as the primary location for story, we explore the potential to create an emotionally connected performance by inhabiting a heightened expressive gestural language. Even though, as modern theatre makers, we may no longer use the mask in our portrayals of Greek tragedy, perhaps we ought not lose our eloquent bodies to tell these stories.

Suggested Music

Gabriel, Peter. 1989. *Passion – Music For The Last Temptation of Christ*. Box: Real World Studios.
Quartet, Kronos. 2014a. *A Thousand Thoughts*. New York: Nonesuch Records.
Quartet, Kronos. 2014b. *Kronos Explorer Series*. New York: Nonesuch Records.
Riley, Terry, Kronos Quartet, and Wu Man. 2008. *The Cusp of Magic*. New York: Nonesuch Records.

Notes

1. The qualities of time and space are inspired by Viewpoints developed by Anne Bogart and Tina Landau, who, in turn, took inspiration from choreographer Mary Overlie's work as originator of the Six Viewpoints.
2. Gesture is one of the nine Viewpoints developed by Anne Bogart and Tina Landau. There are two types of gesture: behavioral and expressive. For the purposes of this exercise, we will only look at expressive gesture.

Bibliography

Beardsley, Eleanor. 2021. Interview with Colette Maze. "This French Pianist Has Been Playing for 102 Years and Just Released a New Album." *Deceptive Cadence. NPR*, September 20. www.npr.org/sections/deceptivecadence/2021/09/20/1036622670/107-year-old-french-pianist-colette-maze-new-album.
Bogart, Anne. 2013. "Heat." *SITI Blog*, June 27. https://siti.org/heat/.
Bogart, Anne, and Tina Landau. 2005. *The Viewpoints Book: A Practical Guide to Viewpoints and Composition*. New York: Theatre Communications Group.
Burrows, Jonathan. 2010. "Form." In *A Choreographer's Handbook*. Abingdon: Routledge.
Fleischer, Mary. 2016. "Theatrical Stillness." In *Movement for Actors*, edited by Nicole Potter. New York: Allsworth Press.
Golder, Herbert. 1996. "Making a Scene: Gesture, Tableau, and the Tragic Chorus." *Arion: A Journal of Humanities and the Classics. Third Series* 4 (1), *The Chorus in Greek Tragedy and Culture, Two*. www.jstor.org/stable/20163587.
Lehmann, Hans-Theis. 2016. *Tragedy and Dramatic Theatre*. New York: Routledge.
Mee, Charles L. 2005. "The Culture Writes Us." In *Divine Fire, Eight Contemporary Plays Inspired by the Greeks*, edited by Caridad Svich. New York: Black Stage Books.
Sophocles. 2014. *Seven Tragedies of Sophocles*. Edited by Robin Bond. New Zealand: University of Canterbury. http://hdl.handle.net/10092/9681.
Svich, Caridad. 2005. "Divine Fire: The Myth Origin." In *Divine Fire, Eight Contemporary Plays Inspired by the Greeks*, edited by Caridad Svich. New York: Black Stage Books.

12
NAUGHTY, BAWDY CHARACTERS AND COMEDY OF MANNERS

Candice Brown

Approaching a character in a comedy of manners play is deliciously fun. Characters are artfully revealed by embodying the text woven into the world of a play. Full of intrigue and satire, wit and folly, characters are thrust into a hollow, feverish, ceremonious, bespangled, glittering, heartbreaking, fashionable world. They share secret commentary with the audience, poking fun at societal manners while simultaneously tearing away social constructs, scattering the rules of polite society into disarray (Maybank 2018).

The design of Restoration comedy, including architectural lines present in the sets and costumes, are often inspired by the feminine silhouette of the day. The "s" curve and hourglass shape of the female body are often overemphasized. The acting style is an explicit, promiscuous romp filled with sexual innuendo and mannered intrigue at every turn of the story. Costumes emphasize a more than sizable erogenous zone by accentuating the feminine bosom with a plunging neckline and an overly corseted waist. Costumes for the female characters in this period widen the hips with panniers and bum rolls and add long sensual trains of flowing fabric. The swarthy rake character might just start offering up kisses to dainty lace-decorated wrists, the forearm, and inevitably an inviting bosom. And speaking of that rake, their own entrance is usually preceded by the enlarged bulge in the pants and by the presentation of a balletic calf perfectly turned out and poised to invite attention from all sexes. Lace drips onto the wrists and gallantly wide hats cover long, feminine curls, all reflecting the influence of the French court and Louis XIV, who was himself known as the "sweetest smelling king."

With all the intrigue, plotting, decadence, artifice, and sensuality woven into these plays like layers of icing and decoration on a cake, where does one begin building a character? Comedy of manners falls within the Restoration period,

DOI: 10.4324/9781003204060-15

historically referenced as the years between 1660 and 1710. This period refers to the time following the restoration of the Stuart line in the English, Scottish, and Irish monarchies under the rule of King Charles II. Charles was exiled for a period of 18 years, during which Oliver Cromwell and the Puritans ordered all London theatres to be closed. When King Charles II returned from France after the English Civil War, he immediately began to rebuild the English court, and theatre was to have an important role to play.

Playwrights were inspired by exciting advances in theatre design and technology, including moveable scenery, candlelit chandeliers, and footlights. On stage, the puritans of former rule portrayed as hypocrites bent upon spoiling innocent fleshly pleasures. The plays were bawdy and risqué, especially the comedies, and they ridiculed upper-class society's manners and rules of behavior, providing a kind of tabloid commentary on class, desire, and the business of the marriage market. The tone was cynical and satirical, and both language and actions were sexually explicit. Characters were driven by lust, greed, and revenge, and their goals were fraud, courtship, gulling, and cuckoldry.

Audiences came to the theatre in droves to see themselves reflected in these plays, but the disreputable nature of the profession, especially for women, meant that actors were recruited from the poorest social groups. Intensive training was required to accurately mimic upper-class speech and adopt the correct mannerism with swords, hats, fans, and greetings. In staging these plays today, the considerations are similar in that actors still require physical alacrity and vocal specificity to create characters who display appropriate mannerisms with swords, hats, fans, and social greetings, but these skills are learned today in order to reflect the time period of the play and underscore the restrictions and boundaries inherent within it.

Today the actor's training is more geared to mimicking the acting style of the time, Restoration period, rather than being a question of the actor being from a poorer social group; it's more to do with moving away from a more contemporary casualness with manners and etiquette.

The following exercises are presented to help cultivate this precision in actors as they develop and embody characters in comedy of manners plays. In addition, you will want to examine the language. Vocally explore words and phrases in the text by investigating the impulse to breathe, connecting a new pitch to every new thought, noticing the rhythm and rhyme in the verse line, varying the tempo of a phrase or word within a phrase, or exploring the emotional quality released in a vowel or the intellectual component of a crisp or explosive consonant. Discover the effort or ease required to release a word or thought phrase, which syllables are stressed and which are unstressed in a word or an entire line of text. All of these ingredients can be used to create specificity and enhance the merriment, underline innuendo, and uplift the comedy while you bravely explore the language in the play.

Impulse, Thought, Breath, Action

As you explore the voice of your character and embody the text in movement, you will find it is helpful to initiate both sound and movement from impulse and breath. Both in life and on the stage, an impulse occurs in the brain as a response to our senses or a feeling or a need, like an electrical charge in motion. Your character then has a thought, so you inhale in order to speak or move, thereby connecting the thought to breath to voice, and movement to action. For example, these might be the steps in that process:

1. A character is spoken to, and in response, something is required of that character. They either do or speak back. They have an impulse to respond vocally, or physically, or both. The reaction begins with an impulse moving through the feeling center in the brain to respond to the situation.
2. Both speaking in response or moving in response requires breath. It is a primal reaction to the impulse. *Impulse leads to inspiration/breath, speech and movement.*
3. When breath is fueling speaking/sounding and/or movement/action as a result of an impulse, then *breath leads to sound/speech and action. This is the natural order of full embodiment of the text.*

Make sure that the impulse to respond first leads to breath, otherwise there will be a disconnect between receiving the impulse and the actual speaking. An easy way to spot this is that the actor will hold their breath or run out of air before the end of the line/thought or movement requirement. Or the actor may forget their line entirely. Sometimes an actor will sigh out the breath before speaking the line in response to the impulse. If this is habitual, it leads to acting before delivering the line and telegraphing the character's intentions instead of acting on the line as it's spoken in the present moment with immediacy, which is essential for comedy, especially with heightened or poetic text. Holding the breath as the character might be useful for certain moments in the play. Perhaps a character needs to hold their breath as a response to an impulse. Perhaps that is the appropriate response to being afraid or to fuel an actual hesitation to speak. That is great, if it is actually a conscious choice for the actor or by the character. It only becomes problematic when holding the breath is unconscious or habitually inhibiting response or unhelpful in terms of execution of sound or full complete responses, thoughts, emotional expression, or vocal freedom or movements.

Embodiment is when *impulses lead* to *breathing/inspiration*, in order that both the character and the actor are able to be immediately responsive with voice, text, and movement. This will inform the way an actor uses and plays with the sounds of the words and also the way they move their body with that sound and text. Respond with full heart/feeling/impulse and mind, awake to the absurd restrictions of society and structure of imposed manners, even while enjoying the *fun* of breaking those same rules of polite society.

Let's examine the sequence outlined previously through this exchange between Lady Sneerwell and Maria from *The School for Scandal* by Richard Brinsley Sheridan (1891, 1.1).

Lady Sneerwell is a sharp-tongued, hypocritical schemer and gossipmonger. She is the center of a group of high-society men and women who spend their time gossiping and creating scandals. She ruins reputations by submitting stories to the gossip columns and by paying others to forge incriminating letters. In love with Charles Surface, Lady Sneerwell conspires with Joseph Surface to prevent an engagement between Charles Surface and Maria.

Maria is a recently orphaned young woman. She is the ward of Sir Peter and heiress to his fortune. She is in love with Charles Surface but is also being courted by Joseph Surface and Sir Benjamin Backbite. Maria is portrayed as being very moral and sensitive. She hates gossip in particular and therefore finds the conversation of the gossips who congregate at Lady Sneerwell's house appalling.

Maria: *For my part, I own, madam, wit loses its respect with me, when I see it in company with malice.*

Lady S: *Pshaw! – there's no possibility of being witty with-out a little ill-nature: the malice of a good thing is the barb that makes it stick.*

Imagine the character of Maria has an impulse to actively defend her point of view, to argue and prove that someone who is unkind in the way he speaks, even as he is trying to be clever. She acts within the parameters of her station – good manners and societal norms intact. She breathes in on an impulse to defend (or prove) first, and that breath sends her into embodied vocal and physical action as she says her line.

Lady Sneerwell, however, may have the impulse to correct Maria for what she views as impudence from a morally sensitive orphan who has no experience in the world. Defying the manners and restrictions of polite society, she takes a big breath to expel an expletive – *Pshaw!*–before another quick breath to correct or educate this audacious girl.

Flirting With the "S" Curve and Laban's Effort Shapes

It's useful to begin this improvisatory work individually before working with a scene partner and, eventually, in small groups as if the characters were at a ball or cocktail party or in the lobby of the opera or ballet at the interlude. This latter option will be elaborated upon later in the chapter.

Draw an imaginary "s" in the space in front of you with your finger, wrist, hand, or forearm. Let it be sensual and light, playful, mischievous. Let it lead your

Naughty, Bawdy Characters and Comedy of Manners 135

imagination toward an opening, flirtation with another character, an invitation, a question that cannot be spoken. Trace the "s" shape in the air or run the finger along the body or a piece of furniture. The "s" curve also offers a pattern to travel across the floor within blocking while weaving through the room from place to place. It allows for a full show of tailcoats and the beautiful train that flows from costumes.

Next, progress to an investigation of the Laban effort shapes. Explore the effort shapes first in a separate rehearsal or class and then bring them into the exercise or take this moment to introduce Laban's work with effort shapes. This is a deeper movement study for actors, but it can be broken down into smaller parts for these specific purposes.

Laban's eight effort shapes are *flick, dab, glide, punch, press, wring, slash,* and *float*. These movement dynamics help us move through space with effort or lack of effort. Be sure to experiment with the effort shapes in both the body and with the text. For example, let us continue our exploration of the "s" curve with the effort shape *flick*:

- Flick someone's hand from your shoulder, or pretend to flick paint from your finger to the wall or another person across the room.
- Explore using different parts of the body to flick: the wrist, the head, the shoulder, the toe.
- Allow the movement to travel through space. Flick above your head while standing on tiptoe, down on the area just above the ground, in the medial in front and in back of you. Flick behind, above, and on the diagonal.

When the body has been explored thoroughly for possibilities with the effort-shape *flick*, begin to layer in sound. Start with a particular vowel or consonant sound that illustrates or makes muscular the effort shape, then continue into an entire word, then phrase, then entire line of text. To start, use the sounds within the word *flick* itself. Flick the vowel in the word (the same as in *pin* or *sip*) *using the effort shape*, then add consonants like *k, p,* or *t*, then flick an entire word, phrase, and finally, a line of text.

Returning to Maria's line from *The School for Scandal:*

Maria: For my part, I own, madam, wit loses its respect with me, when I see it in company with malice.

Flick the following words: *wit, its, with, it, in, malice.*
  Then *flick* the phrase: *wit loses its respect with me.*
  Once the effort shape is working well within the movement of the body and in the mouth with words or a phrase, it's time to associate it with a behavioral gesture that marries it nicely to the action or the "doing." Behavioral gestures are

activities like writing with a pen, playing a note on the piano, opening a fan, or removing someone's hand from your shoulder. Practice the gesture on its own first, then speak a sound to go along with it.

Practice with the effort shape while you execute the behavioral gesture of opening a fan after you say the word *malice*. This will help you underscore your point of action with embodied text.

We have examined *flick* here for its light and playful characteristics. *Float* is another effort shape that invites a sense of lightness and is in strong contrast to effort shapes like *wring* or *press*, which involve significantly more exertion, both in movement and text. However, each may be utilized to great comedic effect. As an example, let's return to Lady Sneerwell's line to look at the use of the effort shape *press*:

Lady S: *Pshaw! – there's no possibility of being witty with-out a little ill-nature: the malice of a good thing is the barb that makes it stick.*

The words *Pshaw* and *ill-nature* especially lend themselves to this effort shape. Try pressing them out of your mouth using the length of the vowel sound *aw* and the length of the *l* consonant sounds in *ill-nature*.

Combine this exploration with a behavioral gesture – perhaps standing with difficulty, as if someone is holding you down or preventing you from rising as quickly and lightly as you would like. Or try pressing a cup of tea across the table while saying *ill-nature*, and you may discover a way of embodying both movement and text as they work together in harmony.

Return to drawing an "s" curve in the space with a part of the body and add in the corresponding effort shape that helps to underscore a moment of effort or action in the text/phrase/sound. It might be a single word coupled with a movement dynamic and blocking as in the example in the previous section with **Lady S's** *Pshaw!* If Lady S struggles to stand using the effort shape of "press" at the same time she uses the same effort shape to "press" out and lengthen the sound of the vowel in *Pshaw!* And she makes an "s" curve with her fan in space pointing toward Maria, then the actor has the effort shape working together with the text, the gesture, the dynamic of the gesture, and the sound of the vowel. Embodiment.

Questions for consideration: "Does the effort shape help to underscore the point of view the character is making in some way?" and "Does it underline that point with both gesture and sound?"

Effort shapes are very useful when executed as the physical and vocal punctuation of a line or accompanying the impulse to breathe at the beginning of a line, phrase, or moment. Find an echo of the Laban-infused effort-shape in the body and the way the text is delivered. When the body, voice, and text are working together fluidly and playfully, then add a costume prop such as a writing quill or a fan. Work with a handkerchief, a parasol, a snuff box, a glove, a handheld mask, or even a sword or dagger to help fully embody the effort-shape with the text.

During the group work, you can add in set pieces like chairs, a chaise lounge or blocks, piano benches, walls to lean upon, or screens to hide behind. These become whimsical opportunities to trace out the "s" curve in walking and blocking or while sitting, standing, slinking, maneuvering, lying down, etc.

The Gallery

Here is where the work moves from individual exploration into scene partners or a larger group.

Arrange the rehearsal space or classroom, lining the periphery of the space with props on the tables, and if possible hang photographs of portraits on the walls or prepare a slideshow that can be viewed throughout the exercise. Have several paintings available from the period. Anything that illustrates relationships, decor, or portraiture from the time period can help stimulate the imagination toward capturing the lines found in the architecture, furniture, sculpture, and court life. Lay out oversize art books from the library or hang prints around the space.

As a first step, have participants draw the lines they see as if they are a painter in a studio. Draw the curves of the bodies as they drape across the furniture. Capture the fragility and finery in the decor, furniture, and clothing. We don't have to be good artists to draw lines in a notebook or on large sheets of butcher paper with paint and pens. The experiment is meant to give feeling to shape by exploring movement and capturing similar lines. Notice how artists posed hands, bodies, wrists, fans, shawls, placement of the legs and feet, manners of bowing, placement of the head and – after drawing some of these lines – try to imitate the figures in the paintings. Embody the character's legs, arms, neck, head placement, and facial expression as specifically as possible, trying on the scenes and silhouettes from the portraits.

Practice choosing a specific line or a silhouette from the painting that captures your interest. You might first draw a line in a journal or have paints and paper available to paint lines and curves you observe. Or just trace a line into the empty space before you as you look at each slide or portrait or painting. The oversize art books are great to page through, marking and tagging those that inspire you. Perhaps have specific examples chosen by the design team that are collaborating on costumes and set design if this work is to be used in a production.

Take a silent walking tour through the gallery with a journal in hand. Play music from the period and allow the music to wash over you and place you into the sound of the period as you are moving through the gallery, drawing and notating which of the lines jump out at you through architecture, furniture, costume, bodies, etc. It's also useful to have costume pieces available on racks or laid out on tables to have a tactile experience with materials. Try on different pieces of clothing and if possible help one another to dress, if in a group, getting the sense of what it might have been like to have a or be a ladies' maid or a manservant. Corsets, rehearsal skirts with trains, coats, lace cuffs, bum rolls, ballet slippers, tights, hats, snuff boxes, even hairdressing are all useful in embodying real life behavior for characters. Anything that might provoke your senses, deepening the imaginative elements, and adding both insight and opportunity to embody a character within this world. You might also have lines from the scene printed on little individual pieces of paper encircling the paintings on the table as you move through the gallery walk, asking participants to pick up one or two lines that seem to enchant, or excite, or more deeply connect you to both painting and text.

After the gallery tour, make notes, drawings, write down your impressions, and note how the music and paintings affected you. Find a physicalization from a painting that connects to a sensibility or nuance you are working toward. This moment might happen during a specific scene of the play or it might be less tangible. For example, perhaps a woman in a painting is draped across a chaise lounge with her closed fan sweeping across her lap toward the floor. As you embody this physicality, you might begin to connect to a feeling of disappointment, despair, ill health, or even a sensual invitation to another character in your scene. Find a way to begin and end the moment using your body and text as punctuation. For example, begin with making your way to the chaise and lie down in a silent improvisation or with music playing in the background. Add the breath to the impulse beginning the movement, sighing as you begin to descend onto the chaise, or perhaps sighing in punctuation as you land on the chaise and drape the fan across your lap toward the floor. Or find a way to initiate the breath into the movement as a quick intake of air on a gasp, as if you just remembered something of importance. Begin to add a note of sound or a voiced sigh as you complete the movement. From here, add in improvised text along with the sigh or actual lines from your scene. This is a way to play with tiny moments without having to concern yourself too much with the memorization of individual lines. It can also be helpful to speak the lines of other characters that are spoken *to* your character.

Marination

Now that you have had a chance to explore initial body lines, poses, and movement opportunities by working with the idea of the "s" curve, Laban effort shapes, paintings, breath, impulse, and sound, it's time to incorporate text from selected scenes from the play with a scene partner. When you are ready to engage, play with expressions of the "s" curves and discover interplay with language, and with one another always begin with consent-based practices and make sure to check in with scene partners and groups at the beginning of each session whenever there is possible touch involved or physical contact exchanged in rehearsals or classrooms. You may, for example, use your hand to draw the letter "s" in the palm of your scene partner's hand, across their forearm, onto the thigh, the back of the shoulders, across the lips, the neck, etc. You might also introduce drawing on the body with props (fans, shawls, gloves, handkerchiefs, etc.) or daringly keep it to using your fingertips on one another's bodies. Before adding in touch, it is recommended that you work with intimacy-based consent practices.

Next, introduce another part of the body to lead the exploration and flirtatious fun. Find an "s" pattern with your toe as you express the Laban effort shape of *glide*. Find a way to flirt with your partner, isolating your foot, stopping just before any contact is made with your scene partner's foot. Then, practice this from a variety of staged positions gathered from your gallery immersion, for example, standing next to one another in forbidden conversation, sitting on a bench or in chairs, one person sitting, one standing, one draped across a fainting couch while the other kneels. Some questions you might consider: "What's possible with just my foot?" "Can I add fan language and words to this moment along with my foot?" "How can I use the effort shape of *glide*, *flick* or *dab* with my foot and in my speech?"

Building on this, now invite the "s" curve into the blocking of the scene.

Remain connected to an image from the gallery exploration or choose another. Once you have some blocking evolved from improvisation, augment the physical work with more text exploration. In this way, the gallery improvisation and the communication between the bodies, breath, and text become a launching pad for the scene or a place to move toward in capturing the scene.

Explore more with breath and pitch as the dialogue shifts, introducing each new idea with a new pitch. Or investigate how the breath journey from the beginning of the line is married to the end of blocking shifts. Is the breath sighed out, landing at the end of the thought, or is it broken into many thoughts with short gasps in a flurry in order to support a build and final punctuation with the voice and the physical body? Or you might even go back to the Laban effort shapes and ask yourself, "Am I floating my pitch or gliding from word to word in order to seduce my scene partner?" "Am I flicking my text at my scene partner's character in order to accuse, or do I penetrate with my action?" "How do I find the slippery 's' curve on my tongue while I weave a lie, or in the hissing of my bite, or pressing of the lips, and can it penetrate the length of the vowels, or even as I linger on the resonating consonants?" "How do I pour sexuality into the sound of a 'z' or into the sensuality of the sound of an 's' at the beginning or end of my words?" This practice and improvisation is about possibilities and playfulness while trying to capture a sense of flirtiness and eroticism with the way the mouth licks, plays with, or even uses sword play, slicing and advancing the text. You might consider, what is the subtext of your soundscape? How can you enter the painting moment with the sound of your voice? Is there a way you can grace your scene partner's body without ever making contact with them? Or can you slash them to bits by using the precision of the text like a sword?

Once experienced fully in play, all of these tools can lead to the building of the character and directly affect the quality of action momentum to drive the direction of the entire world of the play. The actor will have considered the thoughts of the character and how they move through the body, the breath, the sound, the length of the sound and how it all connects to the expression of movement of blocking, their relationship to other characters, and their place in the story of the whole of the play. These explorations for comedy of manners plays will offer tools to the actor that will continue to inspire the way movement and sound are articulated throughout the storytelling and create vivid colors once married with costume and design features of the stage in any genre.

The exercises should arouse giddiness, merriment, and delightful naughtiness. They should challenge and add a quality of daring with both body and text. Exploration demands specificity, precision, and deliberate confrontation with the material as well as the other actors on stage. It's serious fun. Audiences can be left breathless with uproarious laughter or confident in a brilliant feeling of satisfied revenge.

References

Maybank, Diane. 2018. *An Introduction to Restoration Comedy*. London: British Library, June 21. www.bl.uk/restoration-18th-century-literature/articles/an-introduction-to-restoration-comedy.

Sheridan, Richard Brinsley. 1891. *The School for Scandal*. Internet Archive. (Printed for Mr. Daly). https://archive.org/details/cu31924013198134.

13

"O, VILLAIN, VILLAIN, SMILING, DAMNED VILLAIN"

Hamlet and the Rhetoric of Repetition

Matt Davies

The Two Traditions

Rhetoric gets a bad rap in the rehearsal room, even the Shakespeare rehearsal room. The study of rhetoric – and more particularly, the rhetorical figures of style that "constitute a vast technical vocabulary naming the ways that both ideas and language have been configured" (Burton 2016) – is widely considered the preserve of the lecture hall or library cubicle, and not the acting studio or performance arena. In Shakespeare's day, schoolboys not only recited hundreds of verbal devices in class but staged plays as part of their rhetorical training. Today's student, exposed to a handful of common figures – alliteration, antithesis, metaphor, and the like – is more likely to analyze a piece of text than perform it aloud, to test its literary components rather than taste its oracular power. Rhetoric has become a predominantly literary – and rarely artistic – enterprise.

Little wonder, then, that today's generation of theatre-makers is inherently skeptical of rhetoric. Over the course of three decades working as both text coach and roving recruiter for the Oregon Shakespeare Festival, Scott Kaiser discerned an increasing disregard, even disdain, for well-crafted language, especially among younger performers. In an era "infatuated with image technology, the very word rhetoric," he notes, "has become a toxic term, signifying speech that is empty, inflated, deceitful, insincere, artificial, and extravagant" (Kaiser 2007, xix). When effective communication is measured in 280-character tweets, fancy talk becomes the preserve of politicians, braggarts, lechers, and we might concede, a certain type of classical actor.

Whether students in general are quite as distrustful of language as Kaiser claims – after all, rap has been getting a pretty good "rep" in the classroom of late,

DOI: 10.4324/9781003204060-16

especially for teaching Shakespeare[1] – today's young actor contends with conflicting training approaches that complicate the authority of the word in defining and expressing character. "The Two Traditions" of classical and modern acting identified by Royal Shakespeare Company co-founder John Barton position a Formalist approach rooted in the text against the psychological realism of the American Method (Barton [1984] 2001, 3), which, drawing upon the writing of Konstantin Stanislavski, has come to dominate actor training over the past century. While the pragmatic Barton attempts to "marry" the traditions (14), for fellow RSC co-founder Peter Hall, the word remains the sacrosanct source of all knowledge: "Shakespeare's beginning is the word; and his end is also the word. He tells you what he means, and therefore what he means you to feel. And – if you're an actor – he tells you how to *shape* the words" (2003, 209). To repurpose Descartes' famous dictum: I speak, therefore I am. Conversely, the Method actor, trained predominantly in a classical canon rooted in the works of Anton Chekhov and modernist theatre, builds a character's inner life as much, if not more, from the subtext as from the scripted words. "It is the manifest, the inwardly felt expression of a human being in a part, which flows uninterruptedly beneath the words of the text" that gives a character "life and a basis for existing," argues Stanislavski in *Building A Character*. "It is the subtext that makes us say the words we do in a play" ([1949] 1994, 113). The stage is set for a civil war of semantics between competing pedagogies with the student caught in the middle. "First comes the form, then comes the feeling," asserts the text coach. "Get out of your head and into your body!" counters the acting teacher. While I exaggerate the dichotomy to make a point, these competing hierarchies nevertheless risk confining text work to the privacy of the study and emotional discovery to the social space of the rehearsal studio.

I want to challenge this (faintly grisly) Cartesian divide between mind and body by illustrating how actors can effectively engage classical rhetoric as a powerful tool to unlock both conscious and unconscious human impulses in the contemporary rehearsal room. In his online resource, "The Forest of Rhetoric," Gideon O. Burton defines rhetoric as both "the study of effective writing and speaking" and "the art of persuasion" (Burton 2016). The study of rhetoric, which discerns *how* language works, identifies critical oratorical skills to improve communication between the performer and their audience. As theatre director Barry Edelstein argues, the phrasing of arguments that in Shakespeare are always arranged "coherently and methodically . . . to be maximally clear" is a skill that "every Shakespearean actor must learn to emulate" (2007, 72–73). Simply making sense, after all, is central to the craft of the classical actor dealing with heightened texts.

But actors are not orators, any more than Shakespeare's plays are formal disputations. For today's classical performer primarily concerned with character, treating oratory as dramatic action – the *why* driving a rhetorical choice – offers the key to activating the academic discipline as a working practice. "We speak in order to bring about a change," writes Giles Block, former text coach at the London Globe, cautioning us to avoid the lyrical by remembering the obvious: "Speaking is an action" (2013, 16). Applied consciously, dramatic rhetoric treats Shakespeare's words as tactical speech acts delivered in the pursuit of desired objectives – the art of persuasion refigured as the precepts of Method. However, unlike its oratorical counterpart, dramatic rhetoric need not necessarily be conscious; it also plays on the effects of involuntary utterance, the speech habits and verbal mannerisms that, often unconsciously, betray social status and personality traits. Certain figures might even operate in different ways depending on their prosodic environment. At times, I shall argue, the impulsive rhythm of Hamlet's iambic verse seems to counteract the self-conscious performativity of his prose to capture the early stirrings of the subconscious.

By the Pattern of Mine Own Thoughts

That's the theory; now to the practice. In the following pages, I model a process of what we might call "embodied rhetoric," which, harnessing the synergies of critical analysis and linguistic cadence, creates a bridge between argument and impulse, a meeting of text and subtext, and, if not quite a true marriage, then certainly a close working relationship between classical and modern approaches to performance. To do so, I shall document rhetorical discoveries made in rehearsals for a recent production of *Hamlet* performed by students in the Shakespeare and Performance (S&P) graduate program at Mary Baldwin University. As part of their textual training, S&P students learn the core figures of speech taught by the early modern grammarians, which, prior to the emergence of directors, dramaturges, or text coaches, the playwrights relied upon to convey information to actors trained from familiar rhetoric manuals.[2] It has become a common practice to teach students of early modern drama how to scan verse texts for rhythm and metrical irregularities that ruffle the iambic heartbeat to reveal a character's unique way of speaking – their idiolect. Yet fully one third of Shakespeare's dramatic language is in rhetorically dense prose, rich with clues to character (Edelstein 2007, 389). To learn how to read these playable figures as embedded stage directions, in both heightened verse *and* prose, is to invite the early modern playwright into the contemporary rehearsal room.

The immediate challenge for today's practitioner is how to identify playable figures from a A[ccumulatio] to Z[eugma] of unfamiliar Greek and Latin terms that, hard to pronounce and even harder to remember, risk alienating the actor and obfuscating Shakespeare's rhetorical structures. Indeed, Scott Kaiser argues that we should do away with such arcane terminology altogether, for engaging Shakespeare's wordplay is less about naming devices than identifying verbal patterns, "audible, discernable, memorable patterns that enter the ear and mix in the brain, giving meaning to the sounds and pleasure to the listener" (Kaiser 2007, xxi). In *Shakespeare's Wordcraft*, Kaiser modernizes such terms – an accumulation amplifies by piling on definitions, and a zeugma "asks one verb to do the work of many in a sentence"[3] –while organizing the devices into nine groups that offer coherence and manageability.[4] Likewise, the education department at our partner institution, the American Shakespeare Center (ASC), which offers in-person and online resources aimed at high school through college students and teachers,[5] has developed a similar, if simpler, taxonomy. ROADS clusters 50 figures under five mnemonic headings: Repetition (figures that harmonize speech and synthesize ideas), Omission (figures that interrupt or encourage meaning), Addition (figures that elaborate), Direction (figures that reorder), and Substitution (figures that represent).

Unlike Kaiser, however, the ASC materials identify devices by their classical names, in the belief that studied familiarity attunes us to perceive verbal patterns that "pop off the page" ("The American Shakespeare Center Study Guide: The Basics," 32). Moreover, interpreting arcane terms that were as foreign to the early modern ear as to modern readers encourages us to engage with rhetoric manuals contemporary to Shakespeare that translate, or "English," foreign words in much the same way Kaiser does. Modern glossaries, such as Richard Lanham's *A Handlist of Rhetorical Terms* and Burton's online "The Forest of Rhetoric," reference not only ancient rhetoricians like Plato and Aristotle but also the late-Tudor manuals, especially George Puttenham's *The Arte of English Poesie* (1589) and *The Garden of Eloquence* (1593) by Henry Peacham, whose popularity reflected the Elizabethan age's interest in a burgeoning English vernacular. Their definitions of common figures offer vital, and sometimes surprising. clues as to how the playwrights and actors of their day might have read and applied these devices in performance. Bringing these classic resources, all of which are available in modern editions, into the rehearsal room cracks a casement into earlier perspectives that often challenge assumptions about familiar Shakespeare characters like the hallowed Hamlet.

The Rhetoric of the Cuckoo

Armed with a slightly narrower list of 40 figures, S&P students begin rehearsals with table work, in which each scene is separately analyzed for scansion, paraphrasing of difficult words, main themes, *and* playable figures, before being "put on its feet." Since, as the saying goes, everything is rhetorical, we encourage actors to identify two or three character-forming devices, a limitation that can enrich a one-act player like the soldier Marcellus but also simplify the awesome complexity of Hamlet, who speaks more than any other character in the Shakespeare canon. Reading through the opening scenes, we noticed a distinctive repetitiveness in the dialogue. Repetition, the first element in ROADS, accommodates numerous devices employed by Shakespeare. While enhancing the lyrical quality of the earlier comedies, for a skilled speaker like King Claudius, Hamlet's treacherous uncle, such devices often manipulate meaning:

> 'Tis sweet and commendable in your nature, Hamlet,
> To give these mourning duties to your father,
> But you must know, your **father** lost a **father**,
> That father **lost lost** his . . .
> (*Ham*, 1.2.87–90)[6]

While the first figure of repetition, a diacope, interrupts a repeated term with a few intervening words, adding appropriate emotional impact to the inevitability of mortality, the subsequent antanaclasis, which gives identical words different meanings, essentially operates as a pun. Claudius uses clever wordplay in a public effort to compel his new son-in-law's allegiance, offering the actor a telling rhetorical choice to blend empathy with mockery. Employing repetition in such varied, significant ways is doubtless why Kaiser dubs Shakespeare "the all-time Master of Repetition" (2007, 67).

However, a less coherent repetition emerges in Hamlet's next soliloquy, immediately following the departure of Claudius' court. Bemoaning his mother Gertrude's too rash marriage to her brother-in-law, Hamlet wishes himself dead rather than reside in the rotten state of Denmark:

> O that this **too too** sullied flesh would melt
> Thaw, and resolve itself into a dew,
> Or that the Everlasting had not fixed
> His canon 'gainst self-slaughter. **O God, O God,**
> How weary, stale, flat and unprofitable
> Seems to me all the uses of this world!
> Fie on't! O, **fie, fie,** 'tis an unweeded garden
> That grows to seed.
> (*Ham*, F, 1.2.127–33)

The three examples in bold identify epizeuxis, which Lanham defines as the "fastening together" (1991, 71) of identical words or phrases with no others in between and with no obvious alteration of sense. "Buzz, buzz" (2.2.330), as Hamlet later says, dismissing the tedious councilor Polonius. Absent of obvious meaning or intention, this seemingly inane figure is hard to interpret as a playable action. Why are there two "too"s? Are there two different gods, different kinds of the same god, or one god who is not answering? Does the addition of a third "fie" intentionally ruffle the meter, or is it merely evidence of actors' vulgar interpolations, as editor Harold Jenkins has argued? To complicate matters, the Tudor grammarians dispute the rhetorical value of the device. Peacham puts a positive spin on a verbal echo that serves "to express the vehemence of any affection, whether it be of joy, sorrow, love, hatred, admiration or any such like" (1593, 52). Yet Puttenham considers the device "not figurative but fantastical." "Englishing" the Greek term as "the underlay or Cuckoo-Spell," after the songbird's "one manner of note, [that it] for haste stammers out two or three [times], the one immediately after another, as *cuck, cuck, cuckoo*," Puttenham dismisses epizeuxis as "a very foolish impertinence of speech" (1589, 3, 285). While Claudius might find his morose nephew impertinent in the modern sense of the word – as in "absurd," "insolent," or "rude" (*OED*, adj. 3a, 4) – to Puttenham and Shakespeare, impertinent meant "not to the point, [or] irrelevant" (*OED*, adj. 1). Why would someone possessing, in Ophelia's tender opinion, such "noble and most sovereign reason" (3.1.156) favor a manner of speech that is at best histrionic, at worst irrelevant?

This question is hardly rhetorical, given the figure's frequency. Having once identified epizeuxis, it indeed begins to pop up everywhere: the insistent call of the cuckoo sounds through Hamlet's Forest of Rhetoric. As Stefan Keller laboriously tallied, it appears 19 times per 1,000 lines (2009, 38). This might not sound a lot, but in a role constituting roughly 40% of the text, Hamlet utters around 65% of all the instances of epizeuxis in the play – once every 30 lines or so. While such statistics clearly identify Hamlet as the play's chief cuckoo, the remaining instances of epizeuxis also indicate that he is not alone. The interplay of this characteristic figure allows us to hear the rhetorical bonds that bind families, friends, and social networks.

We find evidence of this rhetorical inter-relationality when we next encounter Hamlet, as he confronts his father's Ghost on the battlements of Elsinore Castle. Even more verbose than his son, the Ghost, whose time on earth is limited, quiets Hamlet with an immediate repetitive command: "List, list, O list" (1.5.22). Hamlet, of course, has to interrupt – "O God!" (1.5.22) –prompting an exchange in which father and son create a shared epizeuxis as the father reveals the truth of his sudden death:

Ghost: Revenge his foul and most unnatural murder!
Hamlet: Murder!
Ghost: Murder most foul –   (1.5.26–28)

This apparent trait for trifectas, or tricolon repetitions, continues as the Ghost bemoans being poisoned by his brother in his sleep and without sacrament: "No reckoning made but sent to my account/With all my imperfections on my head./O horrible, O horrible, most horrible!" (1.5.78–80). After urging his son to wreak vengeance on the King (but not his mother – "Leave her to heaven"), the Ghost takes his thrice-protracted leave: "Adieu, adieu, adieu, remember me"

(1.5.86–91). Ignoring his father's caution, Hamlet immediately levels his triple barrels at both mother and father-in-law: "O most pernicious woman,/O villain, villain, smiling, damned villain" (1.5.105–6). As he plots his revenge with Horatio and Marcellus, the Ghost's voice returns from the ether (or beneath the stage) to demand their loyalty, calling three times: "Swear!" (1.5.149, 155, 179). Restoring epizeuxis to Peacham's more familiar "double sigh of the heart," Hamlet calms first himself – "Hold, hold, my heart" (1.5.93) – and then his father: "Rest, rest, perturbed spirit" (1.5.180). What we hear in this scene, over and again, is a figural characteristic that is not just Hamlet's but the Hamlets': Shakespeare writes compulsive repetition into the DNA of the Danish royal family.

Tellingly, when the Ghost briefly returns in the third act, so too do the verbal echoes. Confronting his mother in her bedchamber – "Mother, mother, mother!" (F, 3.4.6) – Hamlet demands of Gertrude, "Come, come, and sit you down," to show her contrasting portraits of old Hamlet and Claudius. Hearing a noise behind the arras, Hamlet stabs Polonius – "How now, a rat!" (3.4.22) – before assailing his mother, twin actions that conjure the Ghost. The fact that his mother cannot see the spirit exasperates Hamlet even further: "Save me, save me, you gracious powers above" (Q1, 11:58). His insistent interjections into empty space finally convince Gertrude that "Alas, he's mad" (3.4.102). Hamlet's tendency to compulsive repetition seems so familiar to Gertrude that she even ascribes epizeuxis where none, in fact, exists: Hamlet, she later confesses to Claudius, "Whips out his rapier, cries 'A rat! A rat!'" (4.1.10; see quote previously). Rather than misremembering the event, Gertrude may have diagnosed her son's tendency toward verbal mania.

The issue of Hamlet's mental stability is central to any interpretation of the role and is complicated because the melancholy Prince, playing on court anxieties, adopts "an antic disposition" (1.5.170) as a smokescreen for his investigations. Among various elements Horatio is told to look out for – including moody folded arms and a head shake – Hamlet includes repetitive phrasing: "by pronouncing of some doubtful phrase/As 'Well, well, we know', or 'We could an if we would'" (1.5.173). Emerging in self-consciously metatheatrical scenes featuring his university playmates Rosencrantz and Guildenstern and the city players they overtake on the road to Elsinore, the antic Hamlet deploys epizeuxis every bit as much as in his familial encounters: the question is whether we, or indeed Hamlet, can distinguish between the rhetoric of acted madness and madness in action.

It quickly becomes apparent that when Hamlet applies the figure consciously, he wields epizeuxis less like an expressive device than an offensive weapon. "Is it a free visitation?" he demands of his college pals, turning a playful request into pointed interrogation: "Come, come, deal justly with me. Come, come, nay speak!" (2.2.241–42). The figure becomes cutting and ironic when Hamlet watches the Players perform his adaptation of *The Murder of Gonzago* to trap the conscience of the King: "No, no, they do but jest. Poison in jest" (3.2.228). It also acquires the brute force of a cudgel when Hamlet alienates those closest to him, as when he beats away Ophelia's affection – "Ha! Ha! Are you honest?" (3.1.101) – and later publicly shames her: "You are naught. You are naught" (as in indecent but also a crude sexual pun, 3.2.140). Less immediately apparent, but increasingly significant, is the fact that these metatheatrical scenes are conducted almost entirely in prose, which has the potential to alter the dynamics of repetitive figures.

Freed from the metrical constraints of iambic verse, Hamlet's repetitions become performatively, self-consciously erratic – they put the "antic" in semantic: "My lord, I will take my leave of you," says Polonius, faced with a mercurial Hamlet, to which the Prince replies: "You cannot take from me anything that I will not more willingly part withal – except my LIFE, except MY life, EXCEPT my life" (2.2.209–12; my capitals). Whichever way the actor chooses to stress the epizeuxis, and in whichever order, the same phrase with different operatives creates radically opposing actions: don't take my life; take any life but mine; please take my life! Little wonder Polonius retreats nervously. Detached from a single meaning, repetitive words and phrases become unstable, untrustworthy, dangerous. In our poststructuralist world, today's actor might even be tempted to fracture Hamlet's figural fastenings entirely. "What do you read, my lord?" asked Miriam Burrows's Ophelia in a memorable ASC production of 2011, to which company veteran John Harrell repunctuated Hamlet's response, turning a repudiation of language – "Words, words, words" (2.2.188–89) – into its weaponization: "Word. Sword. Swords." Stressing slippery semantics over cadence, the prosaic Hamlet performs a studied, early modern conception of madness that feels strikingly modern.

In contrast, Hamlet's metrically stressed epizeuxes seem to necessitate a quite different mode of expression. The emotionally fraught exchanges with his mother, with Ophelia, and especially with his dead father reverberate, imposing a compulsive iambic rhythm that frames Puttenham's definition of that "one manner of note . . . without any intermission," less as an expression of rhetorical impertinence than of emotional trauma. Nothing in the early modern writing on melancholia quite captures this notion of insistent repetition as the expression of traumatic memory.[7] As such, the Hamlets' manic repetitiveness perhaps captures something of the "intense feeling, ecstatic or terrible" that T.S. Eliot, in his famous 1919 essay, "Hamlet and his Problem," imagines lying just beyond Shakespeare's comprehension. Judging the play a brilliant failure, Eliot cautioned that to understand Hamlet, we "should have to understand things that Shakespeare did not understand himself" (Eliot 1975, 49). The desire to chart Hamlet's inner life – to *know* Hamlet – places a particular burden on a rhythmical figure like epizeuxis, which has the potential to voice the inarticulate by verbalizing the rhythms of interiority.

Underscoring the modern actor's pursuit of active specificity at all times, celebrated text coach Patsy Rodenburg argues that "because each stage and word of the character's journey is a new pulse to be experienced," no two words are ever equal: "when words or phrases are repeated side by side [they] must be owned and expressed differently even though they are the same" (2002, 177). Yet an approach that works powerfully in prose raises fundamental questions about the autonomous operation of this repetitive figure in an iambic pentameter that imposes its own accentual rhythm. This tension becomes particularly apparent when the metrical pulse is interrupted – "O, that this too . . . too solid flesh would melt" (1.2.129), as is often performed in Hamlet's first soliloquy – or the stress inverted – "O, that this too TOO solid flesh would melt"–as Edelstein scans the line, arguing that all such repetitions are builds: "Like lists, repeats grow in intensity" (2007, 275). As written in the iambic pentameter, however, Hamlet's "O that this *too* too solid flesh would melt" functions not as a correction or amplification but as an echo, a faint signal emanating from the depths of Hamlet's undiscovered interiority. While Edelstein dismisses such regular scansion because "it makes no sense" (275), perhaps this is the point. Hamlet's strange neologism, "*too*-too" – like the bird's "cuckoo" – might not ask to be understood; it simply calls to be heard. Hamlet's enduring fascination is that everyone – actors, directors, scholars, philosophers, and even psychoanalysts – desperately wants to understand him, and Ophelia, perhaps, deserves to more than most. "How does your honour for this many a day?" she asks, yearning to reconnect with her sweetheart, to which Hamlet quietly replies, "I humbly thank you, well, well, well" (F, 3.1.89–90). Such a triple sigh of the heart*beat* tells us – and perhaps all it can tell us – is that Hamlet is not "well" at all.

An Anti-rhetoric for Our Time

In this chapter, I have focused on the operation of one, seemingly benign, rhetorical figure spoken mainly by one character in *Hamlet*. In doing so, I do not hope to add yet another grand theory on how to better understand Hamlet himself – only to offer an alternative lens through which to examine Shakespeare's dramatic poetry. Nor would I wish to characterize a single rhetorical figure as a key to unlocking Shakespeare's play. Like Claudius' sorrows, rhetorical figures "come not single spies/But in battalions" (4.5.78–79); they are cooperative and context-dependent. In any case, rhetoric offers clues for the reader, not keys for the cryptologist. What I have hoped to demonstrate is the invaluable contribution rhetoric can make in today's rehearsal room, not only as a literary skill that helps shape argument, but also as a network of articulated speech actions that create the bridge between thought and event through the intermediary of breath. If cognition is an electrical impulse, its delivery is pulmonary and its articulation rhythmic: fully embodied rhetoric breathes.

The art of dramatic rhetoric, in effect, identifies how certain forms of speech, activated through cadence and rhythm, evoke specific responses in the audience.

"[It] is the rhythm itself which affects something deep inside of us, not necessarily the argument," notes founding RSC text coach Cicely Berry, adding that we may "understand something through that rhythm which may be outside our full literal comprehension" (Berry 1987, 4). As Hamlet says, "There are more things in heaven and earth, Horatio,/Than are dreamt of in our philosophy" (F, 1.5.165–66). This notion of subconscious rhetorical meaning, so powerfully captured by Hamlet's use of iambic repetition, places classical rhetoric center stage in contemporary theatrical practice since it challenges, or at least complicates, the Method dictum that all speech acts are conscious choices pursuing known objectives. Actions are not always conscious, especially repetitive ones. Peacham's definition of epizeuxis applied angrily as a "double stabbe with a weapon's point" implies clear intention, where the lover's "double sigh of the heart" might not (Peacham 1593, 52). Sometimes Hamlet chooses epizeuxis as a command: "On him! On him! Look how he glares" (3.4.122), he cries, seeing the Ghost that his mother cannot. At others, the rhetoric seems to choose him: "No? Why see the king, my father, my father" (Q1 11.77). And intention, as RSC actor Oliver Ford Davies notes, impacts delivery: "Sometimes the actor tries to play one or more repetitions differently, sometimes the bald monotony is more telling" (2007, 51). In these moments, the actor might trust the language to do its own work; the meaning, after all, is in the rhythm. Although, in the mature tragedies that follow *Hamlet*, the repetitive rhythm increasingly becomes meaning*less*.

At moments of overwhelming emotion, Shakespeare's later tragic characters discard figurative language and rhetorical invention for what A.D. Nuttall identifies as an "anti-rhetorical rhetoric" (2007, 51) favoring stark literalism and verbal skepticism. Schemes of repetition that in earlier repetitious characters, like *Romeo and Juliet*'s Nurse or *Henry IV, Part 2*'s Justice Shallow, created "brilliant tricks of characterization [from] the homeliest stylistic materials" (McDonald 2001, 121), begin to sound like disturbing tics of mental deterioration in Shakespeare's darkening tragedies. The limits of language lay bare the psychological torment of characters in distress. "O Desdemon! Dead Desdemon! Dead! O! O!" (*Othello*, 5.2.288), moans Othello, rocking the body of the young wife he has suffocated in a jealous rage. And characters in distress distress their iterative characters: "Then kill, kill, kill, kill, kill, kill" (*King Lear*, 4.5.177), rages Lear against his imagined sons-in-law, as if breaking words on an anvil, to borrow Anne Barton's brutal image, "to determine whether or not there is anything inside" (1971, 26). A "transitional play in the development of the language of turbulent thinking" (Amelang 2019, 27), *Hamlet*'s rhetoric of repetition does not quite reach for the semantically destabilizing effects of Shakespeare's increasingly nihilistic late tragedies. As an indicator of acted madness and madness in action, epizeuxis holds together that which is fractured and fracturing, capturing the Prince's conflicted self precisely because, in Russ McDonald's terms, it is "rhetoric . . . which conceals itself" (2001, 46). But as the first of Shakespeare's plays to portray how repetition works in capturing a turbulent interiority, *Hamlet* broadcasts a pulsating signal that resonates far beyond his work. We hear it in the meandering recitations of Chekhov's lonely souls, in the endlessly diminishing cycles of Beckett's and Ionesco's absurdist dramas, in the threatening tautologies of Miller's and Pinter's interrogators, in the "Rep[etition] and Rev[ision]" jazz refrains of Suzan-Lori Parks. Reverberating across the centuries and the canons of modernist and postmodern drama, classical rhetoric in *Hamlet* never felt so contemporary.[8]

Notes

1. See, for instance, Akala's "Hip Hop and Shakespeare," *TedxAlderburgh Talk*, June 23, 2016; or the numerous lesson plans offered by university courses, such as, "Straight Outta Shakespeare, or Iambic Pentameter," http: tedb.byu.edu, 2015.
2. *The Arte of Rhetorique* by Thomas Wilson, which ran through eight editions between 1553 and 1585, offered arguably the most influential oratorical training for Elizabethan grammar schoolboys, a small cohort of whom, overeducated and underemployed, fortuitously went on to produce the "golden age" of English theatre.
3. As an example of zeugma, Kaiser cites Richard II's line to John of Gaunt, "We'll calm the duke of Norfolk, you your son" (*R2*, 1.1.158).
4. Kaiser divides chapters into Words, Additions, Repetitions, Reverberations, Transformations, Substitutions, Omissions, Order, and Disorder.
5. https://americanshakespearecenter.com/education/educationhomepage/educationhomepage-2/
6. Today's actor generally performs an editorial conflation of three quite different source texts: the 1603 first quarto (Q1), the second quarto of 1604 (Q2), and the 1623 Folio (F). I will indicate where I veer from the Q2 base text in the Arden *Hamlet* (2006) in the citation following a quotation.
7. Two works in particular offer valuable insights into understanding early modern notions of melancholy and mental distraction: Dr. Timothy Bright's *Treatise on Melancholie*, which seems to have been a source for *Hamlet*, and Robert Burton's compendious *The Anatomy of Melancholy* (1621).
8. In *Shakespeare our Contemporary* (1961), Jan Kott's chapter, "*King Lear* or *Endgame*," makes the connection between Shakespeare's late tragedy and Beckett's absurdist dramas.

Bibliography

Amelang, David. 2019. "A Method to His Madness." *Anglia* 137 (1): 33–52.
Barton, Anne. 1971. "Shakespeare and the Limits of Language." *Shakespeare Survey* 24 (November): 20–27.
Barton, John. 2001. *Playing Shakespeare: An Actor's Guide*. New York: Anchor Books.
Berry, Cicely. 1987. *The Actor and His Text*. London: Harrap.
Block, Giles. 2013. *Speaking the Speech: An Actor's Guide to Shakespeare*. London: Nick Hern Books.
Bright, Timothy. 1940. *Treastise on Melancholy*. New York: Columbia University Press.
Burton, Gideon. O. 2016. *Silva Rhetoricae*. Brigham Young University. http://rhetoric.byu.edu.

Burton, Robert. 2001. *The Anatomy of Melancholy*. New York: New York Review of Books.
Davies, Oliver Ford. 2007. *Performing Shakespeare*. London: Nick Hern Books.
Edelstein, Barry. 2007. *Thinking Shakespeare*. New York: Spark Publishing.
Eliot, T. S. 1975. "Hamlet and his Problem." In *Selected Prose of T. S. Eliot*, edited by Frank Kermode, 45–49. London: Faber and Faber.
Hall, Peter. 2003. *Shakespeare's Advice to the Players*. New York: Theatre Communications Group.
Kaiser, Scott. 2007. *Shakespeare's Wordcraft*. New York: Limelight.
Keller, Stefan Daniel. 2009. *The Development of Shakespeare's Rhetoric*. Zurich: Franke verlag.
Kott, Jan. 1974. *Shakespeare our Contemporary*. New York: Norton.
Lanham, Richard A. 1991. *A Handlist of Rhetorical Terms*, 2nd ed. Berkeley: University of California Press.
McDonald, Russ. 2001. *Shakespeare and the Arts of Language*. Oxford: Oxford University Press.
Nuttall, A. D. 2007. *Shakespeare the Thinker*. New Haven: Yale University Press.
Peacham, Henry. [1593] 1983. *The Garden of Eloquence: An English Bestiary*. Edited by Willard R. Espy. New York: Harper & Row.
Puttenham, George. [1589] 2007. *The Art of English Poesy*. Edited by Frank Whigham and Wayne A. Rebhorn. Ithaca: Cornell University Press.
Rodenberg, Patsy. 2002. *Speaking Shakespeare*. New York: Palgrave Macmillan.
Shakespeare, William. 1982. *Hamlet: The Arden Shakespeare*. Edited by Harold Jenkins. London: Methuen.
———. 2006. *Hamlet: The Arden Shakespeare*. Edited by Ann Thompson and Neil Taylor. London: Cengage.
Stanislavski, Constantin. 1994. *Building a Character*. New York: Routledge.
Wilson, Thomas. [1560] 1909. *The Arte of Rhetorique*. Oxford: Clarendon Press.

14

AGAMEMNON'S HOMECOMING

Using Active Analysis to Explore Ancient Theatre

Sharon Marie Carnicke

As a theatre artist, I have come to believe that Stanislavsky's most innovative rehearsal technique, now widely known as Active Analysis, fosters exactly the kind of flexibility that contemporary actors need as they work with different types of dramaturgies from classic plays to postdramatic works and as they move from stage to screen and new media. Through improvisational etudes that explore the interactive dynamics in a scene, actors test their understanding of a play and discover its artistic style before memorizing anything. This embodied exploration allows actors to experience viscerally their characters' circumstances within the performative realities of a specific production with a specific cast in a specific space. Because Active Analysis inverts standard approaches to rehearsal that put memorization of lines and blocking first, actors learn why a play is structured as it is and why their characters speak as they do before making artistic choices that limit their performance options. This process better enables them to adjust to the production's goals and to the individualities of their acting partners.

This inversion of standard rehearsal procedures also makes Active Analysis a valuable pedagogical tool in courses on drama. The word "etude" derives from the French verb "to study," and etudes effectively invite students to study how plays function as scores for performance, rather than as self-contained literary monuments. Etudes can also foster an open spirit of inquiry by "clean[ing] the dust of time off literary works with wonderful images and characters in them" (Knebel' 1967, 485), thus encouraging students to find relevance and take pleasure in plays from distant eras and diverse cultures.

This chapter suggests how the practice of Active Analysis can be adapted for use in dramatic literature courses through a case study on Agamemnon's homecoming in Aeschylus' *The Oresteia*. My undergraduate course on ancient Greek

DOI: 10.4324/9781003204060-17

and Roman drama enrolls theatre majors and minors as well as students from other disciplines like computer science, physics, narratology, and music. The course begins with a history of the dramatic competitions at the Athenian Festival of Dionysius in fifth century BCE and an examination of the architecture of the Greek amphitheater. Only then do I turn students' attention to a close study of Aeschylus' trilogy, and in the fifth session of the course, we turn to Agamemnon's return from the Trojan War to bring Aeschylus' treatment of choral performance and theatrical space into sharp focus.

The Principles Behind Active Analysis[1]

Stanislavsky developed his most innovative approach to rehearsing during his last four years (1934–38), while looking for a way to help actors retain spontaneity during their performances. For more than 20 years, he had begun rehearsals by spending long periods of time with his actors "around the table," examining every facet of the play and researching the history and culture that informed the lives of its characters. This intellectual analysis of plays emulates the process of literary study but tends to overburden actors with too much information, thus dampening their creative spirits. Stanislavsky noticed that after completing such table work, "the actor comes on stage with a stuffed head and an empty heart, and can act nothing" (Stanislavskii 1991, 325–26). He therefore wanted to get actors up on their feet sooner so that they could analyze their roles holistically, thinking with their minds, bodies, and spirits all at once. In a letter to his family from December 1936, he explains that his "new approach to the role . . . involves reading the play today, and tomorrow rehearsing it on stage:"

> What can we rehearse? A great deal. A character comes in, greets everybody, sits down, tells of events that have just taken place, expresses a series of thoughts. Everyone can act this, guided by their own life experience. So, let them act. . . . And when this is done . . . then we can say that the line of the life of the human body has been created. This is no small thing, but half the role.
> *(Stanislavskii 1999, 655)*

He provisionally called this new approach "a method of physical actions," expecting embodiment to trigger the actors' minds and spirits. "The best way to analyze a play," he now insisted, "is to take action in the given circumstances" (Stanislavskii 1991, 332–33).

Because Stanislavsky's experiments with this new approach coincided with the most repressive era in Soviet history, his holistic ideas were strictly censored, remaining hidden until the 1960s, when a thaw in Soviet artistic policies allowed his ardent and most clear-eyed assistant, Maria Knebel, to teach and write openly about his work. She coined the term "Active Analysis" in order to distinguish Stanislavsky's holistic intent from the politically correct and overly materialist "vulgarization" of his work that was being touted by loyal Soviets as "the Method of Physical Actions" (Knebel' 1971, 109 and 121–23).

As an artistic practice, Active Analysis, like any other rehearsal technique, is a process for creating performances that are memorized, blocked, polished, and repeatable. Etudes function as successive "drafts" of such a performance with each draft actualizing the text better than the last (Knebel' 1971, 52). Thus, etudes are not free improvisations but guided studies on the interactive dynamics of the play being rehearsed. Active Analysis conceives of a play as a chain of events that tell a story, with each event a product of the collision between an action (that initiates and impels each scene forward toward an event) and a counteraction (that resists the action's forward momentum). In the professional arena, actors prepare for an etude by reading the scene under study for those specific facts that reveal its interactive dynamics. The actors then test their understanding by embodying the actions and counteractions that they have identified in an etude, using their own words (a paraphrase etude) or dispensing with words in order to isolate the characters' thoughts and behaviors (a silent etude). After completing an etude, the actors reread the text in order to assess how closely they came to the scene as written and whether the event had occurred as a result of what they did. They next make adjustments to their understanding of the scene and try another etude. This pattern of reading, testing their understanding through an etude, and assessing continues until the actors can "clear up . . . what is really happening" (Efros 2006, 44) and experience the scene viscerally. In my experience, actors often reach this point quickly, after three or four iterations of the process. Only then do they memorize their lines and does the director set the blocking.

In my academic courses, however, I do not use etudes to direct but rather to illuminate aspects of plays that my students find difficult to grasp through reading alone. For example, in my course on Shakespeare's plays, students were unable to laugh while reading Dogberry's scenes in *Much Ado About Nothing*. Shakespeare's language simply got in their way. I suggested that a group of students try an etude on act IV, scene ii, in which Dogberry interrogates the play's villains and ends by asking, "Dost thou not suspect my place? Dost thou not suspect my years? O that [the sexton] were here to write me down an ass!" The laughter that ensued from the etude better uncovered the scene's farcical potential than further discussion might have done. I did not ask the students, who volunteered for the etude, to engage in deeper analysis, as I would when working with actors in a rehearsal. I merely asked the students to play the scene in their own words as best they could and have fun with it. In short, I adapted the etude process to the pedagogical need at hand. In my courses, I am constantly drawing upon different aspects of Active Analysis as they are needed. Therefore, the following case study on Agamemnon's homecoming need not be read as a recipe for how to use etudes in academic courses, but rather as an invitation to all actors to experiment.

Preparing a Paraphrase Etude on Agamemnon's Homecoming

Agamemnon's homecoming after the ten-year war with Troy, waged over the abduction of his brother's wife, Helen, occurs in the first play of the *Oresteia* (Aeschylus 1998, lines 773–974). His victory is tarnished not only by the many lives lost in battle but also by his initial decision to sacrifice his daughter, Iphigenia, to the gods so that the war could commence. Upon his return, he is greeted by the elders of Argos and his wife, Clytemnestra, who has been waiting ten years to take revenge for what she considers the murder of her child. To prepare for this etude, students need to understand what all the words mean and consider the nuances behind the ideas expressed. They will also need to identify what must occur for the scene to unfold in accord with Aeschylus' text: the chorus awaits Agamemnon's arrival with anxious ambivalence; he arrives with the spoils of war in the person of Cassandra, who has been enslaved; he tries to calm the elders with humility and a public promise to establish a democratic assembly; and Clytemnestra undercuts all his efforts by persuading him to behave as an autocrat and tread on a royal carpet dyed the color of blood.

Casting

After reminding my students of the circumstances that condition this scene, I ask for volunteers. Two theatre majors immediately choose the roles of Agamemnon and Clytemnestra. When I observe that in our etude, neither Cassandra nor Clytemnestra's two servants need to speak, students from other majors volunteer. Everyone else in the class serves as the chorus.

Reading for the Facts

The first main pedagogical goal for this etude is to convey how Greek tragedy uses "the tension between the collective chorus and the individual hero" as "a structuring principle, visually evident in the contrast between the lone actor on the stage and the group of [choral singers and] dancers in the *orchestra*" (Goldhill 2007, 47). Although tragedy developed from and incorporates choral odes, today's chorus registers as one of ancient drama's most foreign characteristics. As the classicist Simon Goldhill observes,

> Every . . . modern production has to face the acute problem of what to do with a group of people onstage throughout even the most intimate exchanges of husband and wife, a group which has long odes in dense lyric poetry to

deliver between the scenes of actors acting and events happening. More modern performances fail because of the chorus than for any other reason: if the chorus isn't right, the play cannot work.

(2007, 45)

Without understanding how the chorus "has a special charge in democracy" (Goldhill 49), students are likely to skip over the odes as boring poetry that stops the flow of the story. However, once students see the chorus as a collective character with their own stakes in the play's circumstances, tragedy becomes newly relevant.

Therefore, I begin with a discussion designed to unpack the facts in *Agamemnon* that locate the chorus within the story. Who are they, exactly, and why do they greet their leader with such ambivalence? We decide that they are men, and citizens of Argos, who were too old to join the military at the start of the Trojan War: "We are the men without honor,/ our aging limbs incapable of service,/ left behind, propped on sticks,/ our brittle bones/ as weak as children's/ Unfit to serve the god of war" (Aeschylus 1998, lines 72–77). Do they lack honor because they are ashamed of their inability to fight for their country? We look more closely at the textual details in order to get "beyond the obvious," as Anatoly Efros, one of Knebel's most prominent protégés, puts it (2007, 140–41). One student observes that the chorus recounts the story of Iphigenia's sacrifice three times over the course of this relatively short play, suggesting that this repetition is essential for more than the audience's need for exposition. The elders are deeply haunted by the death of Agamemnon's child. We consider why, launching a lively debate about whether sacrifice is holy or murderous.

After some time, I direct their attention to the play's first choral ode (Aeschylus 1998, lines 195–255), calling upon students to read aloud, paying attention to its rich details. The chorus speaks of "the bitter winds [that] blew down from the [river] Strymon" and the "thin" and "rotting" cables on the ships that wait to set sail. They quote Agamemnon's words, when he finally confronts the fact that the gods have placed him in a no-win situation: "An unbearable fate will fall on me if I disobey/ but how can I bear to slaughter my own daughter?" When he then chooses the gods over his child, the chorus reports, "at that very moment he changed." Next, they follow the sacrifice, step by step, from Iphigenia's pleading, to being gagged, bound, and hauled on high, with her "saffron" skirts falling to the ground. The color stands out as witness to the mythic story behind the play, since Greek brides wore saffron at their weddings, and Iphigenia has been tricked into coming to the harbor under the guise of marrying the hero Achilles. The choral passage culminates in the following stunning words: "What happened next, I did not see and cannot tell."[2] The elders were eyewitnesses to Iphigenia's sacrifice. In fact, being the only men left in Argos when she was summoned, it is likely they escorted her to the harbor. Did they know of the ruse that encouraged her to comply? If so, were they complicit in her sacrifice? Or did they honestly believe they were escorting her to her wedding? If so, they – like she – may have been victims of Agamemnon's lie. Both options resonate as unanswered questions in the text. In either case, the fact that the chorus witnessed Iphigenia's sacrifice explains their obsession with her story and their ambivalent attitude toward Agamemnon.

After this "mental reconnaissance," as Stanislavsky calls this process of reading for the facts (Knebel' 1982, 12), each student in the chorus selects a single, emotionally charged word or phrase that expresses either support or condemnation of Agamemnon. These selections will serve as their lines during the etude. They choose: "rage craves rage," "necessity," "justice," "stolen young," "fury," "marriage rites," "child-avenging rage," "good and evil," "I saw," "bitter," "honor," "light of dawn," "with my eyes," "unholy," "unsanctified." As they choose, I suggest how the sounds of the vowels and consonants can be elongated or spit out to express the chorus' emotions. They play with sound for a while, until their soon-to-be-improvised ode begins to emerge.

I now turn to the other roles, and those who have volunteered read the scene aloud to discover the facts that condition their characters' words and behaviors. Cassandra observes that her presence as a tangible reference to the spoils of war is all that is required of her in this etude. "I must just lie there," she says, "and that alone will speak volumes about how victims of war are dehumanized by the victors." Clytemnestra's servants now chime in, saying that their job in the etude will also be easy. "All we need to do is follow Clytemnestra's explicit instructions."

Agamemnon and Clytemnestra begin with long speeches to the chorus. Agamemnon notices that he first prays to "the gods of this land – my allies who help exact justice" (Aeschylus 1998, lines 810–11), justifying his decision to sacrifice his daughter in front of those who helped him do so. He then turns to the chorus in empathy with them: "I speak from experience, how well I know/ the flattering mirror of comradeship" (Aeschylus 1998, lines 839–40). He assures them of his continuing belief in democracy: "We must meet in council and call an assembly" in order to determine how "the sickness in the state must be cut away" (Aeschylus 1998, lines 846–47). Clytemnestra notices that she, too, focuses on the chorus, asking them to sympathize with her by explaining how she endured the last ten years of war. She turns to her husband and speaks in ways that can be interpreted by him as praise and by the chorus as condemnation: "Is he not worthy of praise?" she asks both rhetorically and sarcastically. "Let justice lead him," either as hero or convicted criminal, to her, and "I will set things right" (Aeschylus 1998, lines 903–14). In short, both Agamemnon's and Clytemnestra's speeches are distinctly political because both seek to sway the opinions of the people.

Next, husband and wife engage in a verbal duel with short, sharp lines directed at each other in an exchange known in Greek as *agon*. Their parrying radically changes the rhythm of the scene and culminates in Agamemnon's decision to tread on the carpet that his wife has prepared for him: "Well, if you want this so much," he tells her, then "here, somebody help me off with my boots" (Aeschylus 1998, line 944). In making this decision, he turns a deaf ear to the politically disastrous implications of his choice. While he has spoken as a democrat, in conceding to his wife and walking on a carpet (which is both the color of monarchy and of blood), he behaves as if he were an autocrat. I take a moment to remind my students how ancient tragedy embodies the values that informed ancient Greek society. In this case, Aeschylus treats Agamemnon's walk as a physical representation of *hamartia*. Generally translated as the protagonist's "tragic flaw," the Greek word more literally means "misstep" or "error." In *The Poetics*, Aristotle writes that the audience's "pity is aroused by unmerited misfortune" when "a character . . . is not eminently good and just, yet whose misfortune is brought about not by vice or depravity, but by some error" (Aristotle 1974, 42). Agamemnon's promise to bring the chorus together in a democratic assembly may have been "good and just," offering hope to heal the community, but his literal misstep onto the carpet further fractures the community's trust in him and provides Clytemnestra with a political justification for his assassination. Thus, an abstract idea is physically embodied in a character's movement.

Setting the Stage

My second pedagogical goal in this etude is to convey how the spatial arrangement of the amphitheater was used to induce patterns of movement that enhance the emotional impact of tragic plays. As Goldhill observes, "This space is fully built into the writing of Greek plays" (2007, 7) and "any production that has not explored the symbolics of space and movement written into these scripts will end up struggling with the form and significance of the play" (Goldhill 2007, 44). To bring this notion into our class etude, we review the "essential coordinates" (Goldhill 2007, 10) that make up the ancient Greek theatre:

1. The *orchestra*, where the chorus danced and sang in circular patterns that involved movement to the right, movement to the left, and moments of stasis. In *Agamemnon*, the ambivalence of the chorus can be easily physicalized through changes of direction.
2. The narrow *skene* or low platform for the speaking actors, backed by central doors that could be used in any way that the play demanded. In *Agamemnon*, the doors represent the palace, and entry is controlled by Clytemnestra, making the *skene* her domain. When Agamemnon crosses the carpet and ascends to the *skene*, he enters her realm of control.
3. Long ramps to either side of the *skene* serve as entrances and exits for speaking actors. In *Agamemnon*, the returning king journeys from the harbor to Argos on a wheeled cart that is pulled along one of the ramps.

Students map these coordinates onto our room's geography as best they can. They clear space for the *orchestra*, use the entrance door to mark the *skene*, and employ a table as Agamemnon's war-cart. Finally, they establish the illusion of the ramp by placing the table diagonally across from the door to maximize the expanse of the room. This decision distorts the spatial arrangement of the Greek theatre but significantly enhances the students' opportunities to physicalize the emotional distance between husband and wife and the tension between the king and the chorus, since he must walk through the center of the *orchestra* to reach Clytemnestra. By mapping the Greek amphitheater, however imperfectly, onto the space of our classroom, the class has an opportunity to experience how space becomes a dramatic force in and of itself in the performance of a play.

Rehearsing the Etude

Before the students perform the etude, they mark the movements of the scene in our reconfigured classroom simply by walking through the sequence of what needs to happen for the scene to unfold. In this way, they figure out who has to be where and when from the beginning choral ode to Agamemnon's exit into the palace. Everyone then sits and quietly rereads the scene, reviewing discoveries and allowing any new thoughts to arise. In particular, it is important for the chorus to reconnect with the community's ambivalence toward their leader and for the speaking actors to reconnect with the content of Agamemnon's and Clytemnestra's speeches and their *agon*.

I next ask the students to get up and show me the scene as they now understand it. The first time they do so, they fall into gales of laughter, prompted in equal parts by a lack of self-confidence and an abundance of self-consciousness. I let the laughter play itself out and then remind them of how high the political and personal stakes are for the characters in this tragedy. "Imagine that you have taken a time machine back to the ancient Festival of Dionysius," I say. "Lend yourself as fully as you can to your imaginations, and take everyone in the room there with you." This request concentrates their attention. They grow thoughtful as they again reread the scene quietly for the facts. They take their places, and I call action.

Performing the Etude

Chorus members begin to mill about in the center of the room. One hugs another; most move randomly through the space; a few gather in one corner and look toward the door; another group eyes the table. After a few moments of silent movement, a single voice intones "rage craves rage"; a second bites down sharply on the consonants in "necessity"; a third hisses "justice." As these words are repeated, an improvised choral ode builds as student after student adds to the mix: "stolen young," "fury," "marriage rites," "child-avenging rage," "good and evil," "I saw," "bitter," "honor," "light of dawn," "with my eyes," "unholy," "unsanctified." Vowels resonate harmoniously against the counterpoint of percussive consonants in a singsong manner. An atmosphere of anxious, ambivalent anticipation begins to fill the space. As the ode builds in intensity, the students begin to circle the room. "Fury" sends them circling to the right. On "light of dawn" they circle to the left. With "unholy" they reverse direction yet again.

As the sound and movement continues, Agamemnon and Cassandra climb onto the table. As head of state, he wears heavy boots and stands with his legs apart and his arms crossed. As a captive of war, she lies unmoving in fetal position at his feet, wrapped in a shawl. He watches and listens for a few moments, then stamps his foot, causing the chorus to freeze and fall silent. When Agamemnon sees that he has everyone's attention, he lifts his arms over his head, shifts his gaze upward, and speaks: "I give thanks to the gods for granting us the spoils of victory." Hearing herself mentioned, Cassandra reaches out and grasps his ankle. He ignores her and continues: "And I give thanks to the gods for bringing me home to this blessed land. We were made lions; we feasted on our prey; now we are home to rest with our pride." At his words some in the crowd avert their faces, while others nod in agreement. Agamemnon now lowers his arm and addresses the people: "I have not forgotten you. I understand you." He looks toward one who has turned away. "I understand that success can induce your envy." He shifts his gaze to another: "And your flattery. But we share the same loss and the same victory. Now that I am back, we will meet together in an assembly and decide how best to prosper."

As he speaks, the door to the room is flung open, and Clytemnestra enters with her two servants, carrying a bolt of purple velvet I provided as a prop. She stands with her back to the door, as if barring all entry, and looks past the crowd at her husband. After a long moment of silent stillness, she turns her gaze away from him and toward the crowd: "Honored elders, imagine how hard it has been for me without my husband! Imagine how my heart ached every time I learned of yet another warrior killed in battle, thinking it might be him! I don't know how I held on, praying for this moment when I could offer my great husband the homecoming that he deserves. And you, you . . . You know what he deserves." Turning toward her husband, she smiles. "Welcome home, deeearrr husband," she intones, distorting the word "dear." She nods to the servants, who walk through the crowd, ceremoniously unfolding the bolt of rich cloth, creating an oblique walkway of color that extends from the door to the table. She continues: "Your actions deserve something other than a hero's welcome. Your feet of clay must not touch the sacred ground of your home."

Her request triggers a rapid and intense exchange between the two. He is a mere mortal, he says, not a god. He should walk only on bare earth. He holds firm, even when she asks: "What would the king of your enemies do, if he were you?" But finally, when she kneels and begs him to yield for her sake, he relents and summons the servants to remove his boots. As he sets his bare feet down on the velvet and walks slowly forward through the *orchestra*, some in the crowd reach out in gestures of support. Others turn away or spit in disgust. As he walks, Clytemnestra rises and reaches her arms toward him and intones "come," "come," "come," as if casting a spell that propels him forward. The servants open the door in readiness. From the threshold, he glances back over his shoulder and orders, "Take that woman there on the cart" – Cassandra stirs and looks up – "and be kind to her." Clytemnestra puts her arm gently around Agamemnon's waist and ushers him through the doorway. At their exit, everyone in the room stands silent for a full minute as if awed by what has just occurred.

Assessment

In this etude, students successfully embodied three aspects of Aeschylus' play. First, they physicalized the chorus' obsessive ambivalence by creating a division between those who supported and those who condemned Agamemnon for sacrificing his child to the war. Second, the emotional distance between husband and wife registered as physical space, when Agamemnon and Clytemnestra stood at opposite ends of the purple velvet cloth, strewn through the center of the room. Third, when Agamemnon walked along the cloth, passing each member of the chorus on his way toward his assassination, he became for all of us present the physical manifestation of "a figure who makes the boundaries of normal life problematic; . . . [who] goes too far, and going too far is both transgression and transcendence" (Goldhill 2007, 47).

When we resume class, we read further and discover how the scene culminates in the play's climax, when the chorus hears Agamemnon's screams from the palace as he is being murdered. They can neither run to his aid nor rejoice in his demise. Some seek "to raise the alarm" and "get the people to storm the palace," while others vote "no," let's "wait." Their disunity leads to their paralysis: "I don't know what to do, where to turn" (Aeschylus 1998, lines 346–1358). This collective inaction allows Clytemnestra and the autocrat Aegisthus to overturn democracy.

By using Active Analysis in our course on ancient Greek theatre, students connected Aeschylus' text with performance through the immediacy of interacting with both acting partners and stage space. They experience the play not as an abstract academic study but as a living document. Etudes can bring equal vividness to plays from past and contemporary cultures that might otherwise seem foreign or elusive.

Notes

1. For more on the history and practice of Active Analysis, see Chapter 10 in Carnicke, *Stanislavsky in Focus* (2009), "The Knebel Technique: Active Analysis in Practice," in *Actor Training* (2010), and *Dynamic Acting Through Active Analysis* (2023).

2. While in some versions of the myth Iphigenia is spirited away by the gods, Aeschylus treats her death as actually taking place.

References

Aeschylus. 1998. *Oresteia*. Translated by Peter Meinecke. Indianapolis: Hackett Publishing Co. Inc.

Aristotle. 1974. "Poetics." In *Dramatic Theory and Criticism*, edited by Bernard F. Ducote. San Francisco: Holt, Rinehart and Winston, Inc.

Carnicke, S. M. 2009. *Stanislavsky in Focus: An Acting Master for the Twenty-First Century*. New York: Routledge.

———. 2010. "The Knebel Technique: Active Analysis in Practice." In *Actor Training*, edited by Alison Hodge, 99–116. New York: Routledge.

———. 2023. *Dynamic Acting through Active Analysis: Konstantin Stanislavsky, Maria Knebel, a Guide to their Legacy*. London: Bloomsbury/Methuen.

Efros, Anatoly. 2006. *The Joy of Rehearsal: Reflections on Interpretation and Practice*. Translated by James Thomas. New York: Peter Lang.

———. 2007. *The Craft of Rehearsal: Further Reflections on Interpretation and Practice*. Translated by James Thomas. New York: Peter Lang.

Goldhill, Simon. 2007. *How to Stage Greek Tragedy Today*. Chicago: University of Chicago Press.

Knebel', M. O. 1967. *Visa shin' [All of Life]*. Moscow: VTO.

———. 1971. *O tom, chto mne kazhetsia͡ osobenno vazhnym: Stat'i, ocherki, portrety [What Seems Most Important to Me]*. Moscow: Iskusstvo.

———. 1982. *O deistvennom analize p'esy i roli [On the Active Analysis of the Play and the Role]*. Moscow: Iskusstvo.

Stanislavskii, K. S. 1991. *Rabota aktera nad rol'iu [An Actor's Work on the Role]*. Vol. 4 of *Sobranie sochinenii [Collected Works]*. Moscow: Iskusstvo.

———. 1999. *Pis'ma [Letters], 1918–1938*. Vol. 9 of *Sobranie sochinenii [Collected Works]*. Moscow: Iskusstvo.

CONCLUSION

In many art museums, curators encourage visitors to engage in "close looking" as they move through an exhibit. In this practice, the observer examines a work of art carefully, from many angles, and uses their life experience and critical thinking skills to uncover layers of meaning that personalize their connection to the piece. The process centers the observer as the creator of meaning, rather than focusing on the museum as the authority, or giver, of meaning.

In this anthology, we have attempted to assemble a wide range of approaches for actors and instructors to do some "close looking" (or close reading) of their own. Our book presents a platform to survey some of the current practices in building embodiment and incorporate them into your own teaching or your own process of artistic analysis. By centering the body and voice as the locus of meaning, the actor becomes an active participant in the artistic process, fueling a deeper relationship with poetic text and opening up possibilities for a broader range of interpretation. Inspiration is everywhere: a single figure of speech can inform our artistic choices, if we are willing to look closely enough.

This collection of essays also speaks to the psychology of the self and the profound value of imagination and individual creative spirit. Whatever approach an actor employs as they analyze the world a playwright has created, they must get *inside* their words to experience a character with as much truth as possible. Whether expansively vocalizing the essence of an emotion, devising tableaux, investigating how sculpture, stillness, or physical action can inspire play, or considering how the mechanisms and sounds of speech and language can inspire new meaning, building embodiment brings the world of the play to life.

DOI: 10.4324/9781003204060-18

INDEX

Note: Numbers in **bold** indicate a table.

Abigail (*The Crucible*) 31
absurdism 28, 151
absurd, the 133
Achilles 157
Accumulation Zeugma 143
acting and language xiii–xiv; poetic text and
acting 5–7; body activated for 113; character exercises (natural elements, air, water, fire, tree) 9–20; exercises in xiv
acting as profession: disreputability of, Restoration period 132
acting methods: Outside/In 9–10; realistic 119; substitution method 9; *see also* Adler method; American method; Dalcroze Method; Method Acting; Stanislavsky method; Strasberg/ substitution method
acting style 21, 22, 28; embodied 110; historical changes in 29, 110; Restoration 132
acting techniques: Classical 83
Active Analysis 153; principles of 154–156
actors embodying a character 1–2; centering the voice/body in terms of acting choices 5–6; committing to physical form, importance of 10; Greek tragedy 97; life experiences and interpreting of characters 5; natural elements, using and exploring 9–20; portraying versus experiencing 1–2; *see also* character
actor's block 33
Adler method 33
Adler, Stella 6, 31, 33, 34, 37
Aegisthus 162
Aeschylus 68; *Agamemnon* 70; anti-imperialist anti-slavery culture of 79; cues found in text of 77; *Oresteia, The* 153–154, 156; polis of 75; *Persians* 6, 67, 68, 70
affective language, music as 120
Affective Memory 31
Agamemnon (Aeschylus) 70
Agamemnon (*Illiad*) 78; casting for role of 156; homecoming of 153–163; Stanislavski's "etudes" applied to analysis of 153, 155–159, 160, 162; walk of 159
agon 158
Alexander Technique 98
American College, Paris, France 38
American College Theatre Festival, College Park, Maryland xii
American Method (acting) 142
American Shakespeare Center (ASC) 144
Ancient Greek sounds, rhythm, dance, tone, and quality 111

166 Index

Ancient Greek theatre and performance 96; physicalizing via scaffolding approach to 119–130; *see also* Greek theatre
anti-rhetorical rhetoric 150
Antony and Cleopatra (Shakespeare) 42–43
Archetypal Gestures 21
archetypal imagery 86
Argan (Molière) 22, 23, 24, 26
Argos 69, 157
Aristotle 144; *Poetics, The* 74, 159
Artaud, Antonin 116
Asaro Tribe, Indonesia and Papua New Guinea 28
ASC *see* American Shakespeare Center
Asia 37; "shepherd" as term used in 78
Asia Minor 74
Asian Greeks ("Ionians") 74, 75, 79
Asia Pacific Bond of Theatre Schools 85, 93n5
As You Like It (Shakespeare) 45
Athenians and Athens 67–70, 74–78; Battle of Marathon 69, 78; Festival of Dionysius 154
Atkins, Chet 102
Attica 68, 77
Atossa 69, 72
Australasia 84

balance: exercise 98–99; testing 99 (box)
Balkwill, Peter: on discovering embodiment in *presence* 81, 96–108
Barton, Anne 150
Barton, John 90, 142
bawdy language *see* comedy of manners
bawdy puns 78
Bechtol, Doreen: on physicalizing Greek theatre 82, 119–130
Becker, Jonathan 117
Beckett 151
Berry, Cicely 87, 90, 93, 150
"bite the bullet" 26–27
block, actor's *see* actor's block
Block, Giles 143
Blueprint for Analysis: Shakespeare analyzed using 52–57
body: activated for acting 113; artistic choices centered in 5; being present and centered in 2, 5; breathing body and behavior 113–115; Chekhov (Michael)'s understanding of 21; expansive body 111; expressive 5, 111; getting out of head and into 19; Grotowski's "seeds of organicity" in 34; grounding voice in 60; language located in 112; Leading Center and 23, 25; mind-body connection 86, 92; as primary location of story in Greek tragedy 82, 119–120; *soaring* used to align mind and 100; trusting the body to find truth of the character 36–37; *see also* embodiment; *Ki*
body language xiv, 1, 50; of queen of Persia (*The Persians*) 68, 69, 70, 79
body parts, language sounds connected to 88–89
body posture, historicizing 75
Bogart, Anne 123, 130
breath: acting as study of 47, 48; activating 113–114; actors' failure to fully engage 58; actors learning to fully accommodate 118; actors' mastery of 97; connecting to 87; deep breathing 91; embodiment through 6, 58–66; ensemble work with 102; essential and expressive 111; expansive 116; far focus and 100; line readings and 51; mapping out 59, 62; remind performers to breathe 108; repunctuating for 42; student work with 121–124, 126, 127
breathing on impulse, impulse to breathe 132, 134, 136
Brecht, Berthold 38
Bright, Timothy 151n7
Brook, Peter 48
Brown, Candice: on bawdy language in comedies of manners 82, 131–149
Brutus (in *Julius Caesar*) 17, 52, **53–55, 56**
Buber, Martin 41
Burrows, Miriam 148
Burton, Gideon O. 142, 144
Burton, Robert 151n7

Caesar (in *Julius Caesar*) 17, 52, **53–55, 56**
cadence 87, 143, 148, 149
Caliban (*The Tempest*) 14–15
Cambyses II 69, 72
Carnicke, Sharon Marie: on Active Analysis and Ancient theatre 82, 153–163
Carpenter, Steven xii
Cartesian divide 142
Cassandra 156, 158, 161, 162
Cassius (*Julius Caesar*) 16–17, 52; word chart analysis of speech by **53–56**

Celimene (*Misanthrope*, Molière) 62; analysis of text/speech of 63, 64
chakra focus 108
Chaney, Lon 29–30
character building 23
character development: world analysis as keys to 50–57
character experiencing xiv
character-forming devices 144
character motivation 21
characters: actors' building of 131, 140, 142; actors' emotional connection to xii, xv; actors' interpretations of 5; actors' visualizing of 1–2; bawdy 131–40; core element, tapping into 19; creating inner life of 50–57; Leading Center and Super Objectives to develop 21–28; natural elements used to develop 9–20; Outside/In approach to developing 9–10; Shakespeare's language as clues to 143–144; Stanislavsky method 142; Strasberg/substitution method used to create 9; *see also* truth of a character
character's journey 149
Charles II (King of England) 132
Chekhov, Anton 142, 151
Chekhov, Michael 6, 21–22, 86; Four Brothers 108; Psychological Gesture 117
Chenard, Josh: on Leading Center, Super Objective, and style 6, 21–28
chi 98, 99
chorus *see* Greek chorus
Cleopatra 83; *Antony and Cleopatra* 42
Clytemnestra 70, 156, 158–162
comedies of manners 58, 82, 131–149
Congreve, William: *Way of the World* xiii
connotative meaning and paraphrasing 52, **53–55**, 57
Constance (*King John*) 6
Constantinidis, Stratos: on the Persian Queen in *The Persians* 67–79
Cordelia from *King Lear* 35, 46–47
Coriolanus (Shakespeare) xiii
court life 137; French 131
courtroom 111
courtship 132
Covid-19 xii
crisis, climax, recognition (in plays) 46 162
Crucible, The (Miller) 31
Cromwell, Oliver 132

cuckoldry 132
cuckoo, rhetoric of 144–149

Dalcroze Method 35
Darius I 67–78; ghost of 67–68, 70, 78
Davies, Matt: on rhetorical repetition in Hamlet 82, 141–151
Davies, Oliver Ford 150
decolonizing methodology 85
denotative meaning and paraphrasing 52, **53–55**, 56
Descartes, René 142
Dibble, Susan 115
Dogberry 155
Doric: dress 70, 73, 74; fashion 74–75; pillars 75
Dushyanta (King) 86, 92

Edelstein, Barry 142, 149
Efros, Anatoly 157
Eliot, T. S. 41, 84, 148; "Hamlet and His Problem" 148
Elizabethan: acting processes 29, 30; *Arte of Rhetorique* (Wilson) 151n2; English vernacular 144; typesetters 46
embodied musicality 111
embodied rhetoric 143; *see also* rhetoric
embodiment: actors building of xiii–xv, 2, 82; breath and voice in 58–66; definition of 133; discovering embodiment in presence 81, 96–108; Fantasia on 6, 38–49; idea and definition of xii; Stanislavksy on 154
embodiment of role xiv
embodiment of sound 112
embodiment of text 2, 133
English Civil War 132
English vernacular 144
epizeuxis 145–150
essential and expressive breath 11
etude 82; assessing 162; improvisational 153; paraphrase etude 155, 156–159; performing 160–161; rehearsing 160; Stanislavski's 82, 153; three-dimensional polarity physical etude 115
Euripides: *Hecuba* 82, 110–118; *Helen* 5; *Medea* 29, 30–33
eurythmy 86
exclamation mark 46–47
expansive body 111, 115
expansive breath 116; *see also* breath
expansiveness 14, 97, 104

expressive bodies 5, 111
expressive emotional life, calls on actors to generate 97
expressive gesture 120; creating 126–128; language of 129

Fantasia, Louis: on embodiment 6, 38–49
Far Focus 100
figure of speech 2
Firth, Colin 58, 59
Fitzmaurice, Catherine 104
Fitzmaurice Destructuring sequence 114
Fitzmaurice Voicework 113
Fleischer, Mary: "Theatrical Stillness" 122
fly back, the 56–57
Formalism 142
"frog overlays" 40

Gallery exercise 137–138
germinal idea paraphrase 42, 56, **56**, 57
Gilbert, John 110
Gillette, William 2
Globe Theatre, Shakespeare 38, 42, 143
Goldhill, Simon 156–157, 159
Greek chorus xiii, xiv, 156–160, 162
Greek drama, tragic female roles in 68
Greek epic poems 106
Greeks, the 68–79
Greek scripts and plays 159; actors confronting 29, 106
Greek tragedy xiv, 28, 97, 156; approaching (via *Hecuba*) 110–118; messenger speeches in xiii
Greek theatre: arrangements of 160; audiences 96; characters with treelike characteristics 12; physicalizing 82, 119–130
Grotowski, Jerzy 6, 33–35, 37

Hall, Josephine: on embodiment through breath and voice 58–66
Hall, Peter 142
Hamlet (*Hamlet*) 31, 44–45, 82, 83
Hamlet: Claudius 44, 145–147 149; Fortinbras 44; Gertrude 44, 145, 147; Ghost 44, 146, 147, 150; Horatio 44, 147, 150; Polonius 145, 147, 148; rhetoric of repetition in 141–151
"Hamlet and His Problem" (Eliot) 148
Hamlet and Ophelia exercise 105–106, 107
Harrell, John 148
Hecuba (Euripides) 82, 110–118
heightened circumstances 10

heightened emotion 111
heightened language xiii, 83–93
heightened style (of acting) 116–117
heightened text 6: actors tensing up when confronting 58; defining 30; Greek 110, 112–113; how characters express themselves using 59; poetic xii–xiii, 81, 133; tackling 21, 29–37
Helena (*Midsummer Night's Dream*) 90–91, 94
Helen (Aeschylus) 156
Helen (Euripides) 5
Hello Dolly! (musical) 44
Henry IV, Part 2 (Shakespeare) 150
Henry VI (Shakespeare) 12–13
Hermia (*Midsummer*) 90–91
Herodotus 68, 69; *Histories* 69
hero 111, 156, 157, 158
hero's welcome 161
Holy Ghost 47
Homer: *Iliad* 78
Hunt, Robyn 81, 98; Hamlet and Ophelia exercise 105–106; Slow Ten 104–105; Slow Ten exercise 105, 106

iambic pentameter, Shakespeare's use of: *Hamlet* 143, 148–150; *King Lear* 47; *Macbeth* 42; *Midsummer* 46, 91
Imaginary Invalid, The (Molière) 22–24
India: dramatic tradition of 84; Sanskrit drama based on myths of 92
innuendo 131, 132
Inside/Out approach (to acting) 9–10
Ionesco 151
Ionians *see* Asian Greeks
I/Thou and I/It (Buber) 41–42

Jacques-Dalcroze, Emile 35
Jason (*Medea*) 30–33
Jenkins, Harold 145
Juliet (*Romeo and Juliet*) 41, 86
Julius Caesar (Shakespeare): Cassius' speech 16–17, 52; word chart analysis of Cassius' speech **53–56**
justice: Agamemnon and Clytemnestra 158, 161; cry for 41; foundation of 111; in *Measure for Measure* 45; price of 118; scale of **55**, 57; as theme 5
Justice Shallow (*Henry IV, Part 2*) 150

Kaiser, Scott 141, 143–145, 151n3
Kalidasa (Indian author) 84, 86, 92
Keller, Stefan 146

Index

Kelly, Baron: on multiple layers of meaning in words as keys to character building 6, 50–57
Ki 98; balancing with 99; connecting to 99; exercises with 99
King Agamemnon (*Iliad*) 76
King Charles II 132
King Creon 107
King Dushyanta 86, 92
King Lear (character) 87; actors' challenges in playing 30, 33; Affective Memory used to play 30–31; animal prototypes used by actors portraying 35–36; physicalizing the character of (advice for actors) 36
King Lear (Shakespeare): "nothingness" in 45; punctuation in 43; "space between the lines" in 46–47; "storm" scene in 30
King Nestor *(Illiad)* 78
Knebel (also Knebel'), Maria 153, 154–155, 157
Kopryanski, Karen: on discovering embodiment in *presence* 81, 96–108

Laban Movement Analysis 117
Laban's effort shapes 134–137, 138, 139; eight shapes of 136
Landau, Tina 130
Lady Macbeth (character, *Macbeth*) 26–27; Super Objective of 26–27
Lady M and Mac exercise 105–106
Lady Percy 87
Lady Sneerwell (character, *School for Scandal*) 134, 136
Lanham, Richard 144, 145
LASALLE College of the Arts, Singapore 83–85, 92
Leading Center 6, 21–28, 108
Lear *see* King Lear (character); *King Lear* (Shakespeare)
Lehmann, Hans-Thies 126
Linklater, Kristen 91, 96, 104
Lipton, James 58
literalism 150
Louis XIV 131
Lysander (*Midsummer Night's Dream*) 83, 94n17

Macbeth (Shakespeare) 25–27, 41–45, 47; ambition of Macbeth 45; Banquo's ghost 26; Banquo's Murderers 44; blood in 44; death of Macbeth 44; Duncan 26–27, 43; Lady Macbeth 26–27; Leading Center and Super Objectives of 25–28; MacDuff 26; Malcolm 43, 44; Super Objectives of 25–28; Three Witches 26
Matthias, Teh En 92
Maze, Colette 120
McDonald, Russ 150
McNally, Joseph 85
Medea (*Medea*) 29–33
Meneghini, Tamara: on new translation of Hecuba 82, 110–118
Method acting 142
Meyerhold 116
Midsummer Night's Dream (Shakespeare) 19, 40, 44, 45, 90; Oberon 19, 40, 45; Puck 19; Titania 40, 45, 90
Miller, Arthur 37
Misanthrope, The (Molière) 62–64
modernist theater 142
Molière 28; *Imaginary Invalid, The* 22–24; Leading Center in 22–23; *Misanthrope, The* 62–64; Super Objective in 23–24
Much Ado about Nothing (Shakespeare) 38, 155
Mortimer, Wendy 100
Much Ado About Nothing (Shakespeare) 38, 155
Museum of the Shakespearean Stage 38

natural elements: facilitating embodiment in acting by engaging with 6, 9–20
naturalism 28, 30
Nestor (King) 78
Nuttall, A. D. 150

Oberon (*Midsummer Night's Dream*) 19, 40, 45
Odyssey (Homer) 78
Odysseus 97
Ohta, Shogo 98
opposite vectors 35
Oram, Daren 87
Othello (Shakespeare) 150
Outside/In approach (to acting) 9–10, 20
overlays (analysis tool) 40

paraphrase etude 155, 156
paraphrasing 52–57, 59; connotative meaning and 52, **53–55**, 57; denotative meaning and 52, **53–55**, 56; inner lives of characters discovered using 6; Fantasia's opposition to 39; line 54; *see also* germinal idea paraphrase
Parks, Suzan-Lori 151
Peacham, Henry 144, 146, 147, 150

Penelope (*Odyssey*) 97
Persian Empire 67–79; eagle as emblem of 72, 74
Persians, The (Aeschylus) 6–7; first staging of 67; foundational role of the Queen in 67–79; overview of significance of 67; summary of 68
Phantom of the Opera (film) 29–30
pity 159
Plato 144
Polynices, ghost of 107
presence: awakening to 98; cultivating 97; discovering embodiment in 96–108; essential and expressive breath as pathway to 111
Psychological Gesture 21–22
punctuation: breath and 42; playing the punctuation 43; repunctuation and 42; using the body as 138, 139; vocal 136
Puttenham, George 144, 146, 148

Queen Margaret (*Henry VI*) 12–13
Queen of Persia (*Persians, The*) 6, 67–79

rake (character type) 131
rasaboxes™ 116–117
rasas 108, 116–117, 118
Rasa-Play 116–117
Rayor, Diane 110, 112
Restoration-era: Cockpit stage 39; comedies and comedies of manners 131–132; plays 12, 58
rhetoric: anti-rhetoric 149–151; Burton's definition of 142; classical 142, 151; clues from 77; of cuckoo 144–149; dramatic 143, 149; embodied 141; *Hecuba*'s mastery of 111; study of 141; two traditions of 141–143
rhetorical choice 145; *why* of 142
rhetorical devices 54, 146; in *Hamlet* 82; heightened language and 86
rhetorical figures 149
rhetorical figures of style 141
rhetorical meaning 150
rhetorical structures, Shakespeare's use of 143
rhetoricians 144
rhetoric manuals 144
rhetoric of repetition, *Hamlet*'s use of 82, 141–151
Richards, Thomas 34
Richmond, Hugh 38

ROADS mnemonic 144
Rodenburg, Patsy 100, 148
Romeo and Juliet 41, 44, 51, 86, 150; Juliet 41, 86; Nurse 150; Tybalt 51
Royal Shakespeare Company (RSC) 142, 150

S&I *see* sculpting and imaging (S&I)
Said, Edward W. 85
Salamis, island of 68
Schechner, Richard 116
sculpture and sculptural imagery 82, 119, 120, 122, 137
sculpting in S&I *see* sculpting and imaging (S&I)
sculpting and imaging (S&I) technique 81, 83–93; imaging in S&I 91–92; overview of 84; results 92; sculpting in S&I 88–91
"S" curve of female body 131
"S" curve exercise 134–137; "marination" stage of 138–139
Second Circle energy 100
Shakespeare and Performance (S&P) program, Mary Baldwin University 143
Shakespeare, William 41–45; analysis based on four natural elements applied to four characters of 10, 12–13; *Antony and Cleopatra* 42–43; Blueprint for Analysis applied to 52–57; Caliban in *The Tempest* 14–15; *Julius Caesar* (Shakespeare): Cassius' monologue from *Julius Caesar* 16–17, 52, **54–56**; concept of character in xiv; Constance from *King John* 6; Cordelia from *King Lear* 35, 46–47; *Coriolanus* xiii; equitable and inclusive approach to speaking and performing heightened language of 83–87, 90–94; Globe Theatre 38, 42, 143; Hamlet from *Hamlet* 31, 44–45, 82, 83; Hamlet and Ophelia exercise 105–106, 107; Hamlet and the rhetoric of repetition 141–151; Helena from *Midsummer Night's Dream* 90–91, 94; *Henry IV, Part 2* 150; *Henry VI* 12–13; "inspiration" and 47; insults 90; Juliet from *Romeo and Juliet* 41, 86; *Julius Caesar* 16–17, 52, **54–56**; Justice Shallow from *Henry IV, Part 2* 150; *King Lear* 29–30, 33, 35–36, 43, 45, 46–47, 87; *Macbeth* 25–27, 41–45, 47; *Midsummer Night's*

Dream 19, 40, 44, 45, 90; *Much Ado About Nothing* 38, 155; Museum of the Shakespearean Stage 38; Nurse from *Romeo and Juliet* 150; Othello from *Othello* 150; over-punctuation of 42; Queen Margaret from *Henry VI* 12–13; *Romeo and Juliet* 41, 44, 51, 86, 150; *playing the punctuation* of 43; Royal Shakespeare Company (RSC) 142, 150; sculpting and imaging (S&I) text of 83–93; text and denotative/connotative paraphrasing of **54**; text and generative idea paraphrase **56**; Trinculo in *The Tempest* 14–15; visceral experience of language of 51–52; worldplay in 143; *see also* iambic pentameter, Shakespeare's use of; Kaiser, Scott

"Shakespearean Insults" 90
Shakespeare Paradigm 39
Shakuntala (Dushyanta) 86, 92
Shnker, Ross 52
Sheridan, Richard Brinsley: archaic words used by 59; *Rivals, The* 60; *School for Scandal* 59
Singapore: LASALLE College of Arts 83, 84–85, 92; founding of 93n7; Lee Yuan Kew 85; "miracle" of 1960s and 1970s 85
Skinner, Edith 87
Slow Ten 98, 104–105; exercise 104–105, 106
Smerdis (Emperor) 69, 72
Sneerwell *see* Lady Sneerwell
Soaring activity 98, 100; exercise 100–104; Mortimer's definition of 100; music used for 108n2
Soyinka, [Wole] 86
space: accessible and inclusive 87; awareness of 116, 117; conceptual 97; as dramatic force in itself 160; moving through 124–125; rehearsal 62, 137, 142; symbolics of 159; theatrical 154; white space on the page 46; wrapping up time and space 125–126
"space between the lines" 46, 47
Sparta 69, 75
speech: breath leading to 133; everyday xiii; Juliet from *Romeo and Juliet* 41; Macbeth 42; as primary method of communication among humans 50; upper-class 132; using S&I to activate 86; words and articulation of 113

speech actions 149
speech acts 79; Method dictum regarding 150; tactical 143
speech discipline 51
speeches: Cassius from *Julius Caesar* 16–17; Celimene from *Misanthrope* 62–64; Helena from *Midsummer* 90–91p Juliet from *Romeo and Juliet* 41; Macbeth 25–26, 42; monologues in classrooms 128; Queen Margaret from *Henry VI* 12–13; prose, of Shakespeare 51; Puck from *Midsummer* 19; Queen of Persia from the *Persians* 70–71; rehearsed or apparently rehearsed 5; Titania "forgeries of jealousies" speech 90; Trinculo from *Tempest* 14–15
speech sounds: Received Pronunciation 84
Stanislavski, Konstantin (or Constantin) 21, 23; *Building a Character* 142; etudes 82; on "mental reconnaissance" 158; rehearsal technique of (Active Analysis) 153, 154–156
Stanislavski method 30; American Method influenced by 142
Steiner, Rudolf 86, 93
stillness: acting and 81, 82, 96–108, 111, 120, 121, 122, 124, 125, 126; of air 33; "Theatrical Stillness" (Fleischer) 122
Stone, Peter Allen: on facilitating embodiment in acting by engaging with natural elements 6, 9–20
Stoppard, [Tom] 86
Strasberg, Lee 9
Substitution (in ROADS) 144
substitution method (acting) 9, 33
Susa 69, 77, 78, 79
Suzuki, Tadashi 37, 98, 104
Svich Caridad 120
Syazwina, Miza 92

Tagore, [Rabindranath] 84
Tejas, Hirah 92
Tempest, The (Shakespeare) 14–15
theatre: death of 120
Titania (*Midsummer Night's Dream*) 40, 45, 90
Titans (mythological) **53**
tragic flaw 159
Trinculo (*The Tempest*) 14–15
truth of a character 6; Adler on 31; Grotowski on 33–37
Tuhiwai Smith, Linda 85

Turner, Elaine 38
"Two Traditions" of acting 141–143

vowels 65, 86, 91, 139;
  elongating via singing 65,
  112, 158; imaging of 91;
  physicalizing 86

Walcott, Derek 86
Wanamaker, Sam 38
Warwick University 38
Wilson, Thomas 151n2

wobbling 102 (box)
word charts 52; creating 53–54
word sounds and images 91;
  consonants 59, 84, 87–89, 91,
  112, 132, 135–136, 139, 158;
  vowels 65, 86, 91, 94, 112, 139, 158

Xerxes 67–79

Zazzali, Peter: on sculpting and imaging
  (S&I) the text 81, 83–93
zeugma 143, 144, 151n3